MANAGE TO ENGAGE

MANAGE
TO
ENGAGE

How Great Managers Create
Remarkable Results

PAMELA HACKETT
PROUDFOOT CEO

WILEY

Published by John Wiley & Sons, Inc., Hoboken, New Jersey.
Published simultaneously in Canada.

For general information on our other products and services or for technical support, please contact our Customer Care Department within the United States at (800) 762-2974, outside the United States at (317) 572-3993 or fax (317) 572-4002.

Wiley publishes in a variety of print and electronic formats and by print-on-demand. Some material included with standard print versions of this book may not be included in e-books or in print-on-demand. If this book refers to media such as a CD or DVD that is not included in the version you purchased, you may download this material at **http://booksupport.wiley.com**. For more information about Wiley products, visit **www.wiley.com**.

Library of Congress Cataloging-in-Publication Data is available:

ISBN 9781119773467 (Hardcover)
ISBN 9781119773900 (ePDF)
ISBN 9781119773894 (ePub)

Cover Design: Wiley

SKY10025130_022221

Erika gave strength. Ron gave curiosity. Both gave their time.

Contents

Introduction

You can be anything you want. But if you are going to be something, be brilliant at it, and do it with gusto. Showing up gets you started. Stepping up gets you across the finish line.

—Capt. Ron Hackett, B.E.M. British & Australian Armed Forces, Military Police

The COVID-19 pandemic thrust the world into navigating the largest "work from home" experiment of modern times. Realistically, it is the largest work disruption of any time since Henry Ford designed his first production line. There is no denying that the COVID-19 virus is a large-scale human heartache, a health care crisis, and an economic tragedy. It raged across the globe, spreading sickness, death, and displacement. The double whammy impact on lives and livelihood hit many. The millions unemployed created a new reality overnight, and many of those jobs will not be coming back. Whole industries will have been destroyed, disrupted, or dislocated. Still others changed at speeds never seen before. Some have and will prosper. Perhaps not the masses.

While the threat of automation replacing jobs was the focus of much anxiety over the past decade or so, it proved to be a disease that did the most damage, most rapidly. We all saw how quickly the economy halted, the health care system faltered, people were furloughed or, worse, simply laid off as businesses shuttered closed. The world suffered a global crisis and responded with a country-by country, industry-by-industry, company-by-company, plan. The word *remote* punctuated management conversations, websites, podcasts, and blogs the world over. As the crisis unfolded, discussions ranged from "How do we cope?" and "How do we cut costs?" to "How do you lead?" and "How do you lead remotely?"

The Times, They Are a-Changin'

As the COVID-19 pandemic continued to unfold, a new reality set in and it became more difficult to predict an end. Financial modeling became increasingly difficult and cash preservation developed into the daily norm. The words *no spend policy* became commonplace for many firms.

Many discussions also addressed the issue of change. "We have changed more in a few weeks than in 10 years," said Tesco CEO Dave Lewis as supermarkets needed to step up into essential services. Others said they'd seen 6 years of change in 6 months. Larry Rosen, CEO of Harry Rosen Inc., the Canadian luxury men's clothier, flatly admitted, "We took a whole bunch of guys like me – I'm 64 – and they learned how to shop online during this crisis."

The rate of change accelerated by this virus had a fundamental impact on many workplaces and it provided a crisis playbook to better engage organizations, one we must learn from and carry over to postpandemic times.

Changing Your Advantage

As CEO of Proudfoot, a management consulting company founded in 1946, I too felt the impact of the COVID-19 pandemic. We had spent our history proud of our "boots on the ground" business model, our people shoulder to shoulder with clients, working through their improvement programs and major transformations to realize large-scale results, coaching new behaviors and implementing new processes and systems, not just advising from a distance. We told our clients, *If you go underground we go underground, if your business has a night shift we work night shift.* Well, that all stopped when the pandemic hit. Some assignments were paused as people zoomed their way home. We quickly switched to remote work. Where remote was not an option, our revenues paused. Suddenly, our competitive advantage nearly killed us. My goal was to save as many jobs as possible and maintain the business continuity where that was a possibility. We continued with projects that allowed it and were safe for our teams. We helped our clients navigate through with COVID-19 response planning, sometimes for free, because that was the right thing to do, and other times deferring their payments to the next year, to prevent them from deferring their improvement and transformation programs when they needed it most.

I was also conscious of the health and well-being of my people. Having been one of the early COVID-19 victims in February after three trips to New York as well as France and the UK, I knew what the virus could do. While I was lucky (its impact stopped at what I compared to a very bad flu bug turn into pneumonia), I recall getting out of bed three nights in a row wondering if I would be able to continue breathing. It was early in the pandemic. I didn't realize I could die. Later, the experience allowed me to understand its potential, and therefore I treated it with great respect. This disease was a killer for some, but it was not so bad for me. I was sick but lucky.

Great Things Happen at the Intersection of People and Technology

Both the firsthand business impact and the impact on my health allowed me to realize the empathy you needed during this time for your own people but also for your clients and customers. It also made me focus on the big picture – I needed my teams to feel as safe as they could, and we as a business needed them to remain engaged. This would not be something to navigate through alone. We doubled down on something we call HeadsUp and 1.5.30, a simple but meaningful global movement we kicked off with a rallying cry of "great things happen at the intersection of people and technology," to remind people to prioritize human connection as a way to better engage with their teams, their communities, and society. 1.5.30 is a quick, once-a-day check-in (1), a once-a-week progress chat (5), and a once-a-month development and coaching conversation (30). HeadsUp refers to people lifting their heads from their devices to actively engage and focus on people. At the time we launched HeadsUp, we had no idea a global pandemic would slam the world's doors shut and create a societal need for a HeadsUp movement. As a backstory, we picked the unusual launchpad of Singapore in 2019 to unveil HeadsUp. After all, Singapore is one of the most digitally fluent and innovative countries on the planet, but also, according to a recent Qualtrics study, was one of the laggards in employee engagement.[1] When COVID-19 hit and much of the world went home, HeadsUp was more than relevant. We knew we needed to all remain HeadsUp. We needed to ensure that people lifted their noses out of their technology and connected with other people, albeit through technology

---

[1] Qualtrics, *2020 Employee Experience Trends* (Singapore: Qualtrics EmployeeXM, 2020). https://www.qualtrics.com/m/assets/au/wp-content/uploads/2020/01/FINAL_SG_EX_Trends_Report_Ebook.pdf

when they went remote. But while it is labeled *remote,* feeling remote was the last thing people wanted during this time. After all, remember what you don't do when you work from home: you don't commute. You don't stop and grab coffee on the way to work. You don't stop and say hi to your colleagues at the office kitchen, in the locker room, or on the shop floor. You don't get the human contact you previously enjoyed. You may also be working on your kitchen table, balancing your laptop on one knee while bouncing your baby on the other knee. It's different. After the novelty wore off, we needed to be prepared for the new routine of the new reality. People saw that they needed to better engage. HeadsUp became a vehicle.

Fast forward past the height of the global pandemic, and HeadsUp becomes a mindset dedicated to encouraging better leadership at every level, irrespective of where people work. It's about developing leaders who prioritize connecting with people and human interaction in order to achieve their aspirations and build extraordinary businesses and communities. Great leaders know how to leverage technology to do that. This is a global need in the workplace, at home, and in society in general. HeadsUp is one of many tools that enable you to manage to engage.

Today, HeadsUp is both a business and a social movement. How effectively we do this now will determine how effectively our people, teams, and organizations not only come out of this period but how they show up in the future. Our wellness will depend on it. Our next-generation leaders will follow on from it. Our engagement will hinge on it.

Flat as a Pancake – Not Yet

While the past decade has flattened the organization structure and reduced the need for some managers, the need to create leaders at every level, particularly frontline leaders, has never been more necessary. Whether teams work from home or not. You need leaders not to command and control, but to create a sense of community, convene collaboration, engage people in their work, enable them to achieve their results, and energize them to coach and guide their teams, so that everybody can get up the next day and do it all again, and with gusto. So they will connect and engage.

We need to build engagement into the lifeblood of a leader's role, a performance requirement. The problem? Leaders have been ill-equipped to engage, not knowing the right tools to employ or the right approaches to take. After all, so much is coming at them. How can they stop and engage?

But What if They Could?

There is a way. Leaders often see engagement as the outcome rather than the launchpad to build stronger ecosystems and achieve results. *Manage to Engage* addresses this with simple concepts you will learn about like HeadsUp and the HeadsUp High Five (Presence, Vision, Tech Savvy, Coaching, and Influence), behavior models like active management, and the unique performance improvement tool that engages as much as it brings about improvement and change: 1.5.30.

These are the fundamental tools you'll find in this book, positioned in an engagement framework based on a new scorecard of 2 Fs and 7 Cs – the MI-9 triggers of engagement. Packed with tools and exercises to apply, the scorecard has you addressing performance improvement through the lens of engagement, and I hope energizes you to manage to engage.

But let's stop for a moment and think about where organizations were long before the COVID-19 crisis hit. Before the global financial crash of 2007–2008, we already had a crisis: a people crisis. Surveys the world over reported high levels of underengagement. In fact, almost two-thirds of most workforces around the world were in neutral at work, neither engaged nor disengaged. Then when financial panic set in, they clung to their positions out of necessity, not interest. A decade on, little had improved. We were relying on those same emotionally disconnected people to execute our business strategies. We knew this epidemic of discontent was hardly going to drive innovation in disrupted, highly competitive markets but we still had no solution.

Then a more literal epidemic hit: the COVID-19 pandemic. And the world changed again. This time on a massive global scale. Trust in leaders, business, and institutions was already at an all-time low as we entered the COVID-19 crisis. The virus gave trust an extra kick in the pants. And that neutral workforce either remained in neutral, disengaged, or if you were lucky, engaged to help save their organizations. Still others became essential workers – everyday bus and train drivers, delivery people, grocery store workers, and of course our health care workers. They all became heroes. The question we then needed to ask was, "How would we treat them postpandemic? Could we engage them for the long term to help *build back better?*"

People Are (Still) the Future of Business

We won't recover this time with the same approaches we used coming out of previous crises. This time a radical transformation is needed. We all know people are the future. But this time we need to prove it. Not just unlocking their potential for the company's sake, but allowing people to bring their best selves to work. This demands something new of managers, something that also needs to be measured differently – something more engaging. This book, I hope, will lead you through some suggestions on both.

Prior to COVID-19, a revolution was unfolding at work. People felt we had curtailed the drive to be the best we can be in the pursuit of quarterly results or improved productivity; their organizations had become shackles. People were underengaged. They had not quite self-organized into engagement movements, or anti-management rallies, to oust what they perceived as poor leadership, but the many were growing less tolerant of the few. They may not have taken to the streets yet; they suffered in silence. It didn't mean the urge wasn't there. It's just that they hadn't yet found a way to topple these flawed corporate regimes that did little to inspire us. We had not quite figured out how to rise for a cause. But things were changing. Companies were struggling to find or keep skilled people. People were voting with their feet.

A Moment Can Become a Movement

We're talking about whole workplaces of people and large populations of industries who weren't really there. We were not moving people to do anything special. Is it any wonder that McKinsey touted a change failure rate of 70–80 percent? And according to a Gallup survey, some 60–70 percent of the workforce is underengaged, and, worse still, on average, some 15 percent are disengaged.[2] Does this actually mean we are operating at 20–30 percent of our people capacity?

And then came a pandemic that changed everything. For better and for worse, business models changed. Operating models changed. Our office space

---

[2] Gallup, *State of the Global Workplace Report* (Gallup, 2017). www.slideshare.net/mobile/adrianboucek/state-of-the-global-workplace-gallup-report-2017.

changed. Businesses proved they could create new shift structures, change our health and safety protocols, send large portions of work to people's homes. Even the people whom just weeks prior we pointed to as "difficult to change" changed. The pandemic showed the resilience of people, the hidden heroes among our everyday workers who stepped up. The people we sadly often didn't think about kept our economies, our businesses, our communities, and our homes safe, secure, and with meals on our tables.

We can't waste the moment. It must become a movement. We must remember the sheer force of change that took place during the COVID-19 pandemic. And to do that, we cannot let our workplaces slip back into the underengaged, underenthused leaders and teams from where we came.

Imagine what you could do if you flipped the formula. What if 85 percent were engaged? Imagine your productivity, your profitability, and growth. Imagine the challenges your teams would show up to solve? Imagine the world we could create.

Unless these chronically low levels of employee engagement prepandemic, are addressed, the world's economies surely cannot recover, and transformation failure rates will remain as low. Perhaps plummet further. With these statistics, you surely won't achieve the results you want or need in your improvement programs, let alone the transformations you now need to achieve. And now, with people likely fearing the loss of their jobs even more, their neutral feelings about work will provide little foundation to grow from.

But Does It Have to Be This Way?

As we cycle from recessions to tight labor markets and back again, it's clear that engagement still underpins business success. The COVID-19 pandemic showed us this. How you survive recessions, attract talent, achieve results, and keep your workplace safe are all impacted by engagement. Management practices stand to have the greatest impact on engagement. Better still, those that achieve high engagement have a competitive advantage.

So, *how do I manage to engage?* That's the real question for leaders today. How do I move from a moment like this, a great global reboot, to a positive movement where people volunteer to engage?

You'll notice I used *reboot* and not *reset.* It's an important difference in intent. *Reset* feels too much like it would be OK to go back to the default setting of old – old management models and processes, old organization structures and behaviors, rather than lean forward into a reboot. When you install new software on your computer you are asked to reboot, not reset. The difference? Your computer cycles through a restart but starts up better than when you shut down. New value is created.

So, how do we create that sense of volunteerism we saw in the height of the pandemic, in a postpandemic world of bipartisanism, fear, and distrust?

What Will Our Legacy Be?

We are at a time in business history where leaders at every level, the people who manage the business day to day, stand to have the greatest impact on their business survival and growth, by how they themselves show up and engage – how they build a better business for people. A new people reality.

We even heard the World Economic Forum at Davos 2020 (prior to the global pandemic): "With the world at such a critical crossroad, this year we must develop a *Davos Manifesto 2020* to reimagine the purpose and score-cards for companies and governments," espoused Klaus Schwab, founder and executive chairman, World Economic Forum.[3] The Business Roundtable announced similar statements in August 2019 on the Purpose of a Corporation. It was signed by 181 CEOs who committed to lead their companies for the benefit of all stakeholders – customers, employees, suppliers, communities, and shareholders. All of these statements require full engagement. They require leaders to manage to engage.

Is It Culpability or Capability?

During the pandemic, we already saw that things could be different. Creativity was delivered. Innovation accelerated. People stepped up. Logistics, online retailers, tech firms, health care, food and beverage, and transport found varying degrees of success. But in others we retrenched people and reduced costs. Hospitality, airlines, bricks and mortar anything. Many employees pointed the finger squarely at management and leadership and how they navigated through the pandemic. Others understood that their industries were

---

[3] Klaus Schwab, *Davos Manifesto 2020: The Universal Purpose of a Company in the Fourth Industrial Revolution* (World Economic Forum, 2019). www.weforum.org/agenda/2019/12/davos-manifesto-2020-the-universal-purpose-of-a-company-in-the-fourth-industrial-revolution/

casualties of a pandemic more than management. But all asked, "Where is this multi-stakeholder capitalism now?"

It is here we need to start. This is where the tone and mood are set at work.

You could think it was a straight leadership problem, poor leadership, but as the world continues to change so rapidly and with so much coming at leaders today, it becomes more a question of developing capability rather than assigning culpability. Are we developing our leaders effectively? Do we have the right tools and approaches for today's workforce? Are our workplaces free of the noise that prevents engagement, the politics that stops it in its tracks?

With the best intentions, many managers struggle to engage their people because they don't lay the foundations for a safe, productive workplace. Leaders struggle to free themselves up to think about how their organizations could be better built to engage.

We know how we manage and lead has a direct effect on how people feel at work. We know that people quit *people* more than their *jobs*. We also know that when your systems, processes, and workplace doesn't support you, frustration takes the place of enthusiasm and the camel's back is broken by the last straw that was hanging on to engagement. We switch off, we quit, or worse still, we quit and stay.

So, what if you could bring a different mindset to engagement and apply new tools and approaches to help you enable people to engage? This is not about perks and prizes. As managers and leaders, we have an opportunity each day, each time we interact with people, to change their world of work for the better. Sometimes with small tweaks in how we connect or how our workplace connects with us, other times with large-scale change. All find their roots in engagement. All are necessary now more than ever. We will not build the businesses we all want to work for, the ones people will feel passionate about rethinking, reinventing, and rebooting, until we do.

Engagement, the Quiet Revolution, the Needed Movement

What if we cast a brighter spotlight on the current workplace crisis? It isn't right, nor appropriate, that so many feel so disconnected from something that consumes the best part of our lives: our jobs. And in times of mass unemployment, it's also not right to rely on a loose labor market to motivate people to bring their best selves to work.

Untapped people power is the greatest access to competitive advantage we have ever had. Tap into it and you have the greatest uncapped advantage to leverage of all time.

It is completely possible to make a difference to those around you by the way we manage and lead. So, this is a call to action for the people who manage teams at every level. From the front line to the top dogs. We need to change the way we engage – at a very fundamental level – and this means to manage in order to engage. A reality check is long overdue. We need a reminder of the impact of our workplaces on our wellness, our lives. Our work fills our brains so we can't relax or sleep, affects our health, our happiness, our relationships, our friendships, and our financial security. Underengagement costs us emotionally, personally, and financially. Our engagement levels come with a measurable price tag. This is an economic need, a societal necessity, a quality-of-life issue bigger than any problem business faces today. It affects how we restart from pandemics, bounce back from recessions, deliver our improvement programs, and transform our organizations and cultures. It drives the results of our companies as well as our personal welfare and life satisfaction. Addressing this situation is the greatest change project for the twenty-first century. It propels everything from innovation to survival, and it needs to start now.

We must feel engaged in our jobs. We should be enthused, not jaded; fulfilled, not drained. We are truly "in it together."

How to Engage with This Book

In this book, I zero in on how you can engage your people better, and along the way, I discuss the vital insights that can be applied to your transformation and improvement programs as well.

Here is a summary of the chapters to follow and the tools you might consider taking to your workplace, to better engage.

Chapter 1: People Matter: We Need a Healthier Way of Working

Humanize. Optimize. Digitize. Engagement is the core of all improvement. Billions are being invested by organizations in the name of improving competitive advantage, productivity and profitability, safety, and brand building. Leaders look for ever-expanding budgets for research and development, technology and digitization, plant expansions, and marketing. But, what if you could gain that same level of competitive advantage by how you manage and lead, with little financial cost? Imagine the impact on results. The need to engage your people and teams has never been more crucial. The upside is limitless.

The takeaway: The MI-9 toolkit. The new scorecard. Manage to engage using the 2 Fs and 7 Cs: Fair Trade, Cause, Clean and Meaningful Infrastructure, Confidence, Connection, Collaboration, Community, Capability and Freedom.

Chapter 2: The Ice Age: It's Alive and Well at Work

Engage. Enable. Energize. Three words to warm your world. The world of business has changed at pace, but 2020 saw it change irrevocably. A global crisis unfolded at record speed. For almost everyone. A few months into the pandemic, the UN was estimating almost 200 million jobs could be wiped out. Trust would be erased overnight. Pre–COVID-19, surveys the world over already had people feeling coolly detached from their jobs. As the planet warmed up, an ice age took hold, as their human needs remained underrecognized and unmet in the workplace.

The takeaway: If we don't solve this icy issue now, we will not only have an employee engagement issue, we will have a long-lasting economic issue. It's finally time to solve the problem.

Chapter 3: Manage to Engage: Building Street Cred

To warm up the workforce, managers and leaders must learn to recognize and rapidly adapt to the new world of work. Those businesses who survive will require new operating models (ecosystems) that synchronize the business and allow a new, more robust rhythm to achieve results and engage people in more meaningful ways. And none of this should be hard wired. It should be flexible, agile, calibrated to your needs, creating new management approaches that are relevant and appealing to your evolving workforce, and the individual characters within it.

The takeaway: In this chapter we explore what going HeadsUp really means and how it applies to everyone. We introduce the HeadsUp High Five.

Chapter 4: Fair Trade: An "F" You Should Be Proud Of

Fair trade: allowing people to feel that they exchange a fair day's work for a fair day's return. While much needs to change in the way we manage, one aspect retains its importance: fairness. Being fair to people won't give your organization an advantage: it's a fundamental expectation. It's the cornerstone of a great mindset. Without it, you may as well pack up your toolkit and go home.

The takeaway: Learn how to be *fair dinkum,* a great Aussie term for authentic. Learn what "color your day" is, and the eight active management behaviors that help you create a fair trade.

Chapter 5: A Common Cause: Collecting Volunteers to Create a Movement

Why don't we feel as good about work as we do about the causes we volunteer for? What would make us jump out of bed each morning and run to work? *OK, maybe not run.* As leaders, our ambition is to have people feel they have a stake in the success or the outcome of our business, right? Yet we struggle to do that. We know having a purpose creates a whole new meaning around our work. When we feel engaged in a meaningful cause, we're happy to contribute and be more productive. Knowing what is expected of you is a table stake. Knowing how you fit is an engager.

The takeaway: When you break a movement down into its building blocks, you see a theme, a way of engaging people in a cause. In this chapter, you learn the backstory of a movement, a way to create that same feeling of a social movement in your own teams. You learn how to help connect people to a cause.

Chapter 6: Cleaning Up Your Workplace

Taking down silos, removing unnecessary structures, delayering authority matrices that delay decision-making, and eliminating unnecessary work can positively impact engagement – it can address what cheeses people off and it can fix the bad hair days. We must build healthy workplaces that are physically efficient. Like pay and rewards, providing people with a clean infrastructure may not engage us, but if it doesn't work for us, it will certainly disengage. Processes that produce high waste are not just costly, they also impact the environment and create unnecessary frustration at work.

The takeaway: Enterprise aerial mapping allows your team to look for opportunities to clean it up, remove barriers to success, connect better, and build your ecosystem into a high-performing operating model. This includes crowdsourcing ways to build clean workplaces; hacking processes to build work that is fit for people to be productive.

Chapter 7: Out Your Doubt and Boost Confidence

Extraordinary leaders bring certainty to uncertain times in how they show up. Out the doubt! Doubt is a killer of confidence at work. Removing doubt and negativity can build people's confidence – in their managers, the business, each other, and their own future. Confidence helps people engage. In a post–COVID-19 world, confidence builds trust, a requirement to demonstrate we work for the right leaders and the right firm.

The takeaway: Checking in is not about checking up. 1.5.30 Connect encourages you to prioritize people in your day and check in routinely. The ability to build confidence through visibility is vital: your own visibility, information visibility, and being transparent.

Chapter 8: Building Connections: Can You Hear Me?

People are hardwired to be social and form connections; our general well-being depends on it. This applies at work, too. The better connected we are, the healthier our relationships and the higher quality of our working life. Additionally, the better our own performance, our teams and our organizations performance. Productivity is stifled when we don't have connection. Great managers and leaders foster strong connections with and between people, recognizing that engaging with others involves people more deeply at work.

The takeaway: If being better connected to your people is the cornerstone of engagement, employee relationship management must have its emphasis on the word *relationship*.

Chapter 9: The Strength in Numbers Is Collaboration

Welcome to the new cooperation. It's bigger, better, and more meaningful. Collaboration is the new teamwork. It's more productive and more innovation inspiring. Boundaryless collaboration speeds up problem solving and learning. It also enables improvements in business outcomes from productivity to innovation, revenues to retention. When you look over the fence, connect and then collaborate with your coworkers, your customers, your suppliers, perhaps even your competitors, you get a multiplier – a performance multiplier. People engage and the business benefits. Competitive advantage kicks in. The deeper the connections, the better the collaboration. This goes beyond teamwork: super collaboration allows for input from nontraditional sources. Great leaders manage at the fringe as well as at the core of the business.

The takeaway: In this chapter, we dig deep into the need for collaboration and take it beyond borders and into powerful partnerships. Further, faster, together, safely. Knock down silos and open the doors to other teams – inside and outside your business.

Chapter 10: Building Community: 1+1 = 3

The more connected we are, the more we collaborate, the more we yearn for communities of practice and communities of kindred spirits. We feel and perform better when we are part of something. Community brings engagement into the lifeblood of the business and your teams, enabling them to see past the immediacy of today's issues and into the future. Community creates an army of engaged minds striving for a common outcome – great results from great work.

The takeaway: When companies view community building as a steppingstone to engagement and therefore as a way of creating new levels of performance, it's a sign they have recognized the power of the "home-team advantage." Communities lift everyone up, together.

Chapter 11: Growing Capability: We Yearn to Learn

Continuous learning isn't just good for business; it's good for people's health and well-being and a key to life satisfaction. It's also good for continuous improvement. When managers and leaders learn how to coach, they enable and energize others, and you've got a cultural change that can turn into a movement. Coaching is another multiplier. It enables skill development, transformations, performance improvement, and engagement. Giving people opportunities to learn through experience and coaching can provide the learning element that they are thirsty for.

The takeaway: The 1.5.30 is a powerhouse tool for capability development, but coaching is king. Gone are the days of annual performance reviews. Routine check-ins build routine coaching into your culture. Ask all your people before they go home each day: Did you learn anything new today? Make sure they did.

Chapter 12: Freedom: The Great Facilitator

The most engaged people at work are those who have freer rein to do what needs to be done, without having to automatically defer to someone else. In the past, this has largely been the privilege of entrepreneurs and senior leaders, and their engagement scores showed. A truly HeadsUp manager's challenge is to step back and give people the freedom to think, to decide, to try, and to grow. Being a manager without taking a sense of freedom away from others is the challenge of the future. Manage to engage.

The takeaway: Check in rather than check up to create freedom rather than boundaries. The intersection of people and technology can absolutely free up people to be remarkable.

Chapter 13: Making a Difference: Engage. Enable. Energize.

Because every organization and workforce are different, and no two employees are the same, you need the right techniques for your workplace.

The takeaway: HeadsUp and the engagement scorecard of 2 Fs and 7 Cs offer the unique tools that engage, enable, and energize your organization. Together, these become the bedrock for long-term business prosperity as the outcome of engagement.

Conclusion

It's up to us, as leaders and managers, to understand and accept that everything we do influences engagement and, drawing on the HeadsUp tools, the toolkit of 2 Fs and 7 Cs, find new ways to explore and bring to bear the meaningful work experiences our people need. Now more than ever, we will reap what we sow. Let's sow the seeds of positive engagement so we can truly flourish in the future.

CHAPTER 1

People Matter: We Need a Healthier Way of Working

Having an engaging environment goes far beyond the workplace itself. When people feel a connection to their jobs, they are more willing to embrace bigger visions, ones that require them to take a leap of faith. They feel a part of something bigger than themselves. They engage in shaping the future. It's the great leader that makes that happen.

—Lorena Schoenfeld, Proudfoot chief of staff and executive director

Prior to COVID-19, and if you look closely at the cover page of Gallup's State of The Global Workplace report[1] published in 2017, in tiny print it says 85 percent of employees worldwide are not engaged or are actively disengaged in their job. With that bleak statistic, it's surprising that companies got any work done at all. Although increasing numbers of companies realize that what's good for people is good for business, something was clearly still amiss. During my 30 years of management consulting, I have pored over

---

[1] Gallup, 2017. *State of the Global Workplace Report.* https://www.slideshare.net/mobile/adrian-boucek/state-of-the-global-workplace-gallup-report-2017

study after global study looking for what is wrong – what businesses across the planet are doing (or not) to create and foster a happy, satisfied, and high-performing workforce. Sadly, the picture that emerged was anything but heartwarming: rather, we appeared to have been living through (and barely surviving) a continued Ice Age – categorized by disconnects, disenfranchisement, and disgruntlement; an epidemic of underengagement and ineffective management solutions. For the billions spent on engagement efforts, organizations had failed to engage with their people. As a result, people were not exactly chipper about showing up at work each day. Many had mentally checked out. We had an army of the "quit but stayed."

In early December 2019, when the pandemic was still nothing but an isolated bug, Klaus Schwab, founder and executive chairman of the World Economic Forum, was busy rallying his Davos cohorts into backing the Davos Manifesto 2020: The Universal Purpose of a Company in the Fourth Industrial Revolution.[2] He acknowledged that we needed a more all-encompassing declaration that included all stakeholders, not just shareholders, and the planet. This followed the Business Roundtable, announcing a few months earlier the release of a new Statement on the Purpose of a Corporation. It was signed by 181 CEOs who "commit to lead their companies for the benefit of all stakeholders – customers, employees, suppliers, communities and shareholders." Something was abuzz. "The American dream is alive, but fraying," said Jamie Dimon, chairman and CEO of JPMorgan Chase & Co. and chairman of Business Roundtable. The Roundtables website continued with the rest of his quote: "Major employers are investing in their workers and communities because they know it is the only way to be successful over the long term. These modernized principles reflect the business community's unwavering commitment to continue to push for an economy that serves all Americans," or the world, you could continue. This was being espoused from the highest echelon of corporations.

By mid-2020 when the pandemic had taken hold of the world economy and impacted the health of some 16 million people, Gallup,[3] the analytics and advisory firm, reported employee engagement at an all-time high: some 40 percent of employees surveyed, reported to be engaged and 13 percent were

---

[2] Klaus Schwab, 2019. *Davos Manifesto 2020: The Universal Purpose of a Company in the Fourth Industrial Revolution* (World Economic Forum, 2020). www.weforum.org/agenda/2019/12/davos-manifesto-2020-the-universal-purpose-of-a-company-in-the-fourth-industrial-revolution/

[3] WORKPLACE JULY 22, 2020 U.S. Employee Engagement Hits New High After Historic Drop BY JIM HARTER: https://www.gallup.com/workplace/316064/employee-engagement-hits-new-high-historic-drop.aspx

said to be actively disengaged. The headlines espoused the unusual jump in engagement. Unusual scores for unusual times. There was just one problem. A whopping 60 percent were still underengaged. And the numbers trended down again as the pandemic continued.

No Connections in Range

Our connectivity levels, a precursor for engagement, are far from ideal. The research shows that people are not willing to invest discretionary effort at work. Our internal sensors are continuously searching for and failing to find a connection, and this is costing businesses billions – in poor productivity, lost profits, accidents, theft, weakening brands, and lost opportunity. It's also costing people their emotional well-being. People feel they are flatlining at work. This disconnect to the world of work is a crisis of epic proportions. Whole populations of underengaged employees are sapping our economies, our health and their own happiness, and ultimately our success as individuals, communities, and even countries. While we know deep down that well-being at work affects every aspect of our lives, the answer to improving it remains elusive.

This must change. We cannot come out of a global economic meltdown and health crisis with a workforce feeling this underenthused. We can't change it if they remain that way. After the 2007–2008 financial crisis, our global business environment had fundamentally changed. And it has continued ever since:

1. *We must run leaner operations and be more innovative and creative to address business and customer needs concurrently.* An attitude of spending money consciously must be built into the fabric of an organization. Innovation and creativity demand this too. Focusing solely on cost-cutting and productivity has come at the expense of engagement. It cannot: a balance must be found. Maximizing all value must be the mantra.

2. *The workforce itself is a force of change.* Different employee values are emerging. The employee-employer relationship has changed. We must work with people differently as a new connected generation emerges and old work values disappear. Post a health crisis of the magnitude of COVID-19, the workforce is thinking fundamentally differently about work.

3. *Learning how to collaborate with new and different partners within and outside the organization is driving change, with new sources of value creation and new structures.* And yet, many of our businesses remain rigidly attached to the traditional structures. Companies have been drawn into a more collaborative world, an engagement economy where managers are no longer gatekeepers but guardians creating the context in which connections are formed.

4. *Growth has slowed in many traditionally high-growth markets, and it may not recover for some time (if at all).* The pandemic stopped growth in its tracks for many industries. This environment changes the way that consumers act, employees behave, and companies compete. How you engage employees in this conversation will plot your next trajectory.

5. *More stringent regulatory conditions and transparency requirements will persist as the world continues to adjust to the fallout of the 2007–2008 global financial crisis.* Risk management topped the business agenda at every level and function. We see this again. We know we must be more flexible and collaborative in both business and management models but still deliver on what feels like ever more constraining regulatory controls. These two opposing forces must be reconciled.

6. *We must rebuild confidence and trust within and outside our businesses.* Our personal and professional reputations require it. It is not just about the "greening" of businesses; we must be socially responsible to each other – doing good by doing right by people and the planet.

7. *Sustainability has become a common operating term, but many companies still need to learn how it will affect their businesses.* We know we must have a demonstrable social conscience. In that vein, engagement becomes a societal problem, and while the biggest consequences are felt in businesses (where it's easier to assign metrics), the deeper consequences are felt by people in their health, happiness, and well-being at home.

These are fundamental changes, not cursory adaptations. They will continue to deepen, and new, more pervasive issues will arrive. We must accept today is different. It is a new reality and less a new normal. With these changes, we must change the way we manage, lead, focus, and inspire our people. The way we engage must be different. Our management models, the way we motivate, connect, collaborate, define our strategies, develop our objectives, and make our decisions, must change.

Seeing People as Value and Valuable

We expect the underengaged people who routinely live through tumultuous times and crises to be the same people to lift us out of crises and deliver better results in this changing world. These same people are the silent workforce who kept our world moving, delivering our day-to-day needs such as health care, groceries, and bus rides so we could stay home and stay safe when so much had shut down during the great rolling lockdowns. They stepped up when the chips were down.

Unless we want a world in which people feel grossly undervalued, we must build businesses that are fit for people, where people can thrive. We need to manage to engage.

In this emerging "engagement economy," creating value may be the key to financial success, but making people feel valued at work is the key to unleashing passion – that raw ingredient needed to spur individuals' willingness to help their companies bounce back from recessions rapidly and build future success. Managers must help people invest their discretionary effort.

This book aims to help managers do that. It aims to help you routinely tap into people's discretionary effort – the effort employees consciously volunteer at work, to create value in your business. It is a call to action, a reminder that the future of business is (still) people.

We Need a New Scorecard That Drives Results

I will explore this through a formula that I call MI-9 tools of engagement: the nine key drivers available to a manager to manage to engage, improve their team's performance, enable people to do great work, and achieve remarkable results.

- MI is an acronym for Management Innovation but is also MY because only we can control how we manage to engage.
- The 9 refers to nine tools that are at our disposal daily to trigger engagement. They are not just required in organizations to improve results, but also necessary for people if everyone is to bring their best to work each day. Importantly, they mostly cost nothing but your time.

Seen through the lens of engagement, these nine tools help us look at what switches people on and off day to day. Seen through the lens of performance improvement, they help us see the connection between how we run our businesses, people's engagement, and the results we achieve:

1. Fair trade
2. A cause
3. Clean and meaningful infrastructure
4. Confidence
5. Connection
6. Collaboration
7. Community
8. Capability
9. Freedom

If people really are our greatest assets in business, our management models must reflect this; in other words, the way that we manage must lead to engagement. The result should be that our management models (how work is led – the practices and processes we use to manage and lead) become a source of competitive advantage. Our management models must deliver results, just as we expect our business and operating models (how work is done), to do so.

Interestingly, these nine tools of engagement, which we can harness as the fuel for transformative results, are available with almost no financial cost. All that's needed is management effort – our effort.

Work: A Four-Letter Word

For the majority of the population, work is a four-letter word – a cuss word. It is something we feel forced to do rather than a choice. Combine this sentiment with the current business environment and the drive to cut costs during and after the pandemic, and we have the perfect storm to create an even greater disengaged workforce – one that is least likely to deliver the productivity gains we need, the turnarounds and business recoveries we strive for, and the business growth and innovation organizations crave. Just as we engage in productivity drives, we must manage to engage. Businesses must put serious backing behind their belief that their people are their greatest assets, by creating businesses built with people in mind. Businesses fit for people. In the organization of the future, productivity and engagement will go hand in hand.

The MI-9 tools must be the foundation for any management model if we are to resolve the chronic lack of engagement in people at work. We must build them into the way we manage and lead. Companies that don't practice collaboration or help their people connect productively at work; that don't recognize the need to engage their people in meaningful activities and help them find a truer purpose; that haven't found a way to manage their business to bring out the best in their people, will surely fail.

Soul-Destroying Survey Findings

Let's step back in time for a moment. In 2003, Proudfoot released the results of its Global Organization Assessment Survey.[4] At the time I was president of the firm's People Solutions practice, so I led the compilation of these surveys and saw the results firsthand. They were anything but encouraging. Combining the responses of over 5,000 people surveyed at the launch of their change programs, from a range of industries, the survey's top-line findings highlighted a startling trend that transcended national boundaries: a global, fundamental development need to address our ability to engage people. When the same survey was conducted seven years later, Proudfoot saw much the same results. Fast forward another seven years, and although some of the survey questions had now been modernized to unpack what people needed to better engage in business, the results were still dire.

The 2018 research confirmed five things:

1. *Changes at work are not managed smoothly.* This was the conclusion of three-quarters of the 2018 survey participants. Organizations were clearly failing to prepare people for – and execute – change. Respondents certainly saw the need for change, but less than 40 percent were confident this would happen. Even relatively straightforward changes to processes or procedures – the fundamental building blocks of any company – were a bumpy ride (just 28 percent said these went smoothly). If we can't get things right at the process level, what hope is there at an organizational level?

---

[4] Proudfoot, 2003. Global Organization Assessment Survey.

2. *The billions spent on infrastructure were not working for people.* Despite the billions invested worldwide in process improvement, technology, and HR, and in systems to report information and enhance communication between people, the research suggested these were not having the desired impact. Half reported they did not have the skills and knowledge they needed to continually improve their performance. Organizations had focused too much on implementing technology and not enough on the impact on people or enabling them to use the technology. Worse still, they had not engaged people in the technology changes early or often.

3. *Communication was still ineffective.* "The many" saw communication (external and internal) continuing to need dramatic improvement. From the 1970s, when communication was first ranked highly on the list of "change disarmers" to 2018, surveys found our ability to communicate information effectively throughout an organization was poor. In many organizations, nothing had changed. Without great communication, how could you possibly engage? Without understanding the role communication has in building employee confidence, you would not engage.

4. *It is a two-way street.* Almost two-thirds of mid-level managers saw a lack of input from "the many" in strategic priorities. Participation was absent. Too often we still operated in a top-down world. The few dictate the future of the many; people removed from the guts of the company were deciding the business's future. Decision-making was hampered by overly complex processes and a lack of freedom to make and act on decisions, and more than half believed getting things done depended more on who rather than what you knew.

5. *80 percent of people lacked faith in leadership.* Further supporting the finding that lower tiers of employees too often feel left out of the loop, survey respondents generally felt leaders' communication effectiveness to be poor, while a third couldn't confidently say that their immediate superiors were preparing their organization effectively for the future. This dismal result is depressing for management teams, to be sure.

The surveys continued to tell us, we'd yet to get it right. The many were still managed by the few, and most were pretty rankled by it. This was a people crisis 100 years in the making, from the time modern management was born. Alexander Proudfoot saw the same issues in 1946 when he founded Proudfoot to address these concerns. As a McKinsey consultant, he felt it was time to move from strategy consulting to implementation consulting – how to get the many on board with the few. The difference this time round (postpandemic) is the urgency needed to address it. Unless we do things differently now, this people crisis will slow the recovery of future economic recessions and crisis, and revisit us with monotonous regularity. Huge proportions of our working populations will mentally and emotionally shut down.

The Problem with Organizations Is O-r-g-a-n-i-z-a-t-i-o-n

Studies such as these highlight the many reasons for underengagement at work. Think of the word *organization*. It projects associations with orderliness, buildings filled with the rank and file of people doing as they have been instructed to do.

The way work is done lacks humanization. Much of a company's focus has been on organizational characteristics and outcomes: the stuff that makes an organization fit. But what about the healthy side? The ability to create a workplace and culture that brings out the best in its employees. Something I think many managers and leaders want to create and inspire, but struggle to find the time and energy to work on once the "day to day" job is done. Or they simply do not know how. Health is not embedded in the DNA of a firm the same way fitness is required.

I Love Being Managed! Not

How often do people get home from work full of enthusiasm for how they've been managed that day? Shouting to their families how much they enjoyed being managed today? Probably rarely! We have built our businesses around management models built for the exception rather than the rule – people needing to be coerced and policed into doing a good job, needing to be structured and controlled. People hearing avoidance management, "I need you to do this because my boss needs it," rather than "We need to do this because the business requires it," or better still, "because it's the right thing to do."

In reality, few people actually need to be managed this way, and even fewer work well under its dark shadow. In the new engagement economy, people become remarkable when they feel well prepared and know what's expected. We have seen during the great lockdown that work continued unsupervised. Our businesses had whole management teams stay home, and the organizations remained standing.

Volunteerism: The New Competitive Advantage

Today, businesses filled with engaged people – those whose people voluntarily invest their discretionary effort at work – are still the exception. But we know that those who achieve volunteerism hold a strong competitive advantage, while their more traditional peers continue to lose ground, as their employees defect or continue to take a salary without giving their all. It's quite astounding how many businesses are still tethered by inertia to the old ways of managing people.

Clean and Meaningful, Not Lean and Mean

Gone are the days of a strictly ordered workplace where a productive and efficient workforce clocked in, did what they were paid to do, and clocked out again. This low baseline had all but vanished years ago. Fast forward to the COVID-19 pandemic, and we saw whole teams rise up to challenging times, to change needing implementation overnight. They proved they could do it. Those underengaged people whom many managers believed were change resistant or fatigued made a world of difference. The danger is, of course, that the businesses will revert to type. They will fall back into the slow-move world. But where's the incentive to keep the new world and not slip back? We must create one.

Engaged people will willingly lead their companies out of economic holes. They will innovate and create. Engaged people will be at the finish line (if such a place exists); they will also have the reward of working for a fit and healthy business, even a happy one.

Sadly, most businesses have been far from this ideal: the environment they fostered does not inspire people to innovate and help inspire the future. One must ask the question, did the quest for productivity cost us the hearts and minds of our people? The survey results reflect an astounding yes. That could cost companies a great deal more than just the loss of their soul.

Consider a trip down the corporate history lane with the well-known story of 3M. If you were in business at the birth of the Post-It note, you might remember 3M as a business built on novel ideas. But that wasn't the case when James McNerney took the helm in 2001. While the former General Motors executive was able to rejuvenate 3M's share price, it's widely believed that he failed to reenergize its people. After a transformation program built on downsizing and efficiency gains, innovation had all but come to a standstill. It was only after George Buckley replaced McNerney in 2005 and reestablished people as the key drivers of success that it began to report record results once again. The contrast is stark: people as part of a systemic, process-driven culture versus people as the force of a culture that respects the use of processes but isn't a slave to them. In the latter case, the organizational infrastructure works for people, freeing them up to be remarkable – and creating a human competitive edge. This is just a great baseline example of a business that has now lasted the long tail and survived the ups and downs of another decade and a half. It's this leg work years ago that provide for the stories of corporate longevity.

Of course, today everybody talks about Google's 20 percent time, allowing people to work on their own ideas. But it doesn't have to be this big. It can be day-to-day actions, within the day-to-day role of people, that can bring about remarkable changes in results.

If the Pants Fit, Wear Them

A fit business is a healthy workplace comprising collaborative teams, which are powered by common sense, common values, and trust – energized by initiative at every level, and aware of what they're aiming for, and how to use their business infrastructure to best advantage.

A fit business has a highly engaged and collaborative leadership team whose members are in sync with one another and their teams. They cultivate a sense of purpose that is greater than profit and financial results. It is a healthy business bubbling with opportunity for sales and human growth, powered by those who show up for work – and who are all in, every day.

In such a business, people feel known, cared about, helped, inspired, led, and mobilized – and have the freedom to act for the good of the organization.

Able to use their own discretion, they in turn volunteer their discretionary effort. Everyone goes HeadsUp. They lift their noses out of their devices and connect with people.

A fit and healthy business is characterized by a different way of managing and a different management model. Managers who can bring focus to people – but will then get out of the way and let them achieve – will win the war on talent.

Fit and Healthy – The Human Competitive Edge

The drive to innovate management practices has been slow to build. The surveys show it. The underenthused demonstrate it. Why? For the most part, businesses continue to recruit, train, structure, lead, reward, recognize, decide, develop, and grow their people in much the same way they did decades ago

It's easy to mistake IT investment and new HR processes for progress. But has anything fundamentally changed in the way a business is run and managed? We haven't invested in thinking about the management models and their ability to promote individuals' discretionary effort – that propensity to go the extra mile. But the model drives management behavior, and management behavior drives employee behavior and engagement. Companies lose out as a result, because this discretionary effort could and should be their competitive advantage.

Imagine the advantage you are sitting on if you address this.

The Chariots Are on Fire

People don't want to be managed the same way we have managed for the past 100 or even 1,000 years. Egypt's pyramids, Rome's Coliseum, and Henry Ford's automotive factory were built by versions of management that are still in use today.

The imperative now is for management innovation – not just product, process, or service innovation. The successful employers of the future will be living, breathing organisms filled with fluid clusters of people – not a series of organizational boxes that can be mapped neatly on a chart.

But before we can reinvent our management models, we must understand what these new models should be inspired by: not shiny new systems and technology, but human emotions and the spirit of what it means to actually be human. Humanize. Optimize. Digitize. In that order. Engaging people to enable results.

Financial Times columnist John Kay has written an entire book on this phenomenon (*Obliquity*): the idea of using a more indirect approach to achieve goals when the parameters are complex.[5] He notes that this can apply when "the effect of our actions depends on the ways in which others respond to them."

Good, Better, Best, Never Let It Rest. . .

Engagement is about people, and wherever people are involved, complexity abounds. So, the aim here is not to prescribe a new management model, but rather to prompt you to see better ways of managing. All too often, we view engagement as an activity – or worse still, the ultimate outcome, when in fact, engagement is the very lifeblood of what should pump through the veins of our organizational DNA. It is the enabler of results, built ubiquitously into our everyday behavior.

In response to talent shortages, or economic fights for survival, and the growing need to build a good brand as an employer, companies have realized that they must now put as much effort into wooing and looking after employees as they do into attracting and nurturing customers. The problem is, leaders have so much coming at them today, they struggle to bring pragmatic people solutions to fruition. Many are wanting to or even hoping they can but falling flat as they try to wrestle the chaos to deliver their day-to-day workloads and engage their people. The two go hand in hand. One begets the other, and that's the problem to solve.

Brand continuity, strategy development, marketing, HR, and operations must come together to bring the employee experience into the same value as we hold the customer experience and shareholder goals.

A lot of work has been done on the customer experience, so now it's time to apply the same effort and innovation to the employee experience: how they experience work in your organization or team. At every level. Because we also know, the underengaged populate every level in the organization. And when we address it, it can't simply be focused on implementing flexible working, bonuses,

[5] John Kay, *Obliquity: Why Our Goals Are Best Achieved Indirectly* (New York: Penguin Press, 2011).

bean bags, and a ping-pong table, but in making people feel valued, inspired, and enabled to make their mark, so they can bring their best selves to work.

The aim of this book is to help you find a way to that point: where everyone in your organization "gets engaged." It's a significant journey: an all or nothing experience. There are no degrees of engagement. Just as with safety, you are either safe or you're not; you either have an engaged workforce or you don't. There are no half measures.

The Workplace Scorecard – Scoring the Top, from the Bottom Up

Let's get back to our nine engagement tools: MI-9. The workplace scorecard of the future will score all nine elements: fair Trade, cause, clean and meaningful infrastructure, confidence, connection, collaboration, community, capability, and freedom.

The vision with MI-9 is that in the future it will be your people who complete the scorecard – the many, not the few. Your organization's score will appear in the annual report. There will be a Quality of Work-Life Index and an Employee Confidence Index. The value of a strong infrastructure that works for people rather than against them will be recognized and implemented. In his book, *Macrowikinomics: New Solutions for a Connected Planet*, Don Tapscott emphasizes the importance of a true "infostructure," which supports better decision-making and capability development.[6] If the goal is to reenthuse people, then the very least we can do is give them the tools to connect, brainstorm, and share ideas in new and easy ways.

In the future, employee advocacy will grow in importance as people are enabled to be their best and feel their best at work. Strong communication; a clearly understood vision; knowing they are making a difference and where their role fits within the grand scheme; feedback on their performance; the ability to play to your strengths; managers and leaders who really listen and care – all of these elements contribute to employee advocacy. All the evidence suggests that a sense of freedom, of control over one's destiny, plays a crucial role in achieving engagement and inspiring that advocacy. It energizes you to go all-in.

---

[6] Anthony D. Williams and Don Tapscott, *Macrowikinomics: New Solutions for a Connected Planet* (New York: Penguin Press, 2010).

But none of these factors in isolation will achieve this. The problem of engagement is so great, the solutions so wide reaching, that all are necessary in some degree, and no single fix will be sufficient.

The MI-9 formula proposed here is a starting point. Those companies that can demonstrate all nine engagement triggers and calibrate them to their people's needs can expect to be able to demonstrate higher levels of connectivity between people, a key ingredient critical to people's success, health, and happiness at work and a critical means to volunteerism and engagement. *Fair trade* will extend beyond the concepts we think of today: to the point that giving employees a fair deal and a good experience at work ranks as highly to outsiders as companies' growth, profit, and environmental and social responsibility credentials, for ESG.

Engage, Enable, Energize. What Does MI-9 Feel Like to People at Work?

To understand what all of this might look and feel like to the people who work for an engagement-focused employer, let's break down the nine engagement tools of the MI-9 formula into the 2 Fs and 7 Cs, looking first at the 2 Fs. Here's how your team might view you through the lens of the MI-9:

1. **Fair trade:** I do a fair day's work for a fair day's return. My return on the discretionary effort I volunteer is rewarded both financially and personally. I know I contributed, I know what I do counts, and I am given a fair go!

2. **Freedom:** I feel in control of my destiny; I can think, feel, and share. I have a voice. I can have an opinion. In my world, I can agree or disagree, but then I commit. I know I am seen as a responsible adult.

These 2 Fs mean that companies will be obliged to engage in fair trade in all relationships across the value chain and beyond. We can expect to see fair trade commissions with a remit as serious as those of human rights and worker rights commissions today. The means will count as much as the end. The businesses of the future must be fit for human consumption, a magnet for talent, ideas, improvement, innovation, and growth, producing better results with less profit consumption. Isn't that the aim? A win-win? And investors will respond accordingly: money flows where engagement goes.

Cs of MI-9 will also be tangible to people in the workplace ᵤᵣ ᵤₑ ₗᵤₜᵤre. Colleagues will be able to vote one another in or out of the company, based on how well they fit the culture and ethos. Underengaged colleagues will no longer be tolerated. Work will be open-sourced: the right people matched to activities and projects based on strengths and capability. The great work will go to those with great engagement. The business of the future will grow because its people are alive and growing, bubbling with enthusiasm to be a part of something valuable and meaningful to them. People will feel valued.

The seven Cs will look and feel something like this to your teams:

1. **Cause:** I have a purpose. I make a difference. I know I'm working for something bigger than profits, productivity, or production. What I do and how I do it contributes to the greater business, to a cause. I know I must make my world a better place – both at work and outside work. I know I need to keep my company fit, to keep my world healthy and my mind happy.

2. **Clean and meaningful infrastructure:** I feel my workplace works for me, not against me. I have clean / perfected processes and policies to help me. Nothing stops me from doing my job well. I have clarity on what's important and what I need to do. I know where to go if I need help. I have an infrastructure built with me in mind. My workplace also fits with the outside world; it is responsible.

3. **Confidence:** I feel my doubts are resolved, my world is transparent, and communication is fluid. I know when things are going well or not, and I know when I've done a great job. People understand me. I trust the people around me. I trust my managers and leaders. I have one foot in the present and one foot in the future; I am set up for success.

4. **Connection:** I am in partnership with my colleagues and peers – we connect. I have a great relationship with my co-workers and managers, my customers and suppliers. I see the connection between the micro vision of my team with the macro vision of our leadership.

5. **Collaboration:** My workplace is a network of alliances working toward one common purpose: to be the best we can be. If one fails, we all fail; together we succeed. We follow the best, not just the boss. We come together naturally to achieve our results.

6. **Community:** I feel I have a network of support. We build communities of practice, of expertise, of problem solving. We are social and professional in our community building. We bring the outside world in,

and we go to the outside world to challenge ourselves to learn and grow from others.

7. **Capability:** I am capable of performing my role, my job. I am learning all the time, from others, from across the business and from the outside. I am surrounded by capable people. Because of this, I feel I am growing, and our results show we are growing. I work for a capable organization. I know we are set up for success.

Fueling Your Fitness Program

MI-9 are the tools to engagement at work; they become the triggers, the fuel for achieving results; when people experience these 2 Fs and 7 Cs, they feel they had a great day at work, achieved what they set out to achieve, learned something new or how to do something better, and laughed a lot. They feel that the discretionary effort they volunteered, the effort they invested, is worth it.

In the business of the future, engagement will grow one person at a time until whole communities of spirit, experience, and accomplishment appear and work in concert with each other. This is a grassroots movement. Everyone will make his or her contribution; companies will engage and succeed because of people who are captivated. The organization of the future will be a living organism fit for people with an engaged state of mind who volunteer their best. What a feeling to aspire to. What a cause for leaders to rise for. What a reason to go all-in and manage to engage.

If you think these MI-9 tools might foster chaos more than engagement, consider this. Engagement need not be monopolized by the nature of a business, nor by its outward appearance of control, because engagement does not come at the expense of control. It comes with the right degree of control for your business to be safe and productive.

And consider Google and what *The New York Times* dubbed its "Quest to Build a Better Boss."[7] In a nutshell, the company's position was that a boss's particular expertise is of little value if their management behavior falls short. And while even they have come under scrutiny, that just reinforces the elusiveness of engagement and the need to continually work for it.

---

[7] Adam Bryant, "Google's Quest to Build a Better Boss," *New York Times* (March 12, 2011). https://www.nytimes.com/2011/03/13/business/13hire.html

The common thread is that people will invest themselves at work and voluntarily give their best when the right engagement triggers are in place and they feel free to do so.

Engagement should be a priority for all organizations and their leaders: there is nothing to lose, but everything to gain. Prioritizing how you bring engagement to your management is probably the single most effective way to change your organizations outcomes and retention. The more you manage to engage, the more you transition from manager to leader.

This period is the most significant opportunity of our lifetime to reboot the end-to-end way we operate. In short, our total operating model, including the processes, capabilities, management tools, technology, and organization structure we choose, as well as how we manage, lead, decide, and how we engage, enable, and energize our teams to deliver our results. Fit and healthy.

The world changed in 2020. Everything about it changed. The question is, "Did you change?" To recover better and with resilience requires different solutions than any other time in your management career and likely in our history. This time a radical transformation is needed. A people renaissance. But unlocking their potential demands something new of managers, something that needs to be measured differently – something more engaging. We need a management model built for a postpandemic world and focused on nine essential ingredients that spark engagement – pragmatic solutions that not only create engagement but become self-sustaining and create better leaders.

---

1. **Start your engagement journey – whether that's across the organization or in a particular department, area, or team. Convene a team being careful to ensure everyone can participate and present a problem statement you want to solve, then free them up to crowdsource the solution.**

2. **Assess your own and your teams' current levels of discretionary effort. How much of themselves are your people giving today? There are no assessment tools for this, just observation and gut feeling. Get out and look, get people to talk about it. Ask them.**

FIGURE 1.1   Things You Need to Do Right Now.

3. Using the following page, take each of the MI-9 triggers and decide how well you currently score against each of them. Invite people to write up their own report cards on your business.

4. Select the most critical of the Fs and Cs to your workplace success. Seek a range of opinions about how to address these in your workplace: ideas of how you can better develop a workplace where people can feel the MI-9 engagement triggers at work.

5. Encourage your team to lead this movement. Let them decide if this is worth pursuing and then try to leave the 'how' to your people.

Score your workplace:

This can be scored in a way that suits your particular workplace. For example, place the percentage of people who you believe would agree with the statements under each dimension. Alternatively, place a percentage that indicates how close you believe your business is to displaying this characteristic: (e.g., 80 percent of my people would agree with these statements; we are probably 60 percent of the way to running our business with this in mind, 'running' being defined as the way we motivate, connect, collaborate, define our strategies, develop our objectives, and make our decisions at work).

Your workplace report card: 2 Fs and 7 Cs

_____ Fair trade: I do a fair day's work for a fair day's return. My return on the discretionary effort I volunteer is rewarded both financially and personally. I know I contribute, I know what I do counts. I am given a fair go!

_____ Freedom: I feel in control of my destiny, I can think, feel and share. I have a voice. I can have an opinion. In my world, I can agree or disagree, but then I commit. I am trusted as a responsible adult.

_____ A Cause: I have a purpose. I know I make a difference. I am working for something bigger than profits, productivity, or production. What I do and how I do it contributes to a cause. I know I must make my world a better place to be – both at and outside work. I know I need to keep my company healthy, to keep myself and my world healthy.

_____ Confidence: I feel my doubts are resolved, my world is transparent, and communication is fluid. I know when things are going well or not, and I know when I've done a great job. I trust the people around me. I trust my managers and leaders. I have one foot in the present and one foot in the future. I feel I am set up for success.

_____ A Clean infrastructure: I feel my workplace works for and not against me. There are clean processes, systems, procedures, and policies to help me. Nothing stops me from doing my job well. I have clarity about what's important and what I need to do. I know where to go if I need help. I am supported by an infrastructure that has been built with me in mind. My workplace also fits with the outside world; it is responsible.

_____ Connections: I am in a partnership with my colleagues and peers; we connect. I feel worthy, I have a great relationship with my co-workers and managers, my customers and suppliers. People understand me.

_____ Collaboration – My workplace is a network of alliances working toward a common purpose: to be the best we can be. If one fails, we all fail; together we succeed. We follow the best, not just the boss. We come together naturally to achieve our results.

_____ Community: I feel I have a network of support with a community spirit. We build communities of practice, of expertise, of problem solving, and involvement. We are social and professional. We bring the outside world in and contribute to the world outside.

_____ Capability: I know I am capable of performing my role, my job. I am learning all the time from others, from across the business, and from the outside. I am surrounded by capable people. Because of this, I feel I am growing, and our results show we are growing. I work for a capable organization. I know we are set up for success.

CHAPTER 2

The Ice Age: It's Alive and Well at Work

There is . . . compelling evidence that work has an inherently beneficial impact on an individual's state of health. In particular, the recent review 'Is work good for your health and wellbeing?' concluded that work was generally good for both physical and mental health and wellbeing. It showed that work should be 'good work' which is healthy, safe, and offers the individual some influence over how work is done and a sense of self-worth. Overall, the beneficial effects of work were shown to outweigh the risks and to be much greater than the harmful effects of long-term worklessness or prolonged sickness absence.

—Dame Carol Black – author of *Working for a Healthier Tomorrow*[1]

In their book *Connected: The Surprising Power of Our Social Networks*, scientists Nicholas Christakis and James Fowler detail the way that people influence each other's happiness.[2] Their research (and our own common sense) tells us that we have a profound influence on one another's behavior, tastes, health, wealth, beliefs, even weight!

---

[1] Dame Carol Black, *Working for a Healthier Tomorrow: Dame Carol Black's Review of the Health of Britain's Working Age Population* (Stationery Office Books, 2008).
[2] James H. Fowler and Nicholas Christakis, *Connected: The Surprising Power of Our Social Networks and How They Shape Our Lives* (New York: Little, Brown and Company, 2009).

My conclusion was also common sense – we should all be much more aware of how we affect others at home, at work and at play. What you say and do affects results – for better or for worse. Each minute you allow your teams to be under-engaged, you create toxins in your business. We all know the impact of a misplaced or poorly expressed thought on one another's emotions. And as humans, we are natural influencers and imitators. If a simple yawn is contagious, think of the effect of your emotions at work.

A Few Bad Apples. . .

Management is an emotional, influential contagion. Hundreds of studies highlight the relationship between a manager and team engagement. Evidence abounds that the manager's state of mind affects a team's state of mind, even their happiness. And don't think happiness doesn't count. It does.

Let's define happiness in this context as a positive mood. Think then of how a positive mood is associated with team performance: productive behavior, increased creativity, and more efficient decision-making. We don't need scientific evidence to confirm that when a leader is in a positive mood, their team's performance improves. People in a positive mood get better results. They are also more likely to be engaged, just as a team drawn down by a negative mood is more likely not engaged. People connect more willingly and positively with happy people. It's human nature to avoid people and teams who are unhappy and negative. The grumpy guy gets left behind or simply becomes team solo, if not, people on the same team eventually opt out – physically or emotionally.

Tony Schwartz reminds us of this in his book, *The Way We're Working Isn't Working*.[3] Sadly, bad always trumps good, and so the unhappy get the upper hand. We humans focus on bad more than good, and negative moods spread like pollutants, more rapidly and more potently than positive moods.

So, it stands to reason that a happy workforce is a better workforce. While happiness in isolation is not the solution to engagement, it can certainly set you on a bright road to a better future.

It really does takes just one bad apple to rot the entire cart.

---

[3] Catherine McCarthy, Jean Gomes, and Tony Schwartz, *The Way We're Working Isn't Working: The Four Forgotten Needs That Energize Great Performance* (New York: Free Press, 2010).

The Freezing of the Global Workforce

It's clear we had problems before the 2007–2008 global financial meltdown and prior to the great 2020 global health crisis. They are bookends to a people crisis evident in both decades. Too many employees, mentally, had one foot out the door, reluctantly sucking it up and soldiering on rather than *showing up* in their jobs. People were frozen in a perpetual state of disgruntlement. The human Ice Age was already upon us.

The pandemic placed us in a precarious position – to once again be pre-occupied by the economy – saving money, cutting costs, heads down. History stands to repeat itself. Our work climate could become all the chillier: connectivity dropping, engagement scores dragging. As Gallup points out, the average percentage of engaged employees worldwide is just 13 percent in their 2017 State of the Global Workplace, leaving 87 percent of us who are just going through the motions![4]

If the best we can hope for is that just 13 percent of the workforce around us is fully tuned in and passionate about what they're doing, it's going to be an uphill struggle to push past the emotions of the neutral and disengaged and feel good about our work to the point that we're inclined to give more, or give a hoot.

A survey of 3,300 employees across 14 countries by Dale Carnegie Training in 2016 found that 40 percent of all employees were poised to leave their jobs within a year. In February of 2020, prepandemic, according to a *Forbes* article referencing the 2020 Engagement & Retention Report from Achievers, that number was 64 percent. And the hardship for employers is that the best performers usually move on, taking their skills, knowledge, and enthusiasm with them. If unemployment is high, this should be a frightening statistic – what if the underengaged have no other option but to stay?

A World on the Run

Let's face it: Today, we're continuously up against some form of challenge. We work in a cyclical world of ups and downs. Businesses must weather recession, recovery, and postrecessionary times. Now health pandemics as well.

---

[4]Gallup, 2017. State of the Global Workplace Report. www.slideshare.net/mobile/adrianboucek/state-of-the-global-workplace-gallup-report-2017.

But whatever the financial climate, the importance of good people remains constant. The two challenges – financial and human sustainability – have to be balanced. The second cannot be overlooked in favor of the first.

Yet too often this is what happens. While many businesses may voice the importance they place on improving employee engagement, few have discovered (new) ways to address it, opting for what they can affect rapidly like perks, incentives, and policies. And many firms may think they are impacting engagement, when all they have really done is improved employment terms or introduced a new wellness program – whatever is in vogue.

But if someone feels unhappy, overlooked, and undervalued at work – which, when you scratch beneath the surface of the surveys, is often the root cause of underengagement – band-aids aren't going to heal the wounds.

As managers and leaders, we need to keep evolving our own skills to keep pace with the changing mood at work and make progress on reversing the general disgruntlement still seen in most workplaces.

Navigating the Perfect Storm

In the past, employers worked hard at trying to solve the revolving door of employee attrition, forever looking to find ways to plug the holes that leaked people. Companies faced a perfect storm: a need to keep costs down; the potential loss of top talent; and the prospect of being left with disengaged, poor performers who have nowhere else to go. All this at a time when markets were being disrupted left, right, and center, and businesses were supposed to be transforming and innovating – something that demands passion and commitment! Here we go again. The storm has taken on a new shape, but the outcome is the same – a virtual landscape of disenchanted. The statistics show it and the conversations in private chatrooms are saying it.

Skill Up or Sink

If you are relying on a disconnected and disgruntled workforce to restore, reinvent, repurpose, reposition, or any other r word for your post–COVID-19 business, you need to be a skilled manager to achieve these ambitious goals – especially given all the other workplace pressures of safety, health, cash, and costs.

The cynic in me sees a *back to the future* new reality:

- *It's an edgier workplace.* Feelings of disconnectedness are compounded by rising anxiety levels caused by continued swings in the economy. Emotions are high, uncertainty and apprehension rule, creating an edgier workplace where conflict and discontent thrive.

- *As a manager in this underengaged workplace, you'd better love conflict and negative contagions, because that will continue to be your world unless something gives.* In this tough world, you need more tolerance, less cynicism, better control of stress levels, and exceptionally sharp connectivity skills. You need to be able to diffuse issues rapidly and arbitrate disharmony with ease.

- *There are silent soldiers at work.* People's confidence in the institutions that employ them is at an all-time low. The workforce is more pessimistic. Disgruntlement is compounded by the stress in businesses. As a result, people are becoming silent soldiers who no longer question or suggest better ways of doing business.

- *Energy zappers are draining work's life force.* It's the energy zapper managers should fear most. Those who sap the energy of others, who dismiss each new initiative, person, or idea because they're too jaded and cynical to welcome any kind of change. They see a problem to every solution. Far from being benign, energy zappers are a force of destruction halting employers' efforts to improve. They turn good news into bad and bad news into another reason why they should be disgruntled.

Managers must find a way to deal with these people. They must seek them out and give them a platform to engage or say goodbye. They must pee or get off the potty – you can't afford to waste energy on these people. If you handle this well, it will send out a strong (and positive) message to others. Netflix has led the way – brilliant jerks are not welcome. You respect everyone when you get the right people on the bus.

A Breath of Fresh Air

Let's talk generation "Why?" Much has been written about the impact and expectations of millennials in the workplace. Compared to Generation Xers, upcoming generations think, work, network, and communicate differently.

They're influencing the way we do business and are influencing other people in our businesses. They should influence you, as a manager and a leader today. They can bring new energy.

Although it's dangerous to generalize too far, millennials are often characterized by a particular blend of confidence; they also have more vehicles to voice how they feel and expect to challenge the status quo and question decisions. But before you try to bring this dynamic force under control, or any cohort trying to affect change, consider their willingness to challenge what's come before them could be a springboard for positive change and a new era of engagement.

The challenge for established managers is learning how to give these forces of energy just enough of a steer to keep the ship on course while enabling the exceptional, unexpected results that can come from bringing different people to problems and diverse approaches to solutions – bringing many viewpoints to old problems to generate new solutions.

In my business, I've cut through several layers to work directly with these team members, and I love it. They have little concern for position and more concern for contributing. They speak up and step up when needed. What they lack in knowledge and experience they make up for in curiosity. What young next-gen leader doesn't want to sit on a team that includes the CEO or upper manager?

Second Acts

Energy flows best across mixed teams, where different ages, gender, ethnic groups, and perspectives complement each other to create something greater than the sum of the parts. In addition to race, age, or gender, diversity is a thinking issue. The ability to bring many points of view around a challenge. Longer-serving team members in the final stages of their careers are important assets and could help younger team members propel new ideas forward because they know how things work. Many also want to leave a legacy. Managed the right way, an organization's next superstars could emerge from your more mature ranks.

I'm Gonna Make You a Star

Some employees will be with you all the way, fighting to turn the business around or maintain its current position in the continued market turbulence.

They are likely to bring you the next great idea, work with you to develop the next success story, and execute to make sure the business survives and thrives against the odds. They are the people who bring energy to adversity, who encourage those around them, who leave the gossip and politics to the disaffected. They agree or disagree but commit because they know that leaning forward is better than standing still or worse still, sitting back.

These are your stars. Make sure they know it. Find out who they are, and fast. These are the keepers – those who need your encouragement and support to continue to work as hard and as thoughtfully as they do during the rough times, surrounded by energy zappers and silent soldiers. They lend their discretionary effort easily and voluntarily. But be warned. This isn't a burgeoning population; in fact, it's very scarce.

Don't Forget to Look at Yourself

A more sobering thought is how the picture looks from the top. Without engaged motivated leadership from above, how likely is it that people will find new passion in their work? Yet people feel jaded at all levels of organizations, which makes it doubly hard to drive change.

Coincidentally, while I was writing this, I opened my Facebook page to see a status update from an old colleague, a senior executive reporting directly to his chief executive officer. It said: "It's only Monday, can't wait for the week to end." No one is immune to feeling dead behind the eyes at work. What goes around comes around if we don't stop the vicious circle now.

So How Do We Break the Cycle?

As Chip and Dan Heath, the authors of *Switch: How to Change Things When Change Is Hard* note, facts don't change people – feelings do.[5] The facts surrounding engagement have been buried in the headlines for decades, but the feelings are living themselves out in your workplace right now, and it's costing

---

[5] Chip Heath and Dan Heath, *Switch: How to Change Things When Change Is Hard* (New York: Broadway Books, 2010).

your business in cold, hard results. It's the reason your transformations fail and your people give up.

So, although the world of business has spent vast amounts of money on HR programs, on training, on employee benefits, it looks as though investments have been in the wrong areas. We must discover the real triggers of engagement in our workplaces and remove the things that don't engage. Like the naysayers and naggers, our businesses are punctuated with roadblocks and barriers to achievement. It's too easy to complain; for many of us it's second nature. We gripe about our bosses, our colleagues, and if we're managers about the people who work for us. Policies, politics, or processes – we moan about them all. About how hard we work or the hours we put in. The people who wrong us, or don't notice us, or don't pull their weight. But perhaps that's because we see ourselves on the outside. It's easy to complain about something being done to us; something we don't feel responsible for, or in control of. And misery loves company, hence all the muttering that goes on in bars after hours, or more recently, in private video sessions and What's App. One thing human nature has taught us is that we are encouraged (or not discouraged) to focus on the bad, we perpetuate negative situations. Sometimes it's almost as though we welcome something to gripe about: self-fulfilling prophecies of doom and gloom.

This is what nags away at culture, at the newbies on your teams, at the guys who are borderline. It can become the reason your engagement remains low – there is a glass ceiling erected by a core group of gripers who keep the lid on and prevent others breaking out and getting engaged. Do something about it. Do it now. If you read nothing more, break the glass.

Start with Common Complaints That Undermine Employee Confidence

If we break down the most common employee gripes, we see familiar themes emerging which significantly affect people's confidence at work. Together, these provide important clues about how to reengage people. Each of them obvious but often overlooked yet needing to be eliminated:

1. *Energy-zapping employees are cultivated rather than removed.* They drain motivation of those around them, planting seeds of discontent. They reflect badly to those who keep them. This suggests that standards in the company are so low that it will keep just about anyone. Don't.

2. *Ridiculous policies and procedures are commonplace.* Too often, company policies and procedures seem to exist to manage the lowest common denominator – a small group of individuals with poor work practices. Whereas people thrive with clear expectations and freedom, they're more likely to rebel if this is curbed. Ask yourself why you need this – and if the answer is that your people require it, change the people.

3. *Dirty processes, systems, and structures get in people's way.* Infrastructure designed so people can do their jobs effectively can become clogged and dirty over time, impeding progress. You need to review your infrastructure routinely to be clean and meaningful.

4. *Disappointing moments create despondency.* When something that ought to be a great positive becomes a great disappointment, this can severely undermine motivation. It might be a fantastic new piece of equipment that doesn't work as it should or a great bonus system that rewards bad performers. These barriers to engagement must be addressed.

5. *Basic human needs aren't being met.* If the washrooms are always filthy, if the cafeteria food is terrible, or if the values of your colleagues, bosses or company as a whole are at odds with yours, you'll soon feel disconnected, eroding engagement.

6. *Politics, bragging, and extreme competition reign.* Politics usually has its roots in competition, which is why rivalry within teams is unhealthy. Keeping that person who is always trying to one-up others is a negative. Create an environment where more people can excel and feel energized. Lose the losers.

7. *Good role models are scarce.* Too often, people have no faith in anyone but themselves: teams fail to inspire employees' confidence; and leaders communicate poorly and fail to provide clarity. As Patrick Lencioni noted in his book *The Five Dysfunctions of a Team*, a business with a dysfunctional top team struggles to function.

8. *Bosses misuse their power.* Errant bosses include micromanagers; credit stealers; those who start from a position of distrust; who avoid the hard decisions; those who work around others. Angry managers commanding power through position, meanwhile, are simply highly paid energy zappers. Inappropriate leaders must be dealt with – otherwise, what hope is there for anyone else?

9. *A lack of common sense prevails.* If actions and behaviors seem to have no rhyme or reason, employees will lose confidence. Examples include

hiring back poor performers; tolerating underperformance; rewarding the wrong things; promoting bad products. All of this must be tackled to maintain credibility and employee support.

10. *Key colleagues are too wrapped up in themselves.* These include multitaskers who seem busy but achieve little, and those who can't spare the time for others and seem distracted by their own interests. It is hard to feel motivated in the company of people who can't be in the present.

11. *Social ineptitude weakens connections.* Companies that have not yet recognized the power of communities at work (and outside of work – with partners, suppliers, and customers) are closing themselves off from something important. These may be communities of practice, or social networks whose purpose is to promote connections.

12. *Purposeless work breeds apathy.* Businesses that have not yet seen how they should be helping people do a great job while also helping people change the world haven't yet understood the power of purpose in our lives. People need to see value in work to feel motivated and engaged.

13. *Anger and resentment are poor catalysts for people's best work.* Companies often fail to recognize and tackle anger in the workplace, which can set a destructive tone and leave resentment festering. No one gives their best when they are inwardly raging. We don't tolerate road rage, why tolerate work rage?

14. *Space invaders sap goodwill.* Invading people's private lives and time unnecessarily should be outlawed. Obvious intrusions undermine how people feel about their jobs. There is a big difference between going the extra mile and willfully stealing someone else's hard-earned free time and personal headspace. Important here is establishing why the extra hours are needed.

These are 14 highly visible and identifiable areas where businesses and their leaders regularly let people down, undermining their confidence in their contribution and worth at work. Put another way, that's 14 tangible areas for improvement that you can impact immediately. *Just stop it.*

Bad News Sells

It's a sad reflection on society that so many of us devour and share bad news rather than celebrate the good. Bad news sells newspapers, attracts the biggest TV audiences, and sells more music. As a French novelist once remarked, "Happiness writes white." Newspapers would be dead if it weren't for bad news. There just doesn't seem as much to say when things are going well.

Politicians play on this with negative campaigning, and at work people too are more likely to rally to the tune of all that's wrong at work, rather than what's going right. This isn't healthy – if a shared experience unites hearts and minds, make it a positive one.

I recall when one of our team scoffed the year we (Proudfoot) were listed as one of the UK's Leading Management Consultancies by the *Financial Times*, a massive accomplishment in the management consulting world. It broke my heart. All those people who worked so hard to be recognized were downplayed in one emotional reaction. When you can't see the good in the great or you invest more time in finding the negative evidence to support your thinking, you need to reboot.

We're All Looking for Value

When you manage to engage, you start with valuing people, and under-standing how to demonstrate that value day-to-day at work:

1. *Engagement comes with senior management's genuine interest in people's well-being.* People have a core emotional need to feel secure, which comes from a sense that their employer cares about and takes an interest in them: that they matter. The way that senior management behaves can reinforce or undermine those security levels. Often when a Proudfoot team arrives at a client site, confidence in the client's management to make change happen is weak. It's why we start every assignment with a people engagement plan.

2. *A genuinely positive relationship with your immediate boss is critical in your intention to stick with your job.* No news here – it is the number one reason people stay or go. Regular, meaningful contact with the boss is vital. Yet studies repeatedly indicate a disconnect between people and their line managers. Leaders and managers need to look for ways – and make the time – to better connect with those who report to them.

3. *Having a voice and feeling heard drives engagement.* Being listened to and genuinely heard goes a long way to making someone feel that their

opinions count. Identifying the difference between the loudest voice and a genuine voice is critical. Who you listen to sends a message.

4. *The reputation of a business as a genuinely great place to work is a critical retention factor.* When people work in businesses known to be great places to work, this automatically reflects on the individuals employed by those companies. If the business is great, you must be great to work there: therefore, you are valuable.

5. *People-based decisions affect staff retention.* Decisions about people show to what extent an organization or leader values its employees, which has an impact on morale. When the right people are promoted, rewarded, and recognized, it shows they count and are valued. How a business manages layoffs and poor performance is watched with a keen eye. This is all about fairness (and fair trade). Leaders must make sure people understand why decisions are made, and help them see the logic. And if a poor decision is made, be transparent and course correct rapidly.

6. *In it together.* When leadership fails to demonstrate they are part of the team by believing the rules don't apply to them, everybody loses. The greatest test on leadership during the pandemic was the fairness applied by leaders to some of the more drastic actions required. Pay cuts, reduced hours, doing more work or taking on more responsibility. Those leaders who did not agree that those situations applied to them lost respect from their teams and their peers. This was impossible to bounce back from. Once a leader showed they were not in it together with everyone else, their teams lost faith in their leadership – the loss of respect moved as rapidly as the virus.

Simple moves to improve on these six common areas of leadership issues can lay the table for engagement. Of course, they remain table stakes and not drivers unto themselves.

People Are a Product of You

While we each have our vantage point, it is influenced by many external factors each day: from the economic environment and job stability; to friends and families' attitudes and what's going on in our home life. Other influences include the 14 things that erode our confidence levels and the six starters (of engagement) above. But it is the boss-employee relationship that has the biggest bearing on how we feel about the job we do, and about coming to work each day.

It stands to reason then that this person has the greatest effect on our willingness to invest our discretionary effort at work, on our state of mind. It's important not to confuse this single individual (a specific line manager) with management more generally. Let's be clear – it's the person we report to that has the most power over us. Higher leadership may be distant, out of touch, and slow to make decisions or take action, all of which also have a significant bearing on engagement, but this does not have as great an influence on retention/churn as that unavoidable direct superior.

The Boss Is Dead, Long Live the Boss

When companies realize this – the scale of impact that managers and leaders have on employees and their engagement at work – their suitability and performance in their roles becomes more important than ever. In fact, it should prompt us to question what the role of a boss is in the context of engagement and how well we train for it. Engagement is vital to results; therefore, the boss is vital to engagement – but not in the traditional management sense.

We might argue that the days of the boss are numbered. While managers and leaders with a recognized ability to encourage discretionary effort at work will have an important role to play, "bosses" have different associations and will become redundant. The role of boss has negative connotations: someone who bears down on people – looking over their shoulder is not the same as lending support. This is not the right kind of person to increase employee engagement! How you show up, how you manage to engage, dictates your results in business and as an individual. How you want "to be" becomes as important as what you need to do. As the self-help author Karen Salmansohn exhorts – you need a To-Be list before a To-Do list.[6] How do you want to be each day? Be a coach. Be a guide. Be a positive influence on others.

It all comes down to how much people feel valued, starting with the people who work for us.

---

[6] Karen Salmansohn, *Bounce Back! How to Thrive in the Face of Adversity* (New York: Workman Publishing Company, 2008).

People Really Are a Product of You

I once did some work for a series of mines across Indonesia – copper, gold, you name it. What was interesting was that these mines were located on the same Indonesian islands as some of the country's most impressive hotels – hotels that boasted five-star service in luxury resorts. Therefore, the labor force for the hotels came from the same labor pool as the mines. Yet company results were starkly different.

The mines suffered a multitude of people issues. Management recounting a litany of problems with productivity, throughput, safety, or various other operating issues. One manager, and not by coincidence the one with the largest employee engagement issues, traced the issue back to the pool from which they could recruit people. This manager felt their payroll included more than their share of lazy people who underperformed and were not interested in improving the performance of the mines.

The hotels, on the other hand, were full of shining stars – people who were attentive, connected, and interested in the performance of the business as well as their own contribution. But consider this: the same people who applied for mining roles were applying for hotel roles. So why were the mines struggling with staff issues while the hotels were not? Why the big difference?

You might blame it on the nature of the work, it's a mine, after all. But many of these mines offer housing, schools, and medical centers that their families benefited from and were far greater benefits than alternative employers. Really, it boiled down to the perceived and expressed value placed on people by line management. In defense of management, many simply didn't know how to show up to get the Indonesian culture to step up. People's direct managers in the hotels visibly valued their employees. The investment had been made in the hotel management training. Training at the mines, on the other hand, had not prioritized their connections and interactions with people. The way the manager treated staff was different. Some mine supervisors and managers spent time on reports and in meetings, taking little time out to walk the floor and connect. Strikes were mounted, performance continued to drop, and people were clearly disgruntled. Our work with the management of the mine not only focused on changing the results but changing the engagement of the people and proved that it was the management and not just the staff that held the key to results – the outcome of engagement, the operating results. People solutions were as essential as technical solutions.

Value Is as Value Does

The picture that is emerging is that, in the new engagement economy, being valued produces value. In the new world of work we need both if we want to increase the level of discretionary effort people volunteer.

This must force all of us to look inside our businesses and ask whether we have done enough to adapt to this expectation. We may talk the talk about transformation, but *transformation* is a strong, active term. It suggests a complete overhaul. If by *transformation* we really just mean operational improvement without the people solutions, or a bit of superficial tinkering with the "soft people stuff," we'll soon be found out.

The Way We've Been Managing Hasn't Managed to Engage

If the present looks spookily similar to the past, we can't hope for much progress in the future. As American author Zig Ziglar once famously said, "You don't have to be great to start, but you have to start to be great." The alternative is to go round in circles getting nowhere: Einstein defined insanity as "doing the same thing over and over again but expecting different results." Today, that applies as much to the way companies view and manage their staff.

To challenge your assumptions, consider how many of the following management processes in your business have altered as a result of the changing environment in which you work – and in what ways have you changed them:

1. *The way your business is organized and how people collaborate.* Is your business built on a boss-subordinate relationship structure? Boxes reporting to neatly organized boxes? Are people instructed and directed? Do hierarchy, egos, and the organization chart determine who speaks and interacts with whom? Do you promote walls and silos without even knowing it by how you are organized? Do you have people who perpetuate old structures by how they manage and what they expect? Or is there a flow of spirit, information, and effort based on the best people to tackle

the work – no matter where they sit – within or outside of the organization? When people own resources in tightly organized structures, sharing is often the casualty. It stops. When they openly and easily network, results improve.

2. *The way you motivate your people.* Do you use traditional tactics such as carrot and stick, reward and punishment, perks and payroll? Or have you sought to shift the emphasis to increase meaning and purpose, development and progress, freedom and autonomy for people? Do you allow people to create new roles or even whole new businesses so they can promote themselves rather than wait for the boss to move on or be promoted?

3. *How you connect with and build connections between people.* Do you know individuals first and foremost based on their performance, their resumes, and their results? Or do you see them as humans whose lives outside work influence their lives at work? Do your people fit the job they do, or do a job they have been fitted to? Do you know which team members are leaders in your communities – scout troop leaders, youth sport coaches, community influencers?

4. *How you define your strategies and develop your objectives.* Is next year's strategic plan and subsequent objectives drawn up in your office for the sake of speed? Or do you invite the wider organization into your strategy process, finding ways to include valuable frontline input? Do you free up people to think laterally and develop new objectives? Do you open the lines of communication to your lines of thought?

5. *How you make your decisions.* Does the boss make all the decisions? Or do you harness the wisdom of the many to find the best solutions, and make better decisions? Not everyone will agree or get a vote, but just being included in the discussion will engender commitment.

As the twenty-first century continues to unfold in unpredictable ways, the way you motivate, connect, collaborate, define your strategies, develop your objectives, and make your decisions at work will define the level of change you make in your business. If you are still using the same management practices and processes of last decade (or frankly even last year), you risk stunting people's engagement in your business, and by extension the company's future prosperity and growth.

Management processes and practices must be dictated by what drives people to perform. They reflect how much we value people. The way we manage and lead will either earn us the 2 Fs and 7 Cs required to engage for business success today, or not. It is important that as managers we also apply the MI-9 scorecard to ourselves as well.

The MI-9 Scorecard Applied to Yourself Consider your current status against each of the MI-9 engagement criteria – this time thinking about yourself as a manager. How well do you score today on a scale of 1–10?	
Fair trade: Are you a fair manager? Are you transitioning from a twentieth-century boss to a true twenty-first-century leader? Are you fair dinkum – authentic in what you do? How do you feel when you hear the need for fairness and sincerity? Do you give people a fair go? Do you feel an obligation to provide people with opportunity?	
Cause: Do your people really know and understand how they contribute to your business? Do you convert vision into verbs? Do you help people see their value? Do you give people opportunities to make great contributions not just do a job? Do you allow people to make their world a better place from where they work?	
A Clean and meaningful infrastructure: Do you really know why people feel cheesed off at work? What's getting in their way, and are you doing anything about it? Are you authentic about removing the barriers that prevent people from achieving what they need to? Do you worry about the quality of people's work lives?	
Confidence: Do you consider it a priority to remove the doubt that creeps into people's minds at work? Do you close the gap on silence? Do you address concerns head on? Are you conscious of your role as chief confidence builder? What in your business is most concerning to your team and what did you do to address those concerns?	
Connection: Do you manage and lead individuals? Do you take the time to really know and understand each person – as well as the team as a whole? Are you a leader of individuals coming together with a common cause? Or do you practice "one size fits all"? How well do you connect with people individually? Can you name one major event coming up in the lives of each of your team members?	

Collaboration: Are you willing to break down the artificial walls in your business, foster wider collaboration, and invite new faces to the table? Do you add genuinely new brain power to old problems, thinking laterally about where you source ideas and feedback? Do you look past relative status, preferring to listen to ideas, see people's skills and ability to contribute? Where in the business are new collaborations springing up?	
Community: Do you proactively look for opportunities to build community into your workplace? Have you sought to create communities of spirit, expertise, knowledge, and practices to give people a sense of belonging and access to expertise, experience, and information? Do you provide nontraditional ways of bringing people together? Today, cross-company, even cross-country teaming is a good virtual start, what's one new community you started?	
Capability: How good are you at letting people learn and at learning from your people? Do you cultivate markets of knowledge ready for exchange, and offer a balance of intellectual stimulation and skill mastery? Do people have the opportunity to learn from each other? Are you constantly on the lookout for future skills, those fit for the world tomorrow and not just today? Can you list them now?	
Freedom: Are you serious about removing the chains that confine people? Do employees have a voice? Better still, does everyone have a voice? Are you ready to empower them with more freedom to think for themselves? Can they access any level of leadership to solve problems, or any place in the business? How are you doing this?	

Coming to a Workplace Near You: The Biggest Change Project Ever

As we've seen over the past years and the decades before that, fighting the epidemic of disgruntlement that is sweeping the business world requires change – not just at the very heart of your business but also in your own personal management and leadership style: You are the greatest trigger of engagement. When employees invest their discretionary effort because they want to, not because they must, you know you are engaging people. But for that to happen, we need to create new feelings about work by understanding the triggers and invoking the MI-9 tools. Together they help you manage to engage.

Connecting with Generation C

When the Arab Spring came to the Middle East, when the prodemocracy movement hit Hong Kong, or Black Lives Matter took hold during the pandemic, the driving force was what came to be known as Generation C – the connected generation. The intention was a nonviolent movement of change. People united for a common purpose: to change their world for the better. It is this kind of movement that businesses need to tap into. It's latent but needs to be released. People at work want a cause worth rising for, worth connecting for, and worth taking to the streets for. When company leaders and managers learn how to harness this energy, their businesses will be energized. What makes your people get out of bed and take to the street that takes them to work? Find out.

1. **Ask a few of your most valuable people to answer these questions about you (refer back to Chapter 1 if you need explanation):**
   - Fair trade: Are you a fair leader?
   - A sense of Cause: Do your people really know and understand how they contribute to your business?
   - Confidence: Do you make a conscious effort to remove the doubts that creep into people's minds at work?
   - A Clean infrastructure: Do you understand what's really holding back your employees?
   - Connection: Do you see and connect with the individuals within the team?
   - Collaboration: Are you willing to break down the artificial walls in your business, open up the business to true collaboration, and invite new faces to the table?
   - Community: Do you look for opportunities to build community into your workplace?

FIGURE 2.1 Things You Need to Do Right Now. (*continued*)

- Capability: How good are you at letting people learn, and are you learning from your people?
- Freedom: Are you genuinely committed to removing the shackles that bind your employees to doing things the way they've always done them?

2. **Which of the following disengagers are currently evident in your workplace? Once you have circled those most evident to you, ask a range of people in different roles what they think:**

   a. Energy leeches and other toxic people

   b. Excessive policies and procedures

   c. Dirty processes, systems, and structures

   d. Disappointments

   e. Basic human factors (hygiene facilities, etc.)

   f. A negative atmosphere

   g. Politics and extreme competition

   h. A poor leadership team

   i. Lack of communication

   j. Bosses behaving badly

   k. A lack of common sense

   l. Feelings of being invisible or ignored

   m. The company's social ineptitude

   n. Purposeless work

   o. A climate of anger and resentment

   p. An invasion of personal space

   q. A failure to change

   r. A lack of enthusiasm

   s. The absence of 'people having one another's backs'

   t. Sarcasm

   u. A lack of spontaneous teaming

FIGURE 2.1 (*Continued*)

3. Ask a variety of people to keep a journal of a few 'days in their lives' at work. No essays required: just a few notes to focus people's minds on what engages them and what doesn't. Then discuss them.

4. Ask yourself these questions:

   - Do you ever challenge the management practices in use at your company, and by you in particular?

   - How would you rate your own level of management innovation: how different is the way you manage today from your approach 10 years ago, five years ago, two years ago?

5. TO-DO LIST (Enter here the action items that surface as you think through these questions.)

CHAPTER 3

Manage to Engage: Building Street Cred

And then, I thought, how could I possibly be better for you? I want to say and sing the right things for you, and I want to make that one melody that really saves your spirit that one day.

—Lady Gaga, musician[1]

Looking to pop icon Lady Gaga as a potential role model for engagement might seem odd. But, if you are serious about transforming your engagement levels at work, you need bold thinking.

Lady Gaga called her multimillion-strong army of fans "Little Monsters" – and they loved it: the definition, that sense of belonging, that confirmation that they have been seen and appreciated in return for their investment of passion. One research study interviewing her monsters found that "Identification as a Monster. . . moves beyond an interest in Lady Gaga's music. . .their interest in Lady Gaga [has become] 'a way of life.'"[2] Because they feel she is interested in each of them, and she creates a feeling of closeness through social connections (reciprocal communication – despite the vast scale), Lady Gaga's fans are among the most engaged of any popular artist. It's the kind of passion and devotion employers and managers dream of.

----

[1] Paula Johanson, *Lady Gaga: A Biography* (Santa Barbara, CA: Greenwood, 2012).
[2] Melissa A. Click, Hyunji Lee, and Holly Willson Holladay, "Making Monsters: Lady Gaga, Fan Identification, and Social Media," *Popular Music and Society* 36:3 (2013), 360-379, DOI:10.1080/03007766.2013.798546.

But perhaps what really sets Gaga apart from her peers is her belief in how she should use her influence, and it is this that makes her an interesting model for engagement. In her early days of popularity, she was often quoted as saying that what drives her is making a difference, rather than making money.

> It's what you do when you're at the top to inspire and influence the people that lift you. . .I have a relentless pursuit in me to give every-thing in me to my fans.

Successful leaders follow the same mantra, understanding that good things will follow if you look after your people. They also understand their people make them successful. It might be common sense and commonly talked about, but it's not common practice yet.

Beware Flying Monkeys!

"Stand back! I have flying monkeys and I'm not afraid to use them!" Remember the flying monkeys from *The Wizard of Oz*? How many times have you felt someone in your organization – a boss or maybe even yourself – threatening frightening consequences if people don't fall into line?

In the not-too-distant past, some managers got their jobs done by using flying monkey power as their primary management tool: the ever-present, seldom-spoken threat that lay before you if you didn't do as the boss required.

Flying monkeys yielded their power using statements beginning with "If we don't. . ." and ending with ". . .then this will happen." Alternatively, they might invoke someone else's flying monkeys: "Sam wants this done (or else!)."

Unfortunately, flying monkeys are still summoned today. But do we think that requiring things to be done because "we report this to our board" or "my boss needs this done so you should do it" will in any way engage them? We know it will not. In fact, each time a manager does this, he reduces his leadership credibility – his street cred. Building street cred is the ultimate compliment for someone who manages to engage.

Volunteering to Do More

If creating volunteerism – getting people to volunteer their discretionary effort – is your aim, flying monkeys are not your allies. During the COVID-19 pandemic, we saw teams come together to do remarkable things for the good of their organizations and their communities. They didn't wait. They felt the call to a cause. We should be looking for ways to create this feeling, this sense of "we're in it together" as a genuine cultural attribute in our businesses all the time. Postpandemic, we want people to step up as they do when they volunteer for causes, charities, or to coach the junior football team – where simply *knowing* they are of value is enough to energize them and unleash their passion to help.

Volunteerism shouldn't need to be coerced.

Engagement Kicks in When Flying Monkeys Are Kicked Out

As we come on to *the how* of engendering engagement with an aim to achieve volunteerism, let's summarize the personal challenges – beyond flattening the flying monkeys – this will involve for managers. Understanding to change the way other people feel about work, you may need to change how *you* feel about work.

- *Be prepared to be engaged yourself. What state are* you *in?* This is paramount. You can't ignite enthusiasm in others if you yourself don't possess the drive for a better work life. You need to lead the way.
- *Consider how others view you. What do they know you for?* What reputation do you think you have as a manager? An easy way to determine what you are known for is to write down what -ability you have – reliability, accountability, dependability, irritability?
- *Be prepared to understand how you influence. Are you guilty of summoning flying monkeys?* Understand that what you do by day goes home with people at night. Your actions as the boss have a greater impact on your people than any other aspect of their working lives, even above pay.
- *Prepare to see work and people differently – change your vantage point.* Whatever is happening in the external market, and however acute the need to control costs, can you accept that a brighter future for the business starts with people feeling brighter about their work? Are you willing to reboot your perspective and discover what you and your team can do for one another?

- *Be prepared to question everything you know and do.* The very nature of business is different today, so the management systems you use, the management processes you rely on, the management behavior you display, even the culture you have tried to embed in your teams, all need to be reviewed.

- *Finally, don't panic.* As much as your panic attacks might have stemmed from pandemic attacks, don't let that be seen. Your calmness is the kindness your teams need.

Engage Yourself

Clearly, it's not just the business environment that has changed. People at work have changed too. While many are weary at what the next crisis might bring, they expect you to be engaged: that you are sensitive and responsive to their needs as *humans*. Positively influencing their experience and contribution, it can't simply be 'you are lucky to have a job'.

At a business level, this means taking these steps:

1. *Look for game-changing ways to inspire rather than manage people.* Remarkable results come from environments that allow people to be remarkable.

2. *Jointly agree expectations.* Decide on performance, targets, mindset, aspirations, together.

3. *Create a culture where people can flourish, not stay in their boxes.* Recognize people for their talents, not their status.

4. *See people for who they are.* People are a product of their environment: the more you learn about people the better chance of helping them thrive.

5. *Invite opinions.* People who are fully present at work won't be passive. Harness their ideas to create better solutions. Check your ego.

6. *Be willing to explain decisions.* People who care about their jobs want to understand and feel part of what's going on. Leveling with people increases their sense of inclusion, understanding, and self-worth.

7. *Reevaluate current levels of influence.* In an online context, vlogger Sarah Austin describes three characteristics of influence: behavior, social capital, and a likable personality. The most prolific test of a leader is

whether, even with no people reporting to them, they can influence people to stand alongside them and achieve remarkable results.

8. *Translate objectives into steps to be taken.* People need to know how to map a route. This is what I call "turning vision into verbs and purpose into plans." Guide the map, but let people be free to determine what needs to be done on the journey.

9. *Adapt to higher expectations.* Employees increasingly know that their employers need them as much as they need the work, and their expectations have risen as a result. Rise up to meet them.

10. *Address attitude and poor performance.* Having a no-jerks policy is one of the single greatest things you can do for your people and your own well-being. Tolerating attitude and toxic personalities are a multiplier in a negative direction.

11. *Realize that employees may actually be ahead of the game.* Employees are often in a better position to see the changes that are needed. So be ready to let your people stride out in front of you.

12. *Move away from the usual suspects.* Invite new faces, front-line heroes, people who don't usually sit at your table or connect to your Zoom room. You get a multiplier: they engage, you learn.

13. *Know when to lead and when to get out of the way.* People need to be free to get on with their jobs. Give clear expectations and let them do their job.

14. *Rethink job titles.* Google didn't have a HR department: it had "People Operations."

15. *Never enact your job title.* Invoking your title is a flying monkey.

16. *Let people have a say about who leads them.* People are more likely to rally around those who make them feel part of something bigger.

17. *Reengineer management indicators and measures.* Include the MI-9.

18. *Lead @ the speed of change.* You need to be dynamic and agile. Moving fast is only bad if your people can't keep up. Then you need to review your people needs – is it a development challenge or are they the wrong people?

19. *Develop a rich sense of community.* When businesses provide an environment and infrastructure where new connections can flourish, the network effect kicks in – multiplying your results.

20. *Use all the tools in the digital workforce box.* Social and collaboration platforms are a must. Self-service platforms can empower and energize.

21. *Rapidly prototype and embrace failure as a learning opportunity.* In an age of rapid innovation and overnight market disruption, businesses are learning that rapid prototyping is a must. Even if only 1 idea in 10 flies.

22. *Provide employee rewards in many forms.* It isn't just money that talks. Personal development, along with a host of other incentives, must be considered and matched to the needs of individuals. But be sure to identify them as table stakes, not engagers. Table stakes rarely engage, but when absent can disengage. Know the difference.

23. *Collaborate across borders.* Market conditions change quickly; companies need to cast the net wide when seeking fresh ideas and new solutions. They must source ideas and abilities from wherever the best fit might be – even if it's outside the business.

24. *Establish closer employee-employer relationships.* They should be less transactional, more meaningful, and more flexible. Certainly, more transparent. Managers need to develop the ability to rapidly reteam and form teams, guide and lead at the fringe, not just the core – and make all relationships significant, to get the best out of everyone.

25. *Make the mission to engage an imperative for everyone.* Everyone stands to benefit, so make everyone part of the solution.

Go HeadsUp

If you really want to build street cred, you've got to go all in, really engage with people. To kick that off is easy – take your nose out of your device and connect socially, even if you need to be physically distant! Go HeadsUp!

The past decade may have flattened the organization structure, reducing the need for traditional supervision, but the need for front-line leaders to connect has never been more essential. HeadsUp leadership is safer, more engaging, and more productive. It's also more human. With the simple 1.5.30 concept at its heart, it teaches leaders that checking in is more valuable than checking up, and routine brings comfort to everyone.

If you want to go HeadsUp and use 1.5.30, here you go:

One: How is your day going? Check in once a day for a quick health check and catch-up. What'sUp? Howzit going?

Five: How is your week going? Meet, Team, or Zoom for at least 30 minutes

once a week. Make this about progre
people need, and how the following

Thirty: How is your job going? Have
once a month to discuss how someone is
and guide on how to keep leaning forward
results.

HeadsUp is a call to action for leaders at every level. It i
essential leadership skills – whether you're leading work from h
your workplace, you need presence and vision, you need to be tech
and to coach and influence. These need to be universally understood to help
people step up in their work and achieve.

When I launched HeadsUp, I wasn't thinking of a global viral pandemic,
I was thinking of a worldwide leadership engagement movement. I sent out a
message to search for and spotlight HeadsUp leaders across the world, setting
up a website **www.headsup-today.com** to capture these leaders and show-
case the human side of the business. But today, it's a necessary movement.
There is a need to look up from our technology, our reporting, and our devices
and connect. We have a need to be socially connected, even if we have to
be physically distant. Together apart. Our wellness depends on it. I'm urging
everyone, get in the game and go HeadsUp.

A Total Ecosystem Approach

To truly and positively impact your teams, they need to behave their way into
engagement. How a manager and leader behave has the most direct impact
followed by the environment in which people work. Addressing the total ecosystem triggers behavior, and then engagement can follow: 2 Fs and 7 Cs.
The multiplier comes from the total ecosystem approach. As we cover each
letter in your scorecard, you'll start to see how they work in concert with
one another to build an operating environment that enables engagement.
In Chapter 4 we'll keep with the role of management as we explore how to
embed fair trade into your business.

hings you can do today to mprove people's quality of life at work

1. **Using the next page as a guide, rate how engaged you feel today as a manager or leader.**

   Now ask your people to do the same.

2. **Review the 'Be prepared' list from this chapter.**

   Where would you say you need the biggest readjustment in your thinking?

3. **Get three of your people in a room or on Zoom.**

   Ask them to review the 'Be prepared' list and have them determine how they think you are prepared

4. **Look at the gap and talk about it.**

   Ask these people which items are the most critical in your workplace and which would make a significant difference to engagement levels at work.

5. **Now review the list again.**

   Which one most concerns you? What will you do about it? And to start the ball rolling, whose help will you enlist?

FIGURE 3.1   Things You Need to Do Right Now.

CHAPTER 4

Fair Trade: An "F" You Should Be Proud Of

We want our leaders to be fair dinkum. As much among us as above us.

—Sir Peter Cosgrove, former governor-general of Australia

I magine how people would *feel* if they felt you were fair dinkum, knew you would give them a *fair go*, and felt they were in a fair trade relationship? Giving people the opportunity to grow and thrive is one of the greatest engagement tools available to you. Beyond the opportunity to be rewarded for work, it means really searching for ways to allow people to truly step up to new challenges – giving a candidate a job, allowing nontraditional candidates to apply for promotions, providing people with experiences to help them grow, or providing opportunity. Providing opportunity is the basis of a fair trade.

Fair Is as Fair Does

Fair trade is about people feeling they exchange a fair day's work for a fair day's return. It's about fair treatment where people's discretionary effort is acknowledged personally as well as financially, so you feel you have genuinely contributed and what you do matters. Giving people a *fair go* means you look beyond the usual suspects and allow people to step up to opportunity and the experiences that are available in your business. Being *fair dinkum* means you are authentic – the real deal. Without these basics, fair trade will not flourish.

As a kid, I worked at McDonald's. Five shifts a week while I was at school. I learned the basics of business before I knew I was learning it. It was there that I also learned a simple concept of management behavior — be firm but fair. Here I sit, thirtysomething years later (OK forty!) and the latter part of that concept – fair – has stuck with me. While *firm* has been the framework of much of my approach to management – standing up for my beliefs and not wavering when things get rough, *fair* has meant the rules apply to everyone.

In life, the feeling of fairness is a prevailing force and so often the cause of discontent. As kids, we expect to be treated fairly by our parents, *"Oh, that's not fair!"* But in business, its often fairness that creeps its way into discussions about promotions, pay increases or bonuses, and the way organizations deal with layoffs, crises, and turbulence. Whether verbalized or not, fairness counts.

Fairness is a basic human desire. It's also the foundation for engagement. Special deals create special agreements. People talk, they trade information, they show off. Next thing you know, that special deal becomes especially painful. You lose people's confidence, and sometimes you lose the people.

You may now be thinking, *"But life wasn't meant to be fair,"* or *"you can't be fair to everyone at work."* Think again. Fairness is the precursor to volunteerism, which is a product of engagement.

Aussie Rules

Australia is famous for its Bring Your Owns (BYOs); bring your own meat to a BBQ; bring your own booze to a restaurant. People bring what they can – and together, it works. In today's business world, we have diverse populations that together create diverse workplaces – different ages, beliefs, skills, and stages of life. So, leaders and managers need to bring a customized approach and management style to the workplace – *one that matches the makeup of its teams* and keeps things fair.

Discovering what fits with your people depends greatly on who they are. Similarly, "fairness" conjures up different things to different people. Take this quote from American author and TV host Dennis Wholey: "Expecting the world to treat you fairly because you are a good person is a little like expecting the bull not to attack you because you are a vegetarian."[1] I would argue that fairness is about treatment, and people do expect to be treated fairly. The tricky part is defining what that means in your world, your business, to your team. Fairness is subjective. Yet when fairness is seen to be absent, greed, jealousy, competitiveness, and protectionism enter the frame – negative qualities that are far from conducive to engagement.

Here's how I view fairness. After much searching for a valid definition, I took to its portrayal in the Josephson Institute's *Six Pillars of Character*[2]. I'd never heard of the Josephson Institute. It is a nonprofit organization dedicated to improving the ethical quality of society, but I found its definition of fairness fitting for a discussion of fair trade within the MI-9 toolkit:

> *Be consistent, open and treat all people equitably. Consider all sides and make decisions on the facts without favoritism or prejudice. Play by the rules, avoid careless accusations, and don't take undue advantage of others. Pursue justice and condemn injustice.*

This puts fairness into the context of character-building and the ability to use character as a compass to guide decisions. While I would remove the word *undue* from the sentence and playing by the rules isn't necessarily an antidote to today's economics, I believe fairness at work comes from your character and helps build engagement – a perfect fit for MI-9.

I also view fairness at work as a trade: a two-way street. Your teams must reciprocate in the trade: transparency, openness, trust, straight speak.

For me, fair trade includes three forms of fairness: the trade of effort with reward no matter who you are (position, level, or diversity we all need to meet our role expectations); giving people "a fair go" no matter their background or diversity; and being *fair dinkum,* our ability to be genuine and authentic at work – these are what growing up Australian leaves you with!

- *Fair trade:* Fair trade is about how you put fairness into action at work – acting equitably as a manager. Engaging in fair trade with employees is about demonstrating that you value and care about the people who work for (with) you. This should be a constant, a default – no matter how

---

[1] Stephanie A Sarkis, "20 Quotes on Fairness," *Psychology Today* (November 3, 2012). www.psychologytoday.com/us/blog/here-there-and-everywhere/201211/20-quotes-fairness
[2] Josephson Institute of Ethics, 2009. *Making ethical decisions.* web.engr.uky.edu/~jrchee0/CE%20401/Josephson%20EDM/Making_Ethical_Decisions.pdf

tough business/market factors become. Fairness should be ingrained. We expect our efforts to be rewarded and recognized, and we expect an exchange of knowledge: to learn routinely and develop our capabilities. We expect just treatment and respect, no matter our backgrounds or ethnicity; to have a voice and to be heard. Whether we are the team leader or the team member, we expect that the effort we volunteer to use at work will count. Fairness is a precursor to feeling valued.

- *Fair go:* "Give us a fair go, mate," as an Aussie might say. Giving someone a fair go is about giving someone a chance to do something, to shine, to excel. We need to feel obliged as leaders to set people up to be great. As managers we need to provide opportunity to our people, opening the door to opportunity beyond your typical circle and setting people up to be successful. When you give someone a fair go, you free them up to be remarkable. You're saying, *"Go on, give it a go. I support you."*

- *Fair dinkum:* This is another great Aussie phrase. It's used as an exclamation or a question after a person describes something that is remarkable. *Fair dinkum!* means "Wow!" Or the rhetorical *Fair dinkum?* means "Really?! Are you serious?" It's also used to reaffirm that something is real or genuine: "It's a fair dinkum deal" For our purposes here, fair dinkum means genuine and authentic. The manager of the future has the mindset: *"I am fair dinkum with people; you can trust me."*

A Fair Go at Work

Some time ago, I was fortunate enough to return to Australia with Proudfoot, to work with one of Australia's leading insurance companies, AMP. The goal was to improve customer satisfaction and reduce costs (spend money wisely), while concurrently increasing employee satisfaction – quite the combination and, to some, the perfect storm. To AMP it was a challenge the business was ready to rise to. And, it was a great example of a business giving people a fair go.

One thing AMP was encouraged to do from the start was involve people in its transformation who were not the usual suspects. They open sourced, inviting people from anywhere in the business to join a project Results Team – with no restrictions. Positions were advertised as "real" jobs for which people needed to apply. It was a fair dinkum strategic need for the business, reinforced by assigning the right level of gravitas to the roles, proving it wasn't a side project. Senior management interviewed candidates, further reinforcing the seriousness with which the company was treating the teams. Additionally, people were told they would receive performance reviews based on the measurable success of the assignment (Proudfoot is exceptionally good at measurement of project results).

This is how you start to go about giving people a *fair go*. We had people from across the business asking to be on the team. Those who made it on the team ranged from front-line employees to senior managers; they included call center operators, administration staff, even the odd techie and IT guy.

Interestingly, once the teams had accomplished their goals, members were to return to their prior jobs. But it became clear this wouldn't be appropriate for many of those involved – as is often the case, they built such new levels of capability it would be a loss not to leverage their newfound skills and place them in roles to leverage these. Call center operators, for example, had displayed remarkable competence, stepping up to the challenge with gusto, and so AMP needed to consider new positions that would provide new opportunity to the individuals and leverage their skills for continued success of the business.

AMP did exactly this, and some of the team members were promoted. These people were given *a fair go*. They had been given an unprecedented opportunity to shine in a different role, and they had grabbed it with both hands.

Other companies might have limited their Results Team positions to those they felt already had the authority or management skills required or to those simply available regardless of skill, but AMP gave everyone a fair go. They brought new faces to old problems. It was a fair trade. The team members were immersed in experiences they would not ordinarily be exposed to, and the company got its results. The return for the risk? The team blitzed the results. The company demonstrated a fair dinkum act of fair trade. They genuinely invested in their people, took a risk, and trusted them to step up. And step up they did.

Fairest of Them All – Give the Gift of Time

You could be forgiven for thinking fair trade is Management 101: the management basics! Instead, think of fair trade as what good looks like. The nuts and bolts of management behavior are the essential launch pad for engagement. In isolation, fair trade may not be enough to secure engagement, but failure to prioritize the obvious is often enough to drive disengagement.

As the pyramid rightly flattens, the challenge in the future will be to find a way to have routine contact with everyone, no matter how large or dispersed the team is – to connect and be active (not busy). This is about management being present (in body, mind, heart, and spirit). It comes back to fair trade, giving people the courtesy of your own engagement – your time. Visibility requires present and active managers – people who are felt, and who understand the nature of their team's work. They practice 1.5.30; they check in, they are accessible and actively involved. Being visible also builds trust.

Practiced wisely, active management demonstrated through 1.5.30 encourages teams to achieve. It isn't what is perceived to be micromanagement; that negative little leprechaun that sits on the shoulders of others telling them what to do, pointing fingers, and checking up on people (not that leprechauns have ever been accused of micromanagement).

Fair Trade in Action: Eight Active Management Behaviors

There are eight active management behaviors (AMBs), and they give insight into the basics of fair management – what a fair trade in behavioral terms looks like. They are also part of the MI-9 toolkit.

Since I began at Proudfoot almost thirty five years ago, active management was defined through eight behaviors, and they remain the cornerstone to achieving results through individuals and teams. It turns out, when applied well, these behaviors were also the bedrock to engagement long before *engagement* as a term was in vogue. Active management was about demonstrating fair trades in the many interactions people have at work each day. It showed managers: care enough to set expectations with their people so teams feel a sense of clarity; check in to see how they can help; and coach to see how they can develop capability. Active management is about being present. No matter the organization, we have found these dynamic set of behaviors to engage, enable, and energize teams to achieve their objectives. How? Using just the right amount of management from leaders to encourage teams and keep them on track.

Businesses are increasingly building supervision into their processes by allowing the right information to surface at the right time, rather than building supervisors into the processes to check and balance other people's

FIGURE 4.1 Eight Active Management Behaviors.

work. On-demand information is crucial to support this, as an integral part of any management process – this is what Dan Tapscott of *Macrowikinomics* calls the *infostructure*.[3]

I'll take this opportunity to share the AMBs with you before we talk a little more about how the best front-line managers spend their days (see Figure 4.1).

The first reaction from clients is always "but these are common sense." Of course, you know the response that is coming. Common sense is not always commonplace. Sometimes the basics are missed. If they weren't, wouldn't engagement scores be higher?

AMB 1: Promote Health and Safety

In the mining world, starting conversations with a "safety share" was common practice for many years prior to COVID-19. I had worked with Rio Tinto in Australia, the US, and Mongolia, and the safety share was a way to bring the safety conversation front and center before any other discussions took place. It worked. A look at their website https://www.riotinto.com/sustainability/health-safety-wellbeing and it confirms what I believe – Rio Tinto puts safety first, it's not just lip service. "In 2019, we experienced no fatalities across our business, with a strong performance in all key safety performance metrics. We improved our all injury frequency rate (AIFR), which was 0.42 for the year

[3] Anthony D. Williams and Don Tapscott, *Macrowikinomics: New Solutions for a Connected Planet* (New York: Penguin Press, 2010).

(down from 0.44 in 2018). However, we know we must do better: we will continue to make safety our number-one goal, with the aim of sending everyone home safely at the end of every shift, every day."

Postpandemic and with the new safety protocols in place within so many businesses across the globe, health and safety got promoted right up to where it needs to be: first among equals in any leader's job, in all businesses. Checking in that your team is safe and encouraging them to discuss their well-being is a must-do table stake today. It is a behavior, not a concept. For example, it's more than asking if a ladder is safe. It asks you to reframe health and safety into continuous improvement conversations. If you want to improve safety, why not ask questions like "Why do we need a ladder?" Couldn't we redesign the process and completely remove the need for the ladder? Why not take it even further? Why not ask if your leadership behaviors are promoting a healthy work environment? The true nature of health and safety is the ability to work with your teams to continuously improve the nature of work and keep them safe. While safety won't create engagement, it's absence will disengage.

AMB 2: Agree on the "What" – Jointly Set Expectations

In a fair trade, expectations are discussed and agreed, and outcomes are clear. Agreeing on *the what* keeps the team focused on the right things. Discussing and agreeing what the work is, what needs to be achieved, and what good looks like enables people to have clear expectations. Both you and your team must be aligned on what needs to get done. This includes how much and by when. It's that simple, yet if this step is missed, so are schedules and cost targets, and you lose co-workers, internal customers, or even your end customer. If people know what's required, they're less likely to let each other down. Once the parameters have been set, managers will get out of the way and let people get on with work.

AMB 3: Support the "How" – Guide, but Don't Drive the Car

You have a general plan for what needs to happen – an outline that still needs to be colored in. People are reassured that you have a roadmap, both near and long term. As a good leader you leave the how up to your people, who want to feel they can add value by filling in the detail. You can entrust this to them with confidence because you know you've hired the right kind of people and paid them well enough to think this through for themselves. They don't need to be policed.

This doesn't mean that managers aren't interested in the finer details; they are simply allowing space for others to think, shape, and thrive – and offering feedback and guidance as needed. It's about providing freedom within boundaries.

AMB 4: Check In – How Are We Doing?

There is an important distinction between checking in and checking up. One makes you interested with a view to remove barriers to achievement, the other has you following up on activity execution. Seldom do we enjoy to be followed up. Instead, consider it about *visiting* progress rather than *managing* it. That is, people should have an ongoing opportunity to discuss their progress on assignments and any needs or issues that arise: a joint progress review at a time interval both parties agree. This contrasts with undesirable shock feedback; it could just as easily happen as part of an informal chat over a cup of coffee, as long as you have data.

Managers struggle most with how often to check in. To help, ask a different question: *"How long can you afford to go before you know there is an issue?"* If the situation was one of life and death, the answer would be, not very long. Similarly, if there are associated high costs, penalty charges for missed schedules, or situations that change rapidly and require constant monitoring, you'll want to check in fairly often. But don't go overboard – if a project has long cycle times and by nature moves slowly, checking in too often becomes excessive follow-up.

1.5.30 is a simple rule of thumb. Recall that it goes like this:

One: Check in once a day (1 day) for a quick health check and catch-up, high-level progress.

Five: Check in once a week (5 days) for a good 30 minutes – make this about how the week progressed, what help people need, and how the following week will go. Now is the time to inject coaching into the conversation.

Thirty: Then have a meaningful conversation once a month (30 days) to discuss morale and performance, as well as offering up detailed coaching and guidance on how to keep moving forward. This is an opportunity to learn, to exchange viewpoints, and ideas. Ideally, it's a development conversation

1.5.30. It's that simple.

Note that taking an interest in people's progress should extend to the *quality* of their output, not simply the quantity. A fair-trade manager will make the effort to appreciate the nature of the work – and the degree of capability of the people doing it – so they can empathize, support, coach, and guide them. If you walk the floor regularly or check in routinely, it doesn't feel like follow up; it feels like you are providing an opportunity for your people to speak up and provide you feedback on progress. This is where you circle back on expectations. If you planned and agreed to achieve something you can now discuss how close you are to achieving it. The difference is the variance. Plan versus actual.

The variance is the conversation. It becomes your continuous improvement plan. The natural discussion is "Are we on track, and if not, why not? What do we need to do to close the gap?" Perhaps capabilities need to be addressed, issues are coming from other parts of the organization, or a team member has been off sick. Without this discussion, schedules rapidly get off track.

Here's where the concept of *shooting for 100* comes in – aiming for best possible, not best practice or benchmarks. Let me illustrate: Teams sometimes decide on a target – they agree what they can achieve, and then that target becomes the standard; we're happy when we hit 80 percent because that's what we agreed last year. But what if you could achieve more than that? When you aim for 100 percent, you open the conversation to the greater discussion around "What's holding us back?" When you aim for 100 percent, you start to think about innovation and continuous improvement, not just process improvement, about the many things that could happen to achieve more, better, different. You open the door to a discussion rather than self-censoring your improvement; we're happy with this number because it's the target, or worse still, we don't even think about improving. Imagine the opportunity if you shoot for 100? Like the old saying goes, you miss 100 percent of the shots you don't take.

AMB 5: Agree on the Progress Made and the Progress Still to Come

Depending on the sophistication of your management reporting, your variance management or plan versus actual discussion can be easy and transparent, or difficult. If you don't have reporting tools that provide that simple data, you will want to reassess your management tools – the dashboards you create and use each day to know how close or far away from the finish line your people are. The Management Operating System, the management tools you use to keep your business humming and bring rhythm to your workplace, is a key adjunct to the behaviors we apply. The tools along with the behaviors can create remarkable results. The more transparent your reporting and the closer it is to the front line, the less you are a micro manager simply wanting to check up on output.

A Tool to Avoid Micromanagement: The Percent Done Conversation

One way to avoid being seen to micromanage people is to talk about the proportion of work that has been accomplished at a given point, so that everyone understands current progress against expected targets. A *percent done conversation* is one that discusses achievement in real time. If there was a forecast for a year, for example, and in November you are just 55 percent of the way there, you know you're in trouble. If you had measured the proportion that had been achieved at the end of each month, week, or other increment of time, and everyone had been aware of this, there would have been no big shock in November: preemptive action could have been taken much earlier to achieve the target.

The important point in AMB 5 is gaining agreement – everyone must agree on the progress that has been made and the actions required to maintain the results, or make changes to get back on track if they are off schedule. Importantly, actions must be *documented* so everyone knows what is happening. Not for HR or to hold it against people, but to capture situations that may be off schedule and record why, so you can track how often something might get in the way of achieving results and then prioritize taking corrective action.

This is where 1.5.30 comes in. It's a checkpoint in time to agree plainly where you are, help people if they are off track, or to congratulate and pat people on that back in real time as they make progress.

There is one other note on discussing progress. Clients have sometimes come back to me and said, "This is all good, but we have really low-level workers at the front line. We can't expect them to be engaged, doing the same menial work each day, so why do we need to check in on them so often?" You couldn't be more wrong. That is the group you want to interact with most and the group who are most impacted by their immediate manager or supervisor. Checking in routinely to coach is a great way to engage, but offering progress reviews to show achievement and how the work counts can really make their day. What if you could truly fire up this workforce? Imagine the difference you would make.

AMB 6: Give Coaching and Support

In reality, all eight behaviors are an opportunity to coach and support, but it's important to call this out. Coaching and support are the backbone of engagement. It's why people want to work for you – or don't. Coaching brings about the fair trade. In a fair-trade scenario, people have confidence their manager will support them in positive ways, including coaching them to help them achieve, or support them to enhance their development.

This is a behavior that helps you manage to engage. When people know they are going to learn something or that you will take the time to directly build their capability or provide the roadmap to make that happen, they engage. Learning is the baseline to opportunity. The more you learn, the more opportunity presents itself.

If criticism or caution *is* needed, tread carefully. Anyone who cares about their work will feel it personally if they are seen to fall short. Feeling criticized can have an immediate impact on our well-being and can trigger emotions that prevent us from thinking clearly. So how a manager handles more negative feedback can have serious consequences.

However, don't mistake this for avoidance. Avoiding providing feedback and living in a world of bright-siding where everything is rosy is to no one's advantage. Deal with it head on, but deal with it with empathy.

And don't forget to praise!

AMB 7: Problem Solve and Decide

In a fair trade, you and your team members work together to solve problems and make decisions. They know you're always on the lookout for ways to do things better, willing to bring people in from anywhere in the organization to help solve problems. Together you find new solutions. In today's fast-changing world, no one has all the answers, so you're happy to enlist the help of other people, no matter who they are or what their status. You give people a go. At the right point, you are ready to move from problem discussions to decisions and actions. Deciding what happens next gives people the confidence that action will be taken.

AMB 8: Datacation – How Did We Perform Overall?

Datacation is reporting (capturing data for decision-making), but this is where reporting comes to life. It's about seeing the story in the data so you can build a better business. It's about trending the data so you can dig into the story to make decisions. It's about reporting the data so you can hold fact-based discussions about it. Capturing the data no matter how simple or complex is a crucial behavior – not for the activity of completing a report but for the action of drawing conclusions from it. If you take the view that people make bad decisions because they don't have the correct facts, it stands to reason that decisions will improve as facts flow more freely. From conclusions come choices – to do something as a result of the data you reviewed and the conclusions you drew. Reporting enables you to make fact-based decisions and take fact-based action.

From Reporting to Collaboration

Before the design and implementation of a new reporting tool, a shift supervisor in a large mining company, would spend two hours completing an email to capture results. It was impossible to print out, made no reference to the shift target, and only included Load and Haul, not Drill and Blast, which the mine supervisor was also responsible for.

The new shift report clearly detailed all targets broken down by loaders and drills. It became a collaboration tool more than a reporting tool, improving communication of results and accountability for their improvement. The supervisor could collaborate with all his teams, and if a target was missed, he could understand the detailed reasons for missed targets from each team and had the information on what actions should be repeated when a target was met – creating a "best possible" discussion. By implementing this tool, total tons increased from an average of 100,000 tons per day to 120,000 tons per day in the first week, which was the highest the mine had ever achieved. By collaborating, the overall morale and alignment within the entire mine network also improved.

Under New Management

Through the lens of fair trade and active management you can see the difference between twentieth- and twenty-first-century management, and the positive results that are possible. Probably the most powerful observation of all is that a *lighter* management touch with deeper connection will mobilize people into positive action. It doesn't mean less management it means a different kind of management – finding the right balance of management and the right style to manage to engage.

There is something very telling about the phrase "under new management" – the emphasis on being *under* the control or status of someone superior. In his book *The Future of Management*[4], Gary Hamel writes about managing less and inspiring more. I call that connecting more. He reminds us that in traditional management circles, passion and management don't naturally fit together. His book was published in 2007. Engagement scores were low then and have only increased by single digits since. In some countries they have declined. In the US as an example, scores changed only 4–5% over the period 2007–2018. We can take some solace in the actively disengaged dropping by 7% in the same time frame.

If good management is more about the ability to connect and release passion from a practical perspective, the leader's legacy becomes more about the ideas they sparked, the minds they inspired, the hearts they stirred, and the spirits they moved – above and beyond the costs saved and increases to productivity. But it's very difficult to manage passion. The emphasis needs to be on *releasing* it, *nurturing* it, and *leveraging* it – very different leadership skills to those of command and control! That's not to say that *management* in the pure sense is detrimental. Rather, it should be about agreeing what is needed for the team, setting the expectations, stepping in when help is required, stepping out when the teams simply need to get on with their jobs, and guiding and encouraging people to think and create along a path that will take the business where it needs to go. That is active management. That is a fair trade.

Keeping this in mind, it becomes clear that when you want to actively manage to engage in a fair trade, it can't be a one-way street. Your employees also need a model of team behaviors to better connect with active managers. This aligns managers and people and promotes accountability and ownership within your teams: Active team member behaviors (ATMBs) must be defined as well. Figure 4.2 shows a peek into those.

---

[4] Gary Hamel, *The Future of Management* (Boston: Harvard Business School Press, 2007).

8. **How did I perform against my targets?** Plan versus actual. Input to reporting & visual management boards

7. **What is wrong & how can we resolve this?** Root cause analysis

6. **How can I improve my performance?** Receive capability development, training, & on the job coaching

5. **What do I change & how to change it?** Agree what I need to stop, start, change, or continue

1. **Am I safe, am I practicing safe actions?** Training, safety procedures, & reporting

2. **Know what must be done?** Expectations, integrated plans, & schedules

3. **How to do it?** Know-how, capability building, instructions, procedures, and team meetings

4. **How am I doing?** Discuss my progress with my team leader. Agree what I need to stop, start, change, or continue

8. Plan vs Actual
7. Provide Input
6. Give & Receive Coaching & Supporting
5. Agree Progress
4. Check-In
3. Understand the How
2. Understand the What
1. Practicing Health & Safety

Eight Active Team Member Behaviors

FIGURE 4.2   Eight Active Team Member Behaviors.

Applying Fair Trade: What Color Is Your Day?

How can you easily self-assess your fair-trade abilities and the way you apply these in your daily life at work? Simple: Keep track of how you spend your time. Keep a fair-trade log to gauge how you are investing your time and how frequently and well you are connecting with the people around you. Assigning a color to the various activities you invest in can build a picture of where your current emphasis is – enriched by notes of what you did, the quality of your interactions with people, and any concerns that emerged – and you will have a clear view of what is important to you.

Proudfoot first designed and used a "Day in the Life of" (DILO) tool to observe how managers invest their time and behavior many decades ago. It recorded everything a supervisor did, as an example, to get the most from staff – from the start of a shift to its end, visually highlighting how they spent their time and to identify issues that people had to face as they went about their work day.

The fair-trade log is a variation on the DILO, focusing on how often managers *engage* with people, color coding and then highlighting daily activities. It can help spotlight where the chances to better connect may be. The bonus is that you will identify operational improvements along the way – the things that get in the way of your people's success.

The Color of Your Most Valued Asset – Your Time

Logging your day as a leader or manager causes you to stop and think about how you invest your time. How you invest your time shows your people what is important. Use the following color codes to chart where your emphasis lies. Ultimately, the aim is to objectively highlight how much time you invest successfully engaging with people. It's a bit like keeping a food diary – once you start keeping a record, it's easier to see the time you've consumed.

- *Green is the color of growth.* This is the time you directly connect with people, whether face to face, by phone, video conferences, or teams. You could be using any combination of the eight AMBs, 1.5.30, or HeadsUp.

- *Purple is the color of calorie burning – look, listen, learn.* Here, you're active and visible, reviewing how well the infrastructure supports people. On the floor, visit stores, walk the factory floor, meet customers, test the product, and see the service delivered firsthand – see how well the processes are performing for your people and customers. You note action needed. You support decision-making with observed facts. This should be a perpetual cycle of observation – of talking, thinking, collaborating, deciding, and acting.

- *Yellow is the color of meetings.* You've done all the right prep work for the meeting; read the materials and rallied support for your ideas. You follow the agenda, you take notes, get action items, and assign follow-up items. As well as facilitating productive meetings, you let constructive conversations take you to places you may not have thought of, encourage debate and check that anything you agree is understood by all involved. Meetings are your friend. You follow Pat Lencioni's advice on meetings (pick up his book, *Death by Meeting*).

- *Pink is the color of planning.* It's the time you invest in mapping out or reviewing the next day, week, month, project, or year; building or reviewing/adjusting schedules, volumes, forecasts, organizing resources or equipment – to be well prepared for people to accomplish their jobs. It is time spent in dialogue with others, discussing what everyone believes is the shape of things to come; learning how the business should organize itself to be more successful. Planning time also includes planning for 1.5.30 time – thinking about people's performance. Effective leaders will build in time to talk about performance routinely, rather than annually or semi-annually. A conversation each week with an individual is worth more than any formal annual performance review.

- *Orange is the color of administration and emails.* I've assigned orange because it can burn up your time if you let it take control – reporting, writing emails, completing endless paperwork. Use this time sparingly and with the full intent to learn from the data and bring the learnings to your next conversation or meeting: datacation.

- *Blue is the color of learning – coaching and collaborating.* This is the time you spend teaching, training, and helping others learn. It's the time you run team or one-on-one development sessions, or when you capture knowledge and spread best possible practices. It's when you implement change and help people acquire new skills, or ease their transition to those new skills. It could be time spent talking to peers or networking across the value chain; seeking feedback from customers and suppliers; or maintaining an ongoing informal dialogue with team members to gauge and influence their ongoing progress.

- *Red is the color of crisis.* It's for unplanned events, crisis activities, and the time you spend troubleshooting when unforeseen issues arise. It also includes time spent unpacking and rescuing work that has gone off track, or assuming tasks on behalf of others. It's the time you might have saved if you'd engaged in discussions with others to arrive at solutions prior to becoming crisis. Red is the time you could be investing in other activities.

When you log everything that happens in your day from the moment you start work, it can act as a wake-up call to how you really engage with your teams. For instance, consider how your typical day starts: responding to emails; compiling or reviewing reports. So far, it's all looking a bit orange. If you're interacting with people through meetings, start to see the difference between yellow (formal) dialogue, compared to green or blue encounters that count more as fair-trade time when you're engaging with people and guiding them to be their best. Time spent on troubleshooting the day's crisis bleeds red – finding out why the shipment is late, a deadline has not been met, a customer has had to call a second time, or where your numbers are. But then you sit back, finding you have a few spare moments to think. So you get yourself a coffee, bumping into one of the guys from dispatch who you invite to join you for a chat. Great – that's green all the way to the bottom of the coffee cup.

The Many Shades of Value

Everything you do can be assigned a color and a value attached. Are you adding value through the way you invest your time? Are you creating value by engaging your people? Are you helping people feel valued? A meeting may add value but the brownie points you scored when you had coffee with the guy from dispatch to help solve his problem creates value for both of you and gets you the multiplier effect.

If spending time with employees is special – something extraordinary, rather than a natural part of your day, then it's time to reevaluate where your focus lies. The more time you spend purposefully engaging with people and keeping abreast of what goes on in their world, the better their workplace and work experience – and the better your results, and sense of reward, as a manager. Meeting people is the job.

Before you start your first log, it's worth taking note of what you *think* the color of your day usually is. Attach an estimated percentage time to each of the colors, based on how you *think* you allocate your time. Prepare to be surprised when you compare to reality.

Your DILO Log

Once you've captured your day in color, ask yourself some questions to see how you feel about the time spent:

- Did you spend the time as you intended?
- Did you spend enough time with your people?
- How much of your time was spent on things you regret, or feel were wasted minutes and hours?

These are all quantitative questions and well worth asking, but here's the qualitative question:

- What did your people learn from you today?
- What new things did you learn about your people today – whether about their life at work or at home?
- Did you help make others successful – remove barriers, jointly solve problems?
- What did you coach people on today?

And the bonus question:

- Did you feel you created value – not just added value but really created value for your people?

In other words, how effective was your day? And, more importantly, how effective were you at connecting with people in a fair trade?

A further benefit comes from identifying how much of your time is spent on things that are unplanned – those things that frustrate people and cause problems in the workplace. The kinds of things that cause people to disengage with frustration, walk out, or quit and stay. We will look at these factors much more closely in other chapters. For now, just consider: if *you* are experiencing those disengagement triggers, imagine how other team members feel!

You Don't Have a Time Machine

Time is the most valuable commodity in the world. You can't buy it, borrow it, or build it. And people hate to waste it. It's our truly scarcest resource. Abundant when you have it, but when it's gone, it has no reclamation process. It simply disappears. Ashes to ashes, dust to dust. And so, in our time-poor world, time management is not the objective; but rather freeing time, releasing it from the guts of your business, by how you and your people invest their time. At the very core of your business is the need to unshackle time from the wasted work effort that sucks your people's efforts and attention away from what counts; delivering safe, productive operations that create value rather than simply use it. Active management can engage people in identifying where they can free up time wasted on rework, recurring issues, and the noise in our ecosystems.

Once you master time, you create capacity for everyone to think, to learn, to act, to give back. To coach. Uptime, meantime, cycle time, ship time, call time, quote time, change over time, or lead time. Whatever is critical to your operations. Once you master time, you add value.

Cut the Passion Police and Create Advantage

Fair trade is the starting point for mobilizing employees, creating people who are passionate about their work. While fair trade is not an advantage, having people with passion is, and one you should take to market. It's the most difficult aspect of business to replicate. The next time you engage with your people, consider as you walk away from them what thoughts you left them with. Did you inspire and excite them, so that their minds are buzzing with great ideas they can't wait to note down? Or are they weighed down with a mental list of things they must do to keep their stress levels down and their boss at bay?

As we work through the 7 Cs and the second F (Freedom) that make up the MI-9 of employee engagement, we will see a clear alternative to management emerge – one that should ensure that, if your people *were* called on to vote for their next boss, they would instinctively choose you.

---

1. **In collaboration with your people, create the fair-trade basics for a fair-trade business**
2. **What should underpin each day regardless of anything else in the business. What are the basic rules of engagement in your workplace?**
3. **Take the fair-trade manager quiz below.**

Answer yes or no. If you answer no to a question, you have some work to do to improve your levels of connectivity and help your people get engaged.

Note: Be honest: it's the only option you have; your people will happily tell you the answers to these questions. Ask them and compare, remembering to take their responses on the chin! After all, we can only learn and improve if we know where we have been going wrong.

1. Are you a visible, active manager?
2. Do you practice honesty, integrity, and sincerity at work?
3. Do you talk about how great the people you work with are?
4. Have you adapted your communication style to suit the nature of people in your workplace?
5. Do you favour plain speaking and make a conscious effort to stay relevant in your communication?
6. Do you use 'You' and 'We' more regularly than 'I'?

FIGURE 4.3 Things You Need to Do Right Now.

7. Are you aware of the words you use day-to-day and how they are received?

8. Have you taken on a more informal approach to working with your people, choosing times to chat, debate, discuss, scheduling coffee breaks not just formal meetings?

9. Do you know the simple 'life facts' about your people – e.g., marital/family status, hobbies/interests, challenges, relatives, living conditions, aspirations? Would you say you know your people well, personally as well as professionally?

10. Do you regularly let people know they have done a great job?

11. Do you consider yourself a good development coach, as well as a manager?

12. Are you well versed in mentoring and helping people succeed who are at the fringe of your business – not just your direct reports?

13. Do you bring all walks of people and their views to your discussions, promotions, special projects?

14. Do you regularly seek people's opinions, input, and guidance?

15. Can you admit when you are wrong and that you don't have all the answers?

16. Do you have 'expectation' contracts between yourself and other people (in all directions)?

17. Do you give people a roadmap with milestones that show progress – i.e., how far or close they are to what needs to be achieved – but leaves room for people to fill in the details?

18. Do you find and talk about what's right before you move onto anything that might be wrong?

19. Do you tell it like it is – and balance this with how it should be in the future?

20. Do people see you as caring and concerned? Do you genuinely help people?

21. Do you deliver on your promises every single time? Do you level with people if you can't?

22. Are you pushing your conclusions or helping people draw their own conclusions?

23. Do you take feedback on the chin – can you take it as well as give it?

24. Do you think other people are on the same page as you?

25. Are you engaged yourself?

26. Do you use technology to your advantage, using the best way to communicate with people or to help your team achieve its goals?

27. Do you see opportunity in challenges?

28. Do you help people partner up and connect across teams or the business?

29. Do you regularly discuss what your people are learning?

30. Do you give people freedom to act?

31. Do you instill a sense of adventure in what people are doing, bring a sense of challenge to their work?

32. Through your discussions, do you help people feel a sense of autonomy – that they can control their destiny?

33. Do you encourage people to volunteer their best effort, knowing that what they do counts? Do people feel that you inspire them to be their best?

How did you score?

If you answered mostly yeses, congratulations – you are connecting! Unless, of course, you answered no to some of the critical questions. Take another look at numbers 1, 2, 5, 16, 23, and 29. These are fair-trade deal breakers. A 'no' to any of these could be having a very detrimental effect on engagement.

If you answered 'yes' to 15–20 of the questions, you're still doing OK – as long as the important ones above are counted. With a bit of thought and effort, you should be able to pinpoint some great additional opportunities to connect more effectively, and increase your fair-trade

FIGURE 4.3 (*Continued*)

rating. Review where your nos are and think about what you can do to turn them into yeses.

If you scored below 15, you're either being more honest than others or you really haven't been connecting well with your people routinely. This probably means you have a lot of disgruntled people at work. It's a common trap: everyday pressures push you into the 'head down' style of management, and the result is a disengaged workforce. Take a breath, think about how you dig yourself out of this hole – and keep reading.

4. Develop your **Management Action Plan** ('MAP' for short). **Jot down the action items that occurred to you as you worked through the questions, and make yourself a list of what you need to improve.**

5. **Consider these additional questions:**

   If they weren't being paid to do it, who – among those you work with – would:

   a. Show up each day? (and would you, if you weren't being paid?)

   b. Attend your meetings?

   c. Speak/listen to you?

   d. Get things done?

6. **Apply the colour-coded management activity log.**

   a. Using the outline offered in this chapter, colour in the log to reflect how you currently perceive your allocation of time in a typical day.

   b. Now complete your target log – showing a more ideal balance.

   c. Then complete the actual log for one full day in your life at work.

FIGURE 4.4 (*continued*)

d. Compare your results with what you thought your results would be – with both your perceived log and your ideal log. Where are the gaps?

e. Complete an action plan to address those gaps, paying special attention to anything that may be discouraging or undermining people's engagement.

Fair trade: 5 things you can do today to improve people's quality of life at work

1. **Think laterally about how you source opinions and abilities. Give people a voice.**

   Look at the projects you currently have underway and those you plan to initiate; the problems you need to solve or the innovations you need to introduce; the meetings you currently hold and those you will run in the future; the decisions you need to make and the performance you need to review. 'Open source' these tasks. That is, include people and from anywhere in the business if you can. Give them a fair go. Let everyone have a voice and let anyone participate if they believe they have something to offer.

2. **Be a listening post and invite input. Stop pushing and start pulling.**

   Use 1.5.30 to engage. Set regular times to 'walk the business'. Once you establish a routine, people will expect your drop-in visit. They'll be more mentally prepared for real discussions with you. Ask people to give feedback on how they feel about their work or the business. Encourage them to speak freely. Any subject should be fair game. Make a habit of asking people what they think of a new process, policy, practice, tool, procedure, change, economic condition, competitor, or product that you are exploring – before you take it to the next step. Work with your critics.

FIGURE 4.4   *(Continued)*

3. **Share management goals – and responsibility for meeting them.**

   At the start of every meeting, ask "How can we improve life at work today so that our people could give their best?" Then ask "What do we want to achieve out of this meeting?"

4. **Thank people and write personal notes.**

   Get personal, take time out to look people in the eyes, shake their hands (or bump elbows), and say thank you for a job well done. Take the time to hand-write a note in your Christmas or Thank You cards to each and every person. Adapt your conversations to the people concerned; let people see that you know who they are.

5. **Go public – update your status, tweet the team's success.**

   Openly express your concerns and your dreams, the results, and the hoped-for changes. Publicly commit to new and different ways of managing, and then let people hold you accountable to those commitments. Tell people what's going on, in timely Yammer updates, LinkedIn blog posts, or bite-sized Twitter feeds.

Rate your own engagement

To create a baseline for yourself, circle the score that best reflects your current state of mind – i.e., your own level of engagement.

10/10: I am fully engaged. I do whatever it takes to ensure we (myself, my colleagues, my teams, my business) are successful. I have one foot in the present and one foot in the future and volunteer my discretionary effort to help make progress each and every day.

8/10: I'm almost there; sometimes I need a little push over the edge when I stumble across an issue or concern; but, for the most part, I'm in top form. Sometimes I end up with two feet in the future, so I may get a little frustrated things aren't moving fast enough to make things happen today.

6/10: Sometimes I have two feet in the present because I'm not always sure how to connect today with where we need to be. I let the energy leeches get to me and slow me down. Occasionally, I think of getting another job; and, if the perfect opportunity came along, I'd take it. I'm tired of hearing other people complain. I do what I need to do to get paid.

4/10: I've got one foot out the door and the other on its way out just as soon as I find a job. I wonder if other companies are run like this one. I keep telling everyone what needs to change, but no one wants to listen. I'm tired of telling them. I'm lucky if I bother to get everything done each day, but why should I? Who cares?

2/10: I have two feet out the door. Other companies can't be run like this one. My brain has already quit. I can't even be bothered to do the work anymore; besides, why would I do anything for this company?

0/10: I have flying monkeys and I'm not afraid to use them. This company doesn't deserve me. In fact, I hope they don't succeed and then they'll know I was right. That will teach them!

If you circled 6/10 or below, you're with the majority of the working population worldwide: under-engaged.

CHAPTER 5

A Common Cause: Collecting Volunteers to Create a Movement

A person needs a job to survive but you need work to feel like you're worth something.

—Robert Jury, writer/director of *Working Man*

The 2020 movie *Working Man* is a chronicle of the value of work in our lives. It tells the story of one man's desire to keep his dignity and his life. It also tells the story of why a job is increasingly so much more important than just its paycheck.

Too often, people feel disengaged at work because they fail to see the wider context of what they do – the contribution they are making and why it matters. People get so bogged down in the day-to-day nitty gritty they can't join the dots to see the bigger picture. Giving people a sense of cause helps to change that. If they understand their purpose – the difference they are making, the value they are adding – they are more likely to volunteer more of their effort. It's not just about what's in it for me. It's about being engaged in something more meaningful than just being productive, and yet if you achieve that sense of purpose, you will be more productive. Needing to know what is expected of you is a table stake. Wanting to know how you fit in is an engager.

Nic Marks, a happiness statistician and a fellow of the New Economics Foundation in London, is a renowned speaker on the science of employee engagement. Among his sage advice is the recommendation that companies stop managing through a lens of fear about the future (if something goes wrong). Rather, they need to offer a vision that people can help make a reality – to feel *inspired* to get involved and give more.

I call this the "What if you could" question. Postpandemic, it's a necessary shift in mindset. When you engage people in a *cause* (rather than instill a sense of fear of what might happen if they *don't* deliver), common sense says people respond more positively, they get to imagine the optimism of what could be, rather than the pessimistic of what might be.

The leader's job, then, is to help people see what's possible – and how each individual can make the possible happen.

Causes Count

In an acclaimed TED talk some years ago[1], Nic Marks highlighted five positive actions that help promote well-being in people. They are to *connect* (foster social relationships); *be active* (the fastest way out of a bad mood is to get out and move); *take notice* (of the world around you); *keep learning* (stay curious); and, finally, *give* (generosity). All five of these actions have a place at work. They fit seamlessly into our MI-9 tools and HeadsUp. And best of all, they cost very little.

Give is a powerful word. Most people feel happier when they give. In his TED talk, Marks drew on the results of a simple experiment to support this point – that if we do something (like spend money) just for our own benefit, we don't feel nearly as good as when we do it for others or, better still, for a higher purpose. At work, when we are contributing to a greater cause rather than just going through the motions of doing a job for a paycheck, it stands to reason that we will feel a deeper sense of engagement.

---

[1] Nic Marks, "The Happy Planet Index," TED.com (July 2010). https://www.ted.com/talks/nic_marks_the_happy_planet_index

Reclaiming Our Sense of Purpose

Unfortunately, for many a sense of purpose has been lost. The business that employs us has become so big, or our role in it seems so small, that it's becoming harder to see why the work we do matters in the grand scheme – it isn't always easy to see what value we add or our special contribution, through the work we do.

Some of this is changing as governments and industry authorities demand more of businesses – for example, by specifying that companies detail their corporate social responsibility (CSR) or ESG commitments as part of their annual financial statements. Such requirements have prompted firms to review their contributions in their local communities and the way that they give back to society. The United Nations sustainable development goals (SDGs), also known as the global goals, are also helping cast a light on the business link to purpose. The SDGs were adopted by all United Nations member states in 2015 as a universal call to action to end poverty, protect the planet, and ensure that all people enjoy peace and prosperity by 2030.[2] They are lofty but practical.

We also saw a massive change in 2020, as the frontline heroes of health care, grocery stores, trucking, transit, or manufacturing were applauded for their ability to work each day so that everyone else could stay home and stay safe. Many risked their lives. Some lost their lives. Suddenly, the cause got real. Everyday people were engaged in meaningful, needed work. They saw the concept of "this is bigger than us" come to life.

Repeated surveys show time and again that finding meaning in the work we do ranks very highly in our happiness and motivation in our jobs. A 2016 global survey of 26,000 LinkedIn members found that 74 percent of candidates preferred to work in a job where they feel like their contribution matters.[3] In an article published in 2018 by ShiftBoard, a workforce technology company, actively disengaged employees cost the US $483 billion to $605 billion each year in lost productivity.[4] That's just the disengaged, not including

---

[2] United Nations, 2015. *Sustainable Development Goals.* Available from: https://sdgs.un.org/goals

[3] LinkedIn, *2016 Global Report: Purpose at Work: The Largest Global Study on the Role of Purpose in the Workforce,* https://business.linkedin.com/content/dam/me/business/en-us/talent-solutions/resources/pdfs/purpose-at-work-global-report.pdf © Imperative.

[4] "The Real Cost Of Employee Disengagement," Shiftboard (February 14, 2018). www.shift-board.com/blog/real-cost-employee-disengagement/#:~:text=High%20Price%20You%20Pay%20for%20Employee%20Disengagement&text=Actively%20disengaged%20employees%20cost%20the,each%20year%20in%20lost%20productivity

trals. Meanwhile, in the UK alone, it is estimated that se their combined value by some £130 billion if they organized around clear corporate purposes that unite s according to a 2016 report by the Big Innovation ... (BIC). It also emphasizes the importance of the evolution of a company's sense of purpose as conditions change – for instance, as a challenger startup company matures and gains direct competitors all offering a similar proposition. "Purpose is a living narrative," the report's authors note. It needs to move with the times and move you.

Research suggests that upcoming generations of employees are increasingly seeking purpose from the outset of their careers. An annual survey of millennials (those born after 1982) by Deloitte, among 8,000 respondents from 30 countries, has repeatedly shown that employer loyalty increases where people feel aligned to the company's values and sense of purpose.[6] No surprise.

Most people want the chance to make a difference. In today's hyperconnected world where communities grow at speed, it is easier to build a sense of conscience, cause, and belonging. Employers can tap into and harness this, not only as an extension of their CSR efforts but as a fair dinkum means of building employees' sense of contribution and achievement. Doing this formally takes businesses into the realm of employee advocacy (unprompted promotion of a firm's brand and values by people who work there), and if causes and purpose are fair dinkum and employees feel aligned with them, engagement can follow naturally.

In the business of consulting, it can be easy to lose yourself in the financial, hard numbers of what we do. So, in 2017 when I became CEO, I took on the task of writing our manifesto, the "why are we here, really?" document. What came to life was how important what we do for clients is. In addition to achieving hugely aspirational objectives, we also enable people to feel they are making a difference to their teams and their business. When we talked about this with our own teams, it became evident how important that was – making a difference to the client leaders, who, in turn, got to make a difference to

---

[5] Birgitte Andersen, Clare Chapman, Alex Edmans, et al., *The Purposeful Company* (Big Innovation Centre, 2016). www.biginnovationcentre.com/wp-content/uploads/2019/07/BIC_THE-PURPOSEFUL-COMPANY-INTERIM-REPORT_15.05.2016.pdf

[6] Deloitte, 2016. *The 2016 Deloitte Millennial Survey Winning over the next generation of leaders Millennial Survey*. www2.deloitte.com/content/dam/Deloitte/global/Documents/About-Deloitte/gx-millenial-survey-2016-exec-summary.pdf

their business and teams. This provided purpose. We had cracked the nut on our real purpose – to make a difference to people by helping others make a difference to people.

In today's world, many millions of people in the workforce also make significant contributions to their communities' and families' well-being, outside of the workplace, from coaches to troop leaders. Add to that the bloggers and social networkers, activists, or hobbyists who make a difference in their worlds, worlds they are totally engaged in. It's how cities get rebuilt after major disasters and how people get on with their lives after catastrophe strikes. We saw it all through 2020 as companies needed people to step up and lead through the COVID-19 crisis. It's through such extracurricular commitments that new policies and bills come into force, that walls come down in communist countries and injustices are resolved. People take action. They help each other. They share and grow their passion in what they believe in. They roll up their sleeves and help others – who in turn inspire and help others.

As employers, leaders, and managers, we need to learn from this. If it is possible to ignite and fan people's passion and sense of contribution and fulfilment outside of work or during crisis, where effort is usually expended for free, surely it should be possible to harness the same momentum at work – if the same sense of engagement and purpose is there. In marketing, they call it B2P: business to people. That's getting close to a better paradigm at work, but shouldn't it simply be P2P: people to people? Your business will move faster when you start with people and ignite their passions. Nothing moves until people are moved.

Volunteering Your Passion

Research confirms that emotions have a strong bearing on engagement, so much so that if someone is emotionally committed rather than or as well as rationally committed to something, it can have up to four times the impact.[7] Poor emotional buy-in, a clash of values, and other negative influencers such as stress and a feeling of failure can erode people's attitude and commitment to their work. A feeling of connectedness and emotional alignment can have the opposite effect – causing people to give more, *because they want to*.

---

[7] Corporate Leadership Council, *Driving Performance and Retention Through Employee Engagement*. www.stcloudstate.edu/humanresources/_files/documents/supv-brown-bag/employee-engagement.pdf © 2004 Corporate Executive Board.

While certain things are beyond managers' control, feelings are a more movable proposition. We may not be able to change what's going on, but we can change how we (and others) respond to it. Could it be that creating emotional commitment is the Holy Grail of engagement? It certainly could, and todays challenges can't be solved by yesterday's underenthused. Our businesses value is in the humans it engages.

Why do people take to the streets for what they believe in, but they find it tough to get out of bed and take to the street that leads them to work? Out in the community, where people are already giving their time and energy freely, there are some good clues about what we need to do to foster the same enthusiasm and drive higher levels of emotional commitment at work. Any one of the national, nonviolent, quiet protests that take place like the Million Women March or Brexit, all show people's ambition to have a voice and rise for a cause. They have something in common: passion.

Where engagement goes, excitement flows. Consider the ways that engagement drives passion:

- *There's a story that gets people talking about a cause worth rising for.* Usually there will be a point of view that gets people interested and talking to each other. People learn about the cause when it stirs their spirit.

- *There's a feeling you need to do something.* The story inspires people to consider how they can help – it's a call to action. There is a sense of urgency that something must happen.

- *There's a champion who inspires you to get involved.* They have information to give you deeper understanding, and they help people connect with the right sources to take action – a resource. They help clear the way to make things happen.

- *Those moved to act mobilize each other.* They spur each other on by adding to the story, they develop an affiliation, they collaborate, and they share a "together we'll get there faster" attitude.

- *There's a trail that's contagious, sparks interest, and inspires people to take action, to go further.* There is usually a path that gets other people interested and sparks more action: there is evidence of progress. You see what you are doing is being heard or having an impact.

- *You build capability as you experience new things.* You learn from others and from your combined experience. New capabilities are developed, new experiences add to your story, you build up your knowledge.

- *There's a sensation that your efforts helped someone today.* Pretty soon, it feels like a movement, building momentum and instilling a sense of accomplishment. Friends, family, and your network, recognize this, too: people think and say, "Wow, what a difference you have made."

This is why volunteer-based charities and organizations have a different level of motivation – it's not about the money – people believe in the work and want to make a difference. These three components – motivation, belief, and making a difference – are the key to engaging people's hearts and minds in a way that paid work has typically struggled to match.

The challenge for employers, as these same people who took to the streets take to their salaried jobs the next day, is to engender the same passion and purpose during work hours.

Users Don't Adopt, People Do

How come management gurus still speak of resistance to change and failed digital transformations . . . yet whole new IT platforms have been rolled out across the globe to billions of people without a memo, a town hall, a training program, an improvement team, or senior leadership support?

Most of us can buy online, check in for a flight, go through automated immigration, use online banking, and many have Facebook, Twitter, Instagram, or any number of other accounts, but it's likely none of us received a memo from a CEO to get on board. Instead, there was a story, early users, influencers, and some common elements to all these examples that created movement – they guide you through your learning and practice: they have user friendly technology, coaches spring up from their new followers, people help spread the word by using the technology and helping others use it. There was also a cause no matter how big or small – convenience, connection with long distance family, sharing experiences. It's not about user adoption, it's about community connection. When you master that, you master not just engagement but transformation.

What we forget is that these same people who are using these technologies at home are the people who come to work each day to participate in digital or operational transformation. The difference? Engagement.

So, what if you could bring that same spirit to work? You can.

Start by taking the happy baggage to work with you:

1. *First, managers need to discover what it is that will get their people out of bed each day.* Having a purpose at work that is greater than the sum of the required tasks is what helps people get up in the morning. When you know you will be operating your machine and acting as coach to a new hire as an example, your sense of fulfilment grows: you have a greater role to play.

2. *Creating community around someone's expertise and practices at work builds interest and buy-in.* Being seen as a knowledge expert, who can help develop skills in others, reinforces our ability, sense of value, and feeling of contribution to the bigger picture. It also encourages togetherness.

3. *Making a difference in the wider community gives additional meaning to people's effort.* How your workplace comes together to give back to the community can lead to more varied and challenging work, and boost our sense of purpose and motivation.

4. *Helping your community grow by growing your business to grow jobs.* The impact on society as people become multipliers.

Starting from Scratch

The good news is that causes can be created. Yet when research spanning Bain & Co, Accenture, and Gallup concurs that up to 60 percent of employees remain at a loss about their company's strategy and purpose, it becomes clear that there is a lot of work to do to give people a higher aim. The bigger the organization, the easier it is for employees to feel disconnected from any higher purpose. Remarkably, these same firms actually have the easiest road to accomplish it. They have budgets and people to work on this.

Gallup is clear that as employees "move beyond the basics of employee engagement and view their contribution to the organization more broadly, they are more likely to stay, take proactive steps to create a safe environment, have higher productivity, and connect with customers to the benefit of the organization."[8]

---

[8] Gallup, *Why your company must be mission-driven*, 2014. https://www.gallup.com/workplace/236537/why-company-mission-driven.aspx

So it's not unreasonable that everyone who works for a company should understand its purpose, goals, and intentions for the long, medium, and short term – its vision. But it's more than that. It's the why behind the vision that opens doors. If employees are to engage and buy into it, and give their best to achieve the aims that have been set out, it helps if they understand what they are working toward and why. So what are the do's and don'ts on the why of business?

1. *Don't rely on numbers to inspire.* The cause cannot be the next cost-saving drive or revenue goal. It also can't be fear based. People don't aspire to do great things because they may lose their jobs or miss out on the next incentive payment. If fear worked, none of us would be overweight and people wouldn't smoke. Even when death is the consequence, it doesn't mean that people will step up and be inspired to do better or different things.

2. *Do use plain speak.* Using *plain speaking* is important, so that people understand what the business does and what it is about, in their own terms – in their own context.

3. *Show how concepts can become doing words rapidly.* Turn vision into verbs, aspiration into action, passion into presence. The vital shift is purpose into plans – demonstrating how our daily activities are connected to our why.

   Telefónica UK (O2) many years ago was already on to purpose. It had a great way of explaining strategy. It started with what it wanted to achieve: "*Fandom — to have twice as many customers who are fans as its nearest competitor by 2011.*" It then went on to explain this to its people. The then-CEO Ronan Dunne explained: "We're articulating the journey to everyone. We're creating visibility across the entire organization regarding decisions, investments, and choices that will define the path we will travel."[9] The company linked the why to the how and showed what they would do to support and align with it, putting money through investment decisions behind specific needs that would reinforce the why.

Have you outlined your strategy in simple terms for your people? Can you point to how your strategy acts as the compass for your decisions? Can you link people's jobs to the strategy, so that they understand the

---

[9] David MacLeod and Nita Clarke, *Engaging for Success: Enhancing Performance Through Employee Engagement* (UK Office of Public Sector Information, 2009), p. 78. https://dera.ioe.ac.uk/1810/1/file52215.pdf

part they are playing and why it matters? Can you link the organizational why to the personal why?

4. *But why?* Too often, we ourselves – as managers and leaders – don't fully understand the bigger picture. So it is hardly surprising that we struggle to communicate it well to those who look to us for direction. An early priority should be to go back to basics and make sure the organization's *raison d'etre*, its purpose, is clear and well understood – from the top down and the bottom up. *This should also be refreshed whenever a major shift in the business occurs.*

Someone who places *why* at the center of leadership strategy is motivational speaker Simon Sinek, the British/American author of *Start with Why*[10] and *Find Your Why*[11]. He goes so far as to argue that it doesn't matter so much *what* you do, but *why* you do it.

5. *Be mission critical.* If the mission is clear from the top, it's much easier for employees to (a) figure out whether their own values and ambitions are well aligned to this, potentially boosting their personal commitment; and (b) understand their role and responsibilities in a new, more meaningful context – which add to their individual sense of value, contribution, and purpose.

Of course, many people often end up in jobs by accident, without any grand plan. When this happens, we are unlikely to take the time to understand what the job *really* is. I became a management consultant over three decades ago because I saw an ad in the *Sydney Morning Herald* for what appeared to be a cool job. It turned out it really was – so much so that I made the profession my career – but I had no inkling of that as I boarded the plane to start work in Mount Isa Mines in far northwestern Queensland, Australia, back in 1987. I didn't even know what a consultant was, let alone what one did or why!

6. *A picture paints a great strategy.* Thankfully, there are some good, solid tools you can use to routinely give employees a consistent message and understanding of your business. I personally swear by *Discovery Maps*

---

[10] Simon Sinek, *Start with Why: How Great Leaders Inspire Everyone to Take Action* (New York: Penguin, 2011).
[11] Simon Sinek, *Find Your Why: A Practical Guide for Discovering Purpose for You and Your Team,* (New York: Penguin 2017).

from a company called Paradigm Learning. Finding your why can come from these creative solutions.

A nice touch is that they build on the influence of the immediate manager, using them to roll out the message through the maps to their teams. This is a smart move – taking advantage of and reinforcing the line manager relationship – something most businesses can learn from. We often hire illustrators to simply visualize the messages.

Context Creates Clarity

Mining is big business in Africa and, in common with many industries, it has been through its ups and downs, pushed to the breaking point as commodity prices dropped in the 1990s and 2010s and bouncing back as they rose again. On a working visit to a copper mine in the Cape of South Africa, one that was struggling with its costs, I will always recall a great "aha!" moment that hit me as I toured the mine site with the operations management team. This mine desperately needed to extend its life or face closure. That day brought me a story I would never forget.

I came upon one of the most interesting workplaces and team of people I'd ever encountered. I was at the point in the copper process (largely manual compared to today) where you saw the molten copper flow, just before it was formed and cooled into a transportable block. I met the *tap-hole operator*. I saw firsthand, in full blazing technicolor, the impact one single employee can have on an entire business. The tap-hole operator had the most dangerous position in the mine – one with a very real risk of death. But also, the most critical impact on costs.

His job was to tap holes in molten metal to separate the copper from the slag — the more slag in the copper, the less pure it was and the lower the price it would command.

Never before had I come across a role with such a significant and direct impact on the total profitability of a business. In my view, this one individual really did hold the life of the mine in his hands. But did the tap-hole operator know and understand the importance of his role? Did anyone ever point this out? No. And why? Because other things get in the way, distracting the manager from offering precious reinforcement of the value of the job being done.

When we're busy, these vital human elements can be forgotten. But, if there's one thing that elevates people's engagement, it's being reminded of how they're connected to everything or everyone else in your business. Context!

7. *A job description is not a call for purpose.* You could be forgiven for thinking that as a hands-on manager you already have all of these important bases covered: "I've given my team their job descriptions; they get a performance review each year; I pin up the weekly numbers and email them fairly regular updates; I've explained how what they do is tracked by the big bosses upstairs, and how their work affects company profitability and customer satisfaction. Surely that's enough?" Well, no, unfortunately – it isn't.

8. *What's the prize?* People want to know how they help win the prize, no matter where they sit in their company. If they can help share in that prize (even if not directly, but through a sense of shared achievement), then engagement builds. You've heard the old story of the maintenance man at NASA helping put the man on the moon. It was updated with complete sincerity during the COVID-19 pandemic, as everyday hospital cleaners and workers could point to how they were saving lives. If you don't link people's contribution, how will they?

9. *Reduce noise.* If work's context and purpose has got lost along the way, this needs to be addressed with simple, direct messaging. Perhaps there is just too much information and complexity. In which case, it's probably time for a good old-fashioned clearout.

What about People in Boring Jobs? How Can They Get Engaged?

There are positions in companies that people feel are just boring – the dirty, tedious, menial jobs that someone has to do. But does this mean they should be disconnected and disengaged? Far from it! Here's a story of my own to illustrate this:

Some time ago, I attended a management meeting in which my client was having a few words with his team. "We need to get people to do their jobs better, no matter how boring the job is," he said. It was said out of concern. In most fields of work, there are laborious, unappealing roles that can only be done by humans. But that doesn't mean the people doing them can't take pride in or feel good about their work.

I started work at McDonald's in Australia when I was just shy of 15. I was busy at school but managed to squeeze in five shifts a week – the equivalent of a full-time job for many people. I started out as a dining-room kid – the person who clears the trays from tables and takes out the trash. I polished the fingerprints off the doors, and cleaned the washrooms. And I loved it! Each day I would arrive, ready to throw on my very ugly and oversized uniform, don my gloves, check my cleaning supplies, and tour the parking lot for trash.

Other kids might have walked the dining area as though they'd been sentenced to life in prison without parole: they would spend each 4–8 hour shift counting each excruciating minute spent wiping tables, mopping spilled drinks, and peeling pickles off the walls, waiting to be promoted to fries or better still, front counter.

For me, it was all about the people and the responsibility. Call me a geek. In my naive fourteen-years-and-nine-months-old mind, I had been entrusted to create a good impression on people, which I took to be quite a responsibility. Occasionally, a crew chief or shift manager came by to see if all was OK, but more often than not I was left alone to chat, wipe, and brush my way from one end of the restaurant lot to the other.

I had proved I could be trusted very rapidly, so no one bossed me around, and I was always looking for a new or better way of doing things to make the dining room look better or to handle the rush more easily, seeing it as a challenge. More than anything, I thought, "Wow – each hour I work is money in my bank, and I get to hang with my friends!" I felt I was adding value, despite merely being the dining-room kid looking after the trash.

I had to be trained to do the job correctly so it must have been important. My attitude to what I did all came down to my vantage point.

There are two things that have always struck me about this first experience of the working world. First, because I earned trust from my bosses, they didn't feel they had to micromanage me. I had built the supervisory process into my own process. Second, I had made the job feel interesting, looking for ways to improve the task or process, or to interact with customers even amid emptying the trash. I also felt that if I did a great job, I might be rotated into a more responsible position – and, lo and behold, that's exactly what happened. Before my fifteenth birthday, I was let loose on the fries' counter!

Coming back to the client meeting I attended where the senior manager was doing his best to encourage those in the most mundane jobs to go the extra mile, the error was now glaring. He framed this negatively; reinforced an idea of some roles being inferior and tedious. Worst of all, no one challenged this statement – not even the head of HR, who was present in the meeting.

Another point of reflection is the type of person often assigned to such roles. Perhaps if we hold certain positions in such low regard, we have low expectations about the people who will want to do them – setting everyone up for failure.

Let's stick with my McDonald's example. If I were running that store today, I'd put my best person in the dining room. Why? First, because it's a visible, front-of-house role that involves close contact with customers. It's also a position that provides broad insight into the business. The dining-room house-keeper is the person who sees what's being trashed and gets to observe customer behavior up close.

So it makes sense to find the right people for the more basic jobs and pay them a decent salary so that they want to stay in the job and do great work. Treat this person well, encourage their progress, and you could have an employee for life – a future innovator and manager. Rather than be apologetic about their role, help them understand how important it is. Perception influences behavior. You might find that your business results pick up and people are a lot more engaged, from the bottom up.

10. *Level with people about what you're doing and why.* Businesses often launch improvement programs yet fail to get people excited because they haven't understood what this means for them. This is one of those *common sense isn't always common,* points: Once people appreciate the need for change and have a clear picture of what difference it will make, they're more likely to get behind it. We've known this for a very long time, and yet, my experience with clients shows that we still often miss this step and forget to help people connect the dots. Sometimes it's simply about a compare and contrast exercise – showing people the difference between where you are and where you want to be.

Channeling Grassroots Success

I once did some work for a major global metals company that owned a mine in the US that was not producing a viable return. Frankly, at that time it could have put the money in the bank and made a better return. The company needed to decide between continuing to invest in an operation that was underperforming (safeguarding several hundred jobs), or cut its losses in favor of something more profitable.

As part of its attempts to turn the situation around, people had been asked to look for cost-reduction opportunities. The results had not been particularly inspiring. The teams weren't well organized; they had little management support by way of real time or attention, and they were populated with people who struggled to do their usual jobs while simultaneously looking for improvement opportunities as a special project.

But actually, addressing business profitability shouldn't have needed to be a special project: surely this is business as usual and everyone's responsibility. The priority was to get the project on management's agenda and show people how their efforts had the potential to have a huge impact on operating results.

Of course, attaching cost to a problem is a great way to get people's attention, but remember: facts don't change people, feelings do. It's not a great way to make change happen. People were well aware of the mine's precarious situation but in reality, little was being done about it. They also couldn't see a way to participate. A double whammy.

It took a new joiner to show that, new or not, he could have a direct impact on the profitability of the mine and make a difference. Within a week of joining the team, he found that $100,000 could be put back onto the company's bottom line, just by changing the way air was put into the tires of its CAT trucks. The new joiner's fresh eyes (and ears) and a new line of sight found the answer others had missed: he saw the possible, where others had seen defeat. A few days later an awareness program was put in place to address a tire overinflation problem. Over the course of the next year, the US $100,000 was recaptured, covering the costs of at least one person on the payroll. If each employee had found their own mini solution, those savings would have added up quickly. If they'd known and understood how their actions added up to a job being saved, perhaps dozens of job sized savings would have been unearthed.

It didn't take long before the buzz of "making a difference" took off. With a little marketing and a lot of discussion, the new joiner's achievement sparked a whole series of conversations across the mine, which in turn led to hundreds of improvement activities at the grassroots of the company being identified. With no lower limit to the scale of improvement, people's imaginations were fired up. Ultimately, several million of recouped dollars were ploughed back into the business before any jobs needed to be lost.

The moral of the story is that even a modest contribution could soon add up – and that their success would be celebrated and communicated to drive more of the same. In the end, everyone benefited from grassroots change.

11. *Beware isolation: people crave connection.* A big trigger for disengagement is when people become isolated at work, perhaps because of their office setup/working hours, an absence of peers in similar roles, or a global pandemic that removed the ability for regular face to face contact to get work done. Of course, it's fantastic if people have more flexibility in how and

where they work, or that we trust them not to need constant supervision, but if connections weaken, people can lose their sense of community, direction, and, importantly, their purpose. Without people on hand to witness or discuss their achievements, their commitment to excelling may be slowly eroded. People like working with people, and enthusiasm is catching. But enthusiasm only works if we can see and be inspired by what each other is doing. We all need validation, others to bounce ideas off, examples and role models of what to aim for. A visible reason to keep going. We learned this throughout 2020. Once the novelty of our great work from home experiment wore off, our need for connection greater than the job being done at our kitchen tables, rose.

There Is No Cause Too Small

A great many businesses and their leaders feel that unless they're actually making a difference in the world on a grand scale (finding a cure for cancer, eradicating poverty), they're unable to help their people connect to a cause. This is untrue. While some firms do have the opportunity to easily make such profound world-changing links, real causes that turn people on at work can be found in everyday work life. You just need to look. The feeling of helping a customer or a colleague to be all he or she can be can have meaningful resonance for those inspired by helping others achieve. Think about it, in the early days of recycling, having recycle bins available at work was a great way of aligning corporate values with employee ethics. We wouldn't dream of not having them today. While each small step may not achieve something monumental in isolation, they all have an impact on employee engagement and help to set the right tone. They send a message.

As the world spins ever more precariously forward, and our world changes ever more rapidly, it's worth revisiting your vision, your purpose, and your plans. Are you translating your vision into the verbs needed for today's world – articulating the company macro vision into your team micro vision? Then take the time to revisit your purpose – does it need to change? And do you have a plan to stay true to your vision and purpose that is clearly understood? Do people know how what they do each day contributes to those plans? Does how they spend their time support them?

We must lead by example – regenerating our own enthusiasm and sense of purpose. Role modeling. Remember that *you* are the one who moves people to do remarkable things; *you're* the passion prophet (rather than the passion police); *you* are the one who must find ways to create passion in others so they want to do remarkable things. Be the leader your people want you to be.

---

1. **Explore the concept of volunteerism and how you can bring it to work for you and your people. How can you use the concept to get better results and, most importantly, instill a state of mind that has people willingly investing their discretionary effort in your business? Would it be beneficial to your workplace or your people? How could you bring it to life in your business?**

2. **Bring volunteerism to work. Consider a critical issue you need people to get behind and expend their discretionary effort on. Try using volunteerism to plan how you will create interest in your issue:**

   a. Build your **story.**

   b. Create a **call to action.**

   c. Find a champion: **the key resource.**

   d. Think laterally about who you assign to the team: find people with a **"together we'll get there faster" attitude.**

   e. Determine how you will **show progress to build interest.**

   f. Look for ways to show the momentum and let the team feel **their bit helped someone today.**

   g. Make sure the team knows that **"It was fantastic of them to help today."**

3. **Think about the people you work with and determine where they would sit on a cause scale of 1 through 10: from (1) I work for a paycheck to (10) I'm committed to the cause! Then ask each in turn the same question. Anything below 10 needs reflection.**

FIGURE 5.1   Things You Need to Do Right Now.   *(continued)*

Cause: 5 things you can do today to improve people's quality of life at work

1. **Distill important explanations into tweet form**

   Take a tip from Twitter. Look at your business and start explaining it in 140-character stories. Your strategy, your dreams, your passions, your team's purpose, their jobs. When you can rewrite job descriptions in 140 characters or less, you know your people will start to understand what they really mean and can stop trying to filter out what's important from amid all the noise. Let people go deeper at their own pace, to gradually build their understanding.

2. **Get good at status updates**

   Create the ability to easily and efficiently provide your people with real-time updates on progress – big picture and little. Set up boards, RSS feeds, Facebook pages, or Twitter accounts; whatever it takes to keep people informed and up to date in real time. Regularly seeing we are making progress helps us engage.

3. **Join the dots**

   Not everyone 'gets it' like you do — some need help joining the dots between what they do and how it makes a difference. Bridge the gap. Tell people the contribution they have made, daily if necessary, until they get it. Help people understand where they fit.

4. **Promote a sense of giving**

   Help people give, at work, or in the community. Each community has things it needs. Find out what your community needs and what your people can give to it, then provide the mechanism to do it. This may be something as simple as setting up a box in your lunch room

FIGURE 5.1 *(Continued)*

to collect toys for charity. Let your teams drive it. Alternatively, let people in on your biggest challenge and ask for their help.

5. **Value volunteerism**

This can be done in many ways. Here are three options for starters. (1) Once a month, allow everyone to volunteer for another job and let them do it for a day. (2) Identify people in your business who want help at work or at home (it could be learning a new skill at work or teaching a child to swim) and open it up to your people to offer that help. (3) Look for community efforts that need volunteers and put the community in touch with your people.

CHAPTER 6

Cleaning Up Your Workplace

To simplify and streamline a business you need a clean sheet of paper – start with understanding the outcomes and then design the simplest operating model to deliver them. If you do this at every level, starting with the big picture view and then narrowing it down to the process level, you end up with a business that regardless of its complexity, is not complicated. And that's important for engagement as much as cost. The bonus? Your people are freed up to think and be their best because they design their jobs to fit the needs of the customer and bring out the best in themselves.

—Jon Wylie, president of Proudfoot Global Natural Resources

Imagine how people would *feel* if there was nothing to stop them being remarkable at work. A cluttered, chaotic, disorganized working environment is the opposite of energizing. Of course, I'm not talking about a cluttered desk. I'm talking about the equipment that's faulty, the processes that don't work as they should, the systems that let people down, the structures that make decisions slow. They are the disengagers, teaching us that silently, each day, there are forces working against your desire to engage, flying in the face of all the great things you're doing to connect better with your people.

Creating a "clean" workplace is about creating an environment, infrastructure, and atmosphere where people feel supported. An ecosystem that works for us. Where clean, clear processes, systems, procedures, policies, and organization design help people achieve and thrive. Cleaning up your workplace is a table stake. Making a clean, uncluttered workplace a priority is one way to unblock employees' creativity and passion, so that they feel inspired to give more to their work. Like most engagers they usually have the added bonus of also helping you run a more cost effective, efficient business so people can be freed up to invest their time in what they are good at – getting the work done, thinking of better and new ways of helping your business win, and creating great cultures.

Sadly, and unwittingly, companies put up a series of barriers that hinder rather than promote employee engagement and reduce best efforts by way of a poorly performing ecosystem. But if you recognize a clean infrastructure makes for an easier world to engage in, you'll also reap the rewards of a more productive workplace.

So how do you assess your business? You'll need to map out your overall business infrastructure, not just your processes. It's the complete ecosystem that drives engagement at work. Consider the following:

- Do you routinely map out the workplace terrain to establish where there are bottlenecks to productive work? Looking at your total operating model through the lens of people, technology, systems, management tools, processes, and structure?

- Do you have a business with sound, people friendly *management models*? How you *motivate, connect, collaborate, define your strategies, develop your objectives, and make your decisions at work?*

- Do we have *clean processes* that encourage the kind of behavior and results we need from people?

- Is your IT and are your digital *systems* still fit for purpose? Are they user friendly and easily accessible?

- Do you have a people friendly, "digital employee workplace" where technology and communication tools are used to better connect people with other people and information?

- Do your *policies* enable and encourage people to do remarkable things? Built for the many not the few?

- Do your *procedures* leave room for people to do a great job, rather than simply "get the job done"?

- Does your approach to *capability development* link to improved results?
- Do you have *data that allows for routine means* to identify and address barriers to productivity and engagement – the things that stop people excelling, thriving, and innovating?
- Does your structure push data and knowledge to the people who need to make decisions. Does it allow speedy decision-making?
- Have you asked what work or processes should be eliminated, improved, simplified, outsourced, automated, digitized, restructured, or sent home – the *eight accelerators of productive work?*
- Are you hacking your work? Looking at it from the outside in.

All of the above impact engagement. Normally, management view these items through the lens of productivity alone or cost reduction. If you focus on engagement, you will reap the rewards of far higher financial benefits, improved operating results, and have engaged people working in a productive culture.

Engaging in Cash, Cost, and Growth

The economic crisis coming out of the COVID-19 pandemic caused many firms to immediately need to protect their cash as business shuttered their windows and closed their doors. Of the three areas that impact EBITDA – cash, cost, and growth – cash and cost obviously became omnipresent in every management meeting. We at Proudfoot were no different, but our advice to our clients was. Our message was not one of reset, nor was it one of convening a new normal. We believed this great human tragedy had to have a silver lining of causing management and their teams to fundamentally imagine a whole new world of work – a completely new reality. A reboot. And an opportunity to truly invent a new way of doing business. One that was clean and meaningful. Smart organizations were asking themselves: What should our working model be post–COVID-19?

Lean Isn't Always Clean

In the Global Organization Assessment Survey mentioned in Chapter 1, two-thirds of respondents felt their systems and processes – the infrastructure of their business – did not support them in effectively and efficiently doing their jobs. Proudfoot has experienced this in the 30,000 client assessments we have completed. Over the years, these results have barely changed – and that's despite all of the reengineering and process improvement programs that have been so popular. More recently, it is despite the many digital transformations underway.

The preoccupation with cost-cutting is the most likely reason for this. Lean is not the same as clean. If the process is efficient but disengages your teams in its execution, not allowing for think time or creating unintended consequences that negatively impact the work environment, you win the productivity game in the short term but lose the war on talent in the long term. Worse still, you may not achieve the productivity gains in a sustainable fashion, providing for only the one-hit wonders that can kill your results and engagement if they are not sustainable. If all of the good stuff, the fun stuff, the creativity has been stripped out of processes, policies, and systems to drive greater productivity alone, something fundamental may well have been sacrificed. Just as measurement is valuable for monitoring progress, if the wrong things are measured, businesses could label any organizational change a success when the reality may be that a much more serious failure is looming as morale dives and employees reconsider their futures. Jon Wylie, president of Proudfoot America's and Natural Resources describes this another way: "Companies that choose to redesign their organization chart rather than redesigning the work can cause disconnects between how work is managed, the organization structure and how work is performed – the work processes – and create alignment and engagement issues, and worse still unintended consequences."

The long obsession with efficiency alone, with finding and squeezing out lost time from our processes without engaging people in their work, has contributed to poor engagement. Business leaders and managers have expended so much on seeking out and eradicating sources of inefficiency and boosting productivity, that they haven't fully appreciated the impact on people's engagement and motivation – on the way people *feel* about the work they are doing.

So when we think about the workplace environment, about the business infrastructure, we need to consider this holistically – and in terms of its impact on people's engagement, enthusiasm and energy that impacts productivity as much as a poor process. This is particularly the case, as so many businesses embrace the need for transformation and product/service innovation. A clean business environment should create room for innovation, support "big thinking" and foster spontaneous collaboration, not just produce an efficient, productive process where no one speaks or engages. You need to be healthy (engaged) and fit (productive).

Humanize. Optimize. Digitize. Healthy and Fit.

It's time to clean up the working environment – the infrastructure that helps us run our businesses – with both fitness and health in mind: productivity and people. Here are a few ways you can do this rapidly.

Step One in the Cleanup: Figure Out What Cheeses People Off

Any day, anywhere in your business, great things are being undermined by great irritating incidents that get in the way of achievement, winding people up until they become distracted and deenergized. People may tolerate these work niggles if they are temporary and short-lived, but when they become the norm, it becomes the culture – a status quo of breakdowns and bandaids, until people's tolerance levels flatline.

Years ago, there was a great Australian show called *Hey Hey, It's Saturday Night* – think of it as a cross between America's *Saturday Night Live*, and any of the late-night shows (*with David Letterman*, Jay Leno's *Tonight Show*, James Corden, Stephen Colbert, Jimmy Fallon, Jimmy Kimmel. . .).[1] Then add a dash of the old *Gong Show*, for those old enough to recall. Throw in the more recent *Survivor*.

One of the funniest segments was "What Cheeses Me Off." People would write in to tell the host what had annoyed them in life that week, and as Sir Arthur Conan Doyle espoused – truth often proved to be stranger than fiction. There were hilarious anecdotes, to which most people could relate – and there was so much passion in the complainants. It's something we can see play out every day in our workplaces. Many employees are so used to airing grievance about work, but often with the knowledge nothing will be done about it. This spiral of negativity is hardly healthy or conducive to inspiring good work. It's a must-fix in your engagement stakes. Find and fix what cheeses people off. Before you even start worrying about who moved your cheese, worry about it

---

[1] Peter Ots, *Hey Hey It's Saturday*. 1971–2010. Australia. Somers Carroll Productions.

going off – the things that cause people to lose faith in the business's ability to support them. The things they think are conspiring against them rather than working for them. These cause motivation to plummet, and so too, engagement.

Think of the employee who's just pulled a night shift to get an order out after a major line breakdown. The only thing she really wants is a hot cup of fresh coffee before she heads home, only to find there's no milk in the staff kitchen. It's the last straw, and she gets in the car feeling drained and despondent. If it happened a few too many times, she may even hand in her two weeks' notice. Not because of the lack of milk, but because of the many times she's been the hero to fix what could be resolved permanently if only we had a way to address it. Then there's the guy who recently fixed that key piece of equipment for the fourth time because the boss wanted to save on maintenance bills. He sees it's broken again and his heart sinks. His instinctive reaction is, "How the heck does this company make money if it can't even keep a simple piece of equipment maintained?" Downstairs, there's an equally exasperated engineer who can't fix a leak in the mechanical room until the new, long-winded purchasing policy has been completed – to authorize the $24.50 needed (delayed for two weeks by the wait for a signature from a manager who's currently on vacation). The futility of it all, as the company drains energy at great expense in the meantime, is soul-destroying. Add these three scenarios together (they could easily be at the same company), and it's easy to see how the tone is set in a business before the manager even gets out of bed. Hardly a motivational, "can-do" environment that inspires people to be their best!

Forget the change management jargon for a moment and think about your own infrastructure. Does it help or hinder people as they go about their daily activity? Asking people to come back with their "what cheeses me off" list is a great start to engage people in solutions. But it's only the start. A long list of issues will simply reinforce the negative. Your role is to spark the solutions. To make sure every problem has one. To crowdsource the answers.

The Hairdryer, the Hotel, and the Bad-Hair Day

With the amount of travel I do (or did – pre-COVID!), I've learned a lot about bad-hair days. And it's the hairdryer and the decisions designers make (or don't) that, from experience, has a lot in common with how we design work.

It is due to poor design choices involving a hairdryer, that I have found my head in hotel cupboards or leaning uncomfortably close to hotel toilet bowls. Beautiful hotels designed for appearance rather than functionality have inadvertently subjugated me to the nooks and crannies of a variety of plush hotel rooms in the pursuit of dry hair. It's a mistake we often make at work, resulting in many a metaphorical bad-hair day.

One of my most memorable hairdryer encounters (for all the wrong reasons) took place at London's Heathrow Airport, Terminal 5. If you experienced British Airways Terminal 5 when it was first opened, you will know it was really a remarkable airport experience. Of note were the BA lounges where you could wine and dine, do last-minute work, surf the internet, catch up on emails, or take a shower between flights. All of which was still quite special at the time. Though commonplace today, it was still a cut above back then. But it was my après-shower experience that brought everything back to zero. Despite the many millions of pounds that had been spent attending to every tiny detail at the then-shiny-new terminal, it was what confronted me as I emerged from the shower that proved to be the one step in the process that drowned out all others. As I stood, wet hair wrapped in a towel after debating whether to in fact wash it, I was faced with what looked like a vacuum cleaner hose – no power to dry, and a hose so short it barely reach my head! Unable to make it work, I reemerged from the shower cubicle, my hair still wet, and coined my new process phrase: "bad-hair day experiences." Of course, I still shower at the terminal, but I never wash my hair.

This kind of scenario is all too common at work. No matter how much money has been spent or how much thought and effort invested in a business's operational design, all it takes is one broken link in the chain to create a bad-hair day. With all the best intentions in newly designed systems, automated or improved processes, a great salary, happy customers, new equipment, and technology, the perfect location, or great employee services and benefits, these can be rendered null and void with a bad-hair day experience. Your what cheeses me off factors become pieces of the infrastructure that don't work for you – a process that doesn't do what it originally set out to do; a policy that in practice can't be adhered to; a system that isn't user friendly; or a procedure that was built for Benedictine monks whose patience is built into their DNA. Bad-hair days make us grumpy and despondent, so that all we see is the negative. They cheese us off.

This despondency, which has a habit of spreading quickly, could persist and become ever more pervasive if the infrastructure failings are not addressed. It creates conversations that distract from the business at hand, building what

I call babble (disgruntlement triggers), and goes home with people – it settles into their daily lives. Before you know it, people are switching off in droves, feeling that they are being blocked from being their best, that their needs are not being taken into consideration, that their input hardly matters.

Recognizing the Signs

If you want to understand the sources of bad-hair days, try tuning in to the babble at work: look closely for changes in behavior – for example, when perfectly good people begin to show signs of boredom, anger, or bad communication. These are early warning signs of people dialing down their discretionary effort, taking the attitude, "Why should I bother? This place sucks!" You'll probably be quicker to notice it among people you don't think are great – but perhaps their attitude has been off exactly because they've felt so ground down by the system, for so long.

So where should you look for sources/causes of babble? Common ones include:

- *Measurement systems*. Wrong KPIs, too many KPIs, bad KPIs, inappropriate frequency of measurement, measurement used to police rather than manage and lead – checking up on numbers rather than checking in.

- *Management models*. How you get work done through people and what you expect people to get done; how you find, select, hire, retain, manage, reward, and lead people; how you organize and motivate your people through to how you make decisions about what needs to be done.

- *Processes and technology*. IT systems and processes including work flows, paper flows and people flows. Do they work? Do they do what they were designed to do? Do they free people up or tie people down? Do they fit with each other?

- *Policies*. Are these built on trust? Do they help people get their jobs done or encourage routine policing? Are they communicated effectively and understood?

- *Procedures*. Are they built with the desired outcome in mind?

As obvious as some of these disgruntlement triggers are, the real cause may be something very simple or subtle. So what unintended consequences might be resulting from your decisions and actions?

- *People become derailed*. Digressions will steal time from work that matters, a situation that will worsen as unchecked grievances start to fester.

- *Wasted energy*. Energy zappers and mudslingers who enjoy a good drama will delight in sucking up people's time as they complain, and make everyone else aware of their frustration because something else is draining their reserves. Worse still, they drain other people's reserves.

- *Unintended crisis*. The trouble with little problems is that they can quickly escalate to become much larger ones if no one is seen to be taking action. Don't let that molehill become a mountain.

- *Bad messaging leads to bad feeling*. This could be the message you're sending out by not acting, or the way you communicate about issues once you do recognize that something is wrong. If you're not clear and conciliatory, you could have a mutiny on your hands.

From Walk-the-Floor to Walkabout

Consider when you last "checked the hairdryers in your workplace" – when did you last take a close and critical look at your infrastructure and the way work happens? Walk the floor, or go on a famous Aussie walkabout? Discover what really goes on at the front line? Look for what cheeses people off and is sapping your people's morale and discretionary effort.

Here's a few tips to get you visible, present, and looking through your employee lens from micro to macro:

1. *Drop in*. Whether it's virtually, in the office or at site, find ways to attend meetings you would not usually get involved in, to join teams in their day-to-day work, to literally walk the floor. When you do this, listen for what is really being said – could issues be solved and resolved if the right people heard about them?

2. *DILO a Day*. Remember the "what color is your day" from Chapter 4 for how you spend your time? Now do it for how your teams spend theirs. Proudfoot launched DILOs in the 1940s, a simple observation technique to see reality where work gets done. At the end of the day, you can see how much time is spent being truly productive versus tripping over the hairdryer moments. In that spirit, ask to spend a day in the life of one of your people. Learn how their day goes. See what they really need to do.

Pick a typical day and shadow your team member. I've done hundreds of these shadows. People forget your presence quickly and get on with their day, dealing with the issues that come at them and prevent them from being great. What better way for you to get a real taste of reality. What you often find is there are many barriers that prevent people from being successful and are out of the control of the team they impact, often repeating themselves day in and day out, creating frustration. These are the hairdryer moments coming to life.

3. *Datacation.* If your operational reporting does its job, it highlights the gaps that exist between what you plan to accomplish (targets) and what you actually accomplish (results). When you review this data and look at it for the story it tells, you can see where you need to look under the hood of your business. It points out what to look for. Much like a DILO, you want to look at the environment wrapped around the data by talking to teams about the results; what's causing the result and what needs to happen to improve them? Conducting fact-based observations validates desktop data analytics. Together, you can identify all the opportunity available to create value, identify risks, and prioritize action. Importantly, you will also be removing the barriers that often disengage.

4. *Create T-Labs.* Mini transformation laboratories right where work gets done. Taking immediate action on what you learn from these first three steps is the kind of thing your teams are waiting for – to see change as a result of your intervention. Identifying opportunity and then ring fencing it so you can rapidly prototype solutions to the problems will go a long way to engaging your people.

5. *Platforming.* This is where you hand over the reins to your teams, having them complete their drop-ins and DILOs to gain a multiplier effect. If you found opportunity, imagine what your people at the coal face will find? You aggregate and prioritize the opportunities to create a real platform for change, accelerating the cleaning up of the workplace. When everyone is in agreement, you launch the new ways for working that are both engaging and more cost-effective because the waste and lost time is eradicated from the business, by the teams who work in the business.

6. *Transforming: Humanize. Optimize. Digitize. Repeat.* This is when your teams can prioritize people over profits and lay a solid foundation so that optimization and digitization flow with engagement. Allow great things to happen at the intersection of people and technology.

From Process Mapping
to Aerial Mapping

Done right, these six items become just a few of the activities in what I call an
enterprise aerial mapping exercise. It goes far beyond traditional process mapping to enable you to map out the entire operation of your business, see what's
working and what's not, and determine how engaging your business really is.

Starting with a bird's-eye view, you map your business, including
processes, technology, functions, reporting lines and interfaces, relationships,
and connections, to understand how work is really performed to uncover barriers to performance.

It sounds like a technical, academic exercise but it's far from that. It's
a wall-to-wall, bottom-up look at your business terrain, building it with
your people. The objective is to improve the way your business works
so your teams can deliver their best work. The outcome? Better, more productive workplaces built for people where safety and efficiency go hand in
hand with engagement.

You zoom in and out, seeing how everything connects and really works,
where the interfaces are between processes, functions, and people as well as
the actual value stream and how the individual processes connect. Throw in
your organization chart, the tools you use to manage the business and make
decisions, how information flows, your reporting, what your customer and
supplier touchpoints are, what regulatory issues and requirements are out
there, what communication points exist, what technologies are in use, and
how they work with the rest of the business, and you have a picture of your
current operating model and what results it's giving you – financially, opera-
tionally, and culturally. Add to it the behaviors people are demonstrating and
their perceptions and attitudes, as well as the results they are achieving
and the cost of any unintended consequences like waste or lost time, then
add safety issues, as well as what's happening beyond your front door in your
community, and you'll get a pretty good understanding of the entire world
your people work in.

It becomes one big engagement canvas. A picture of what can disengage
and where you can better engage, as well as where your costs are. Another
multiplier.

Here are some of the questions I'm asked about aerial mapping.

Couldn't You Just Process Map and Get the Same Understanding?

No. Far from it. Anyone can process map. It's not the same. Process mapping is a linear view of processes, mapped out through the lens of one process. Often, it's made even more linear doing the maps in software applications that show the theory not the practice, which is fine once you completed the exercise, but not before.

Aerial mapping starts with the end-to-end value chain and it can often end in a complex pile of spaghetti we call the real world. Imagine doing 10 traditional process maps, even worse if you do them by 10 different people or teams who don't speak to one another. You'd end up with 10 isolated maps that may not connect – you would lose the "between the cracks" view of the business – where things get really messy and where your advantage in cost, service, or even innovation can be lost.

A great enterprise aerial map is crowdsourced: it's touched by many more people than the traditional process owners. It should be touched by absolutely everyone who in some way has an impact on or is impacted by the work to be done. Everyone is engaged in discussions about what needs to change and where the bright spots are – what is working and can be leveraged. Enterprise aerial mapping is so much more effective than process mapping – it's an employee engagement exercise that creates real business advantage. It encourages discussion, debate, and critique of your current ways of working but more importantly, it focuses on looking at what the future should be. It looks for improvement as well as innovation. Brown paper and white paper mapping.

People really get a WOW from the aerial map. It helps them find a voice to give ideas for how to make a business better. They realize they have never seen their business through this lens. It also gives people a bird's-eye view of where they fit and how they make a contribution or can make better contributions in the future.

Don't People Already Know What Their Business Looks Like?

Not usually. They have an idea and they know how it should look, but sometimes this is the first time employees are able to see how everything connects. You could call it a discovery learning exercise. The outcome is a bit of an oxymoron: big picture detail. You allow people to step back and see the big picture, but get right up close and see the detail concurrently.

Enterprise aerial mapping enables and gives teams a vehicle to reach beyond their normal boundaries. Management can then tap into the employee base to see through their eyes what needs to change.

The completed enterprise aerial map lets you see today's iceberg story – where management only see what's above or a few inches into the water and yet all the activity and issues are far beneath the surface witnessed each day by the people doing the work. The reality is that your people usually see 100 percent of the issues in the business, they just don't have the vehicles to communicate them or the tools to fix them, or they don't have the capacity or reach to address things that are outside their control. The aerial map allows people to identify opportunity – challenges in their workplace and across interfaces. Mapped well, it can identify the downstream challenges needing medication and upstream solutions that give prevention.

Enterprise aerial mapping also allows you to do something bigger than process improvement. It allows you to hack your business. This is where the conversation gets exciting. Plotting where you want to be and then saying how do we get there? No hacker ever worked through the process to get to the answer, they work around the process by looking through a different lens.

How Can We Engage Employees in Change?

Any business that wants to make true transformation – deep change in the way work gets done and the way people are engaged in that work – needs to start with an aspiration and then a picture of where you are against that future. This is aerial mapping. I've seen it used in just about every industry – to analyze from pit to port in an underground mine, to solve logistics issues in trucking, or to map out full wall-to-wall businesses to reinvent and better value the organization ready for an acquisition from the insurance industry to manufacturing. It can be used to identify why new technology is not being adopted or simply to show everyone how work really happens. The applications are endless for improvement projects but with the real spirit of employee engagement at its heart, it can help reinvent whole businesses to build back better and transform.

In Proudfoot's Triggering Transformation Survey, one finding was that the biggest inhibitor of real transformation was not that people were resistant to change but that people don't know how to participate in change. Enterprise aerial mapping gives them the vehicle to do that. It is a powerful way to visually show how people connect – whether across the production line or supply chain or across your business and beyond into suppliers and customers. Aerial mapping shows the networks of people who rely on each other for information sharing and mutual success. Mapping these connections – and getting everyone involved in doing this (pasting and linking pictures of each other) – can help people understand where and how they contribute, and how they are linked to everyone else. Most important, you can return to the map if connections break or fail, to work out what is needed to rebuild them.

Why Is Aerial Mapping So Essential?

Aerial mapping helps you identify where to free up your scarcest resource (time) so you can engage your most valuable resource (people) in the right places, doing the right things. It allows people to identify the bad-hair day moments, what cheeses them off, and the babble at work – all the things that consume time and energy.

Aerial mapping done well releases time. When you release time, you relieve frustration, you release assets, you revamp and innovate your products and processes more often, and you reenergize people. You transform.

Aerial Mapping Giving People Their Life Back

A large part of the startup of a transformation is aerial mapping to enable new, more effective ways of working to be designed – including changes in processes, behaviors, and the design of new management tools. But sometimes it's what happens later that can truly impact someones life as a senior executive with Proudfoot discovered when he revisited the work he had done with a client 18 months after the start of a large scale transformation and it gave a massive reminder of our purpose – to make a difference to people. He interviewed one of the key leaders in a project as a part of a sustainability audit – to ask had the changes stuck? One leader said with the answer was from the heart: "I got my life back. Before, I was always on call, and I had no family life, always worrying about the performance of my asset. Now, I can plan to participate in family events like my kids soccer and cricket games, I know my team is safe and our production levels are stable and predictable." You cannot put a price on that improvement but chances are this leaders engagement levels skyrocketed. This was a quality of life improvement.

How Do We Measure Quality of Life?

When the World Health Organization rates a nation's quality of life, it assesses specific categories to determine overall living conditions – including infrastructure. This makes sense – if citizens cannot do what they need to in their everyday life; if they are not supported by the right facilities and means of making things happen, their overall life experience is negatively affected.

It also makes sense, then, to measure quality of life as an important determinant of the health of a business, and the role and state of our business infrastructure that influences this. The aerial map can help feed this diagnosis and using a societal view on quality of life categories can expand your thinking for your organization.

Here are some of the questions you might ask by categories relevant to quality of life:

1. *Cost of living.* Are your salaries reflective of the cost of living? Do you help enrich your people's lives? Do you value their time. Do you go the extra mile in your HR services – educating people on how to do things like offset their taxes or get the best rates on car insurance?

2. *Culture and leisure.* How do you define and communicate your culture. What can people touch and feel as your culture? How are your people's skill levels? How many people make use of your online platforms? Do you have ways people can connect socially? Do you offer development programs for all your people to access? How many people attend company events? What sort of social, networking, or learning exchanges do you host? How do you help people take a break at work? What causes do you support? How do people connect beyond their usual borders?

3. *Economy.* This should be easy to apply at work. Take any number of your company's scorecards, key performance indicators (KPIs), and financial results and build your own "state of the company's economy." Is your business growing? Is it profitable? Are you creating new jobs? What about innovation levels, new products, new ideas? These all apply under the business's economic indicator. Later in this book, we'll discuss employee confidence. Employee confidence results, as we will see, are a view into the economics of your business: its numbers and leadership. An employee confidence index might fit well here.

4. *Environment.* This is your company's social responsibility score. ESG. What's your carbon footprint? What are you doing to build greener practices into your business? How are you giving back? What greater purpose

do you provide people? What "cause" are people working for? What are the results of your social programs?

5. *Freedom.* We will talk about this in more detail in the chapter about "Freedom," but for now, think about the extent to which your people have a voice and are free to make a voluntary contribution of discretionary effort – something above and beyond their immediate remit. How much of what your people say and recommend does your business act on? The level of engagement of your people and their willingness to volunteer something extra is a meaningful way to score this category; both can be indicators of the level of autonomy people feel at work.

6. *Health.* This category has already made its way into management discussions and employee programs at work. Now, all businesses should be asking the question, "How healthy is your workplace?" And this should go far beyond the basic considerations of a health and safety audit. Also consider: Do you bring health and wellness into daily discussions, and do these discussions provide a departure point for discussions on work-related illnesses? Consider how you would measure the health of your business from a people perspective: Are people learning and growing? Do they themselves help to build capability in others? How is your retention? What is your employee turnover? Do you have a healthy culture?

7. *Infrastructure.* Think in terms of your business infrastructure – the various components at work that enable people to be their best. How clean is your business infrastructure? How effective is your supply chain? What stops people from doing their job? Can you identify inadequate or broken processes, out-of-date policies, systems that don't work, equipment that fails, or management models that are well past their use-by date? All affect engagement levels, if only you were measuring it.

8. *Safety and risk.* A few years ago, these factors may seem somewhat extreme in the average business context, but since the COVID-19 pandemic, they could help highlight risks associated with your workplace. Many businesses have seen the reluctance people had to return to their workplaces, even with worries as simple as "How do we navigate social distancing in lifts (elevators)?"

   Additionally, you should include employee theft levels, fraud, or sexual harassment, bullying, and discrimination. Combined, these factors will shed light on your people's quality of life at work and may offer a direct window into your company's levels of engagement. Theft, for instance, is often associated with an "I'm owed that" attitude from disgruntled employees.

Further risk factors may relate to your financial position and how leveraged the business is. Here you can add commentary on your business's ability to weather a crisis: you could measure some of this risk based on confidence levels. Do you believe the current management team could navigate the company through a storm?

9. *Climate.* Think of climate in the traditional sense of employee or organizational climate, and add your thinking around company culture, management styles, and the levels of fair trade in your business and you've got climate on a score from icy to melt down. All are measures affecting people's quality of life at work, but measures where seldom the link is made.

There are potentially so many factors that relate to our quality of life and our well-being. In designing an index to best suit your business, you are developing a subjective measure; how people feel. That's OK. How people feel about their quality of life at work is a leading indicator in the discovery of how engaging they find their workplace. It can help determine how willingly people might invest their discretionary effort and predict to what extent they will be volunteers.

Well-being and quality of life are not happiness measures. Happiness can come and go, and while it too counts at work, well-being and quality of life are far more stable attributes. They provide a longer-term view on how people feel about their life at work. They relate to our personal satisfaction and our satisfaction within the world we inhabit. When we measure these elements, we're looking for change: Are they improving?

If you're not convinced by a quality of life index, consider the significant results being experienced as companies roll out increasingly imaginative health and well-being programs. A *Fast Company* article published in May 2017[2] highlighted how far initiatives have come – and how laterally companies are thinking now when it comes to the benefits on offer to maintain and boost employee morale. In recent years, options have broadened from encouraging healthy eating, offering free flu shots and getting people cycling, to encouraging and enforcing vacation/rest time and adapting programs to meet the needs of the individual. In France, the government has stepped in to enforce a "right to disconnect,"[3] to remove the pressure employees can

---

[2] Gwen Moran, "This Is The Future of Corporate Wellness Programs," *Fast Company,* May 10 2017. https://www.fastcompany.com/40418593/this-is-the-future-of-corporate-wellness-programs

[3] This came into force in January 2017. Companies with more than 50 workers are now obliged to draw up a charter of good conduct, setting out the hours when employees are not expected to send or answer emails.

feel to read and respond to emails outside office hours. Any company could introduce those terms voluntarily, of course, showing that they respect their employees' rights to a private life and some downtime when they can fully switch off from work.

The upshot is that you don't have to spend millions to reap millions of benefits from a focus on people's quality of life and well-being at work. Helping people focus on their health won't just see a rise in engagement levels; it could also reduce the number of days lost to sickness.

What Does Working Here Really Feel Like?

That's the question a quality of life index would pose – and answer – for you. What if you could produce a quality of living index for your business each month? What if this became one of the indicators used to inform investors, or to determine if you are an employer of choice, or to establish if customers should spend their hard-earned dollars on your products or services? We will see measures like these increasingly become the case in the same way companies are rated for their labor practices across the globe. It adds even deeper meaning to the balanced scorecard and offers an alternative to a plethora of traditional measures we apply at work. At a minimum, it can combine existing measures within a different context, to provide everyone with a bird's-eye view of *what it really feels like to work here.*

Process improvement exercises that focus exclusively on reducing costs and improving profit are out. If you fix the problems that lurk in your infrastructure, preventing people from excelling, it should automatically follow that you will reduce costs, improve productivity, and grow profits. Adding the dimension of engagement can reap more benefits.

If You Must Focus on Cost, Study These Numbers

In the US, unhappy workers were calculated by Gallup to cost US businesses collectively up to $550 billion a year in lost productivity[4]. This is a nation that

---

[4] Gallup, *State of the American Workplace* (Gallup, 2013). https://www.zipperjunction.org/wp-content/uploads/2014/10/State-of-the-American-Workplace-Report-2013.pdf

has traditionally been associated with minimal vacation allowances (compared to many European countries). Meanwhile, in the UK alone, cases of work-related stress, depression or anxiety in 2015–2016 was equivalent to a rate of 1,510 cases per 100,000 workers, according to the UK Health & Safety Executive's Labor Force Survey (LFS)[5]. The total number of working days lost due to this condition in 2015–2016 was *11.7 million days*. In 2015–2016, stress accounted for 37 percent of all work-related ill health cases and 45 percent of all working days lost due to ill health. The main work causes were cited as workload pressures, too much responsibility, and a lack of managerial support.

There is also a marked trend of American employees forfeiting their hard-earned vacation days because they feel too stressed to take them: According to travel company **Priceline.com**, every year, US workers earn more vacation days than they use. In 2019, employees forfeited, on average, about half of their paid time off. That's the equivalent to $65.5 billion in lost benefits. In 2018, they left a record 768 million days of vacation on the table, up nearly 10 percent from the year before, according to research from the US Travel Association. American workers gave up $66.4 billion in 2016 benefits alone, according to a survey by GfK conducted in early 2017 with over 7,000 US employees[6]. This is despite the fact that the vast majority of managers recognize that vacation improves health and well-being, boosts morale, and alleviates burnout, plus allows people to give more when they return to work.

BP is a company that gets it. While it struggled with its external image after the great oil spill of 2010, it endeavored to bolster its internal image with employee well-being initiatives at work and found it was able to reduce employee turnover by 25 percent after implementing a variety of activities. Later in this book, I'll talk about St. George Bank, an Australian financial institution. For now, take note of its retention statistics: it achieved 8 percent employee turnover against an industry average of 25–30 percent by investing in employee health and well-being.

So, however you invest in it, prioritizing employees' health and well-being pays dividends, whereas failing to do this can prove very costly.

---

[5] *Work-Related Stress, Anxiety and Depression Statistics in Great Britain 2016* (Health & Safety Executive (UK) Labour Force Survey 2015–2016). https://www.hse.gov.uk/statistics/causdis/stress.pdf

[6] US Travel Association, *The State of the American Vacation 2017* (US Travel Association, 2017). www.ustravel.org/sites/default/files/media_root/document/2017_May%2023_Research_State%20of%20American%20Vacation%202017.pdf

If you look after your people by removing what prevents them from being successful and provide what is captured in your quality of life index, people will look after your business. That's a step in the right direction to build a business that is fit for people, with less profit consumption and better results.

If you're still not convinced in the value of looking after your people to look after your business, consider Birmingham City Council, a major urban local authority in the UK. Some years ago, it received a dismal two-star performance rating for its service efforts. Additionally, employees didn't feel engaged, and less than half of the staff had confidence in the management.

The Council found that thousands of niggling little things were getting in the way of delivering the levels of service it wanted to provide: bad-hair days and things cheesing people off. To address its service issues, Birmingham CC worked on transforming its back office, finance, and procurement operations while concurrently running workshops with its people to come up with initiatives to improve customer service, partnerships, and teamwork across the organization.

In the first year alone, the Council captured 6,000 service improvement ideas, not only impacting service levels but also giving employee motivation and engagement levels a huge boost. Two years later, 84 percent of employees said they were proud to work for Birmingham City Council, up from 50 percent. People's confidence in the management, initially at 29 percent of the workforce, rose to 68 percent.

It's always worth having a good clean-up. You never know what it might unearth.

---

1. **Put a new spin on process improvement so you get new results – make it about Aerial Mapping and eliminating frustration. Commit to a hairdryer tour. Call these infrastructure reviews whatever you like — 'what cheeses me off' audits, bad-hair day surveys, etc — but make sure you find all those points at work that are stopping people from doing their jobs**

FIGURE 6.1 Things You Need to Do Right Now.

as well as they would like. Here are some ways to get the most out of this exercise:

a. **Involve your top performers:** Have your star performer take you on a tour of your workplace and point out what he or she knows are the most irksome grunt factors, however benign they might seem.

b. **Involve your under-performers:** Now have your poorest performer or most challenging staff member take you on the same tour and give their vantage point.

c. **Be inclusive:** Open the door for anyone to participate in the tour if they feel they have something to say. Create your big, visual aerial map of your workplace, detailing its infrastructure. Have sticky notes on hand and invite your whole team to critique all the different elements. Capture what needs to change. Once you've let everyone contribute, summarize the issues and start to solve them with your people. Implement the changes and, if you like, create a new map showing the new world so people can see their contribution. What better way to get people engaged than giving them a chance to fix the issues with you?

d. **Experience or walk through a day-in-the-life of someone.** Conduct the same exercise as above, but ask your people to map out their day on a huge piece of paper, starting with when they get up in the morning to when they get home at night and capturing everything that happens in between. You could do individual maps or have your people create them together, showing everyone's day on one map. Or you could revisit the simple colour-coding framework we discussed earlier in the book, and have people log how they spend their time through their day based on categories. You want people to identify what negatively impacts them or takes them away from their work unnecessarily. Let people be as creative as they like in this exercise. If they trust you, they'll include valueless discussions with bosses; policies and procedures that don't make sense; and irritating, condescending signs on lunchroom walls that demotivate them. Then it's up to you to work with them to address the issues they raise.

e. **Open your management models to critique.** Invite people to discuss the effectiveness of the management models or management approaches you use to motivate, connect, collaborate, define your strategies, develop your objectives, and make your decisions. Listen to your people very closely. What issues do they raise? Bad hires, wrong people being rewarded, slow decision-making, poorly articulated objectives, inadequate team designs? The message you send out when you reward the wrong individuals will overshadow any good press. Leaders quickly lose their credibility when they back the wrong horse. Look at where your management or measurement systems are failing you.

f. **Critique the killer complaint.** Take the top complaint from the previous list and map it out in much the same way as above, showing how these management models or processes are currently working. Then, get everyone's input to critique them and look for better ways of managing people. For this you need nothing more than an open mind.

2. **Develop your organization's Quality of Life Index. Put a team together to determine the measures, weighting, and methodology to develop a Quality of Life Index for your business. Then start measuring, marketing, and acting on the results.**

Clean: 5 things you can do today to improve quality of life at work

1. **Have a 'bad-hair day' or a 'what cheeses people off' session**

   Have a monthly gripe session to understand what is regularly causing disharmony and disruption at work, ending with a 'what-if' session: i.e., 'What if we did this to solve that?' Let people vent, but rapidly get to the action needed to remove the issue.

2. **Use a Quality of Life Index**

   Agree on how you will measure quality of life and then track it publicly. Most importantly, act on the results. Show people you really want to improve.

3. **Create healthy habits**

   Open source a 'healthy habits' team for your workplace – just like a safety committee, only on health and well-being – and let them lead the way.

4. **Run a 'small' campaign**

   Help your people see how the smallest things can make a big difference. One degree, one inch, one word. Point out the big changes in your business that have come from small beginnings. Then let your people go out and 'think small'!

5. **Introduce quality-of-life shares**

   Encourage people to post one thing they have done each week to improve the quality of life for someone else at work.

CHAPTER 7

Out Your Doubt and Boost Confidence

Most important thing is to get rid of doubt. If you got doubt in what you doing it's not going to work.

—Nipsey Hussle, rapper

I magine how people would *feel* if they were confident they'd succeed. Confidence is a multiplier. With it, great things can be achieved. Without it, very little. Have you ever really performed to your best when you lacked confidence?

Having confidence at work isn't just about our own ability, it's also about having confidence in leadership, peers, and team members that they will be great people to work with or they can do what's expected. The confidence leaders can lead us through crisis and transformative times. We also expect to have confidence in the products and services we offer customers. When you are in a tight labor market with more jobs than talent, employee confidence is a critical index. The same is true in times of high unemployment when people are reluctant to move jobs, having confidence you will keep your job or that the firm will treat you fairly will retain your heart, head, and effort not just your hands and body.

While broad confidence surveys might measure employees' confidence in the economy or their ability to get another job, the key indicator is confidence in their employer – do people trust their employer, leadership, their boss? When we know we can trust the people around us, particularly our managers and leaders, when we know the information we receive is useful and accurate, when we can trust that our work is adding value and is meaningful no matter how menial it can sometimes feel, we gain confidence in our circumstances – and the more confident we are that our job is worth the effort, the more inclined we are to like it. This is all common sense. You don't need a survey to tell you this.

As obvious as this might seem, confidence in leaders has been plummeting. Society as a whole is more questioning of and more determined to make its leaders accountable. So far, the results aren't good. If such a thing as a global leadership confidence index existed (which it does), it would not only show our *trust* in leaders dropping but also our *confidence in their abilities*. One look at Gallup's leadership poll and, with few exceptions, it tells you this. During the pandemic, we also saw leadership satisfaction rise and fall depending on how well our leaders of countries, business, and institutions coped. Angela Merkel, the chancellor of Germany, topped Gallup's polls with German leadership, taking the number one position in 2020 for the third year running, while Jacinda Arden, prime minister of New Zealand, popularity rose to record levels above just about any leader through the pandemic. But, overall, we have been neither impressed nor happy with our political, business, or community leaders, in recent years. We doubt they have the answers to today's questions.

Moving from country to business, Proudfoot has been conducting its Change Readiness Assessment within client firms for several decades. Prior to embarking on a major transformation journey with a client, workforce perceptions of the business are surveyed. Everything from communication, process and system effectiveness, through to confidence in leaders. And while seeing how people behave in their real world is always more interesting than surveying their opinions, this survey has long provided a window into the soul of the organization, giving clues to what needs to change to enable not just engagement to improve but for hard company results to improve. Confidence in leadership has been either a comforting result for the leadership team or gut wrenching, as their people provide their perceptions as to whether the leadership team – the CEO and their direct reports – can make the cut to lead. Long before the crisis of 2020 there was a crisis of confidence in leadership, and it has not been good for anyone.

Engagement cannot follow a lack of confidence.

Business Is Consuming Our Confidence

Gallup monitors Confidence in Institutions annually in the US[1], and for the last few years only a maximum of a third of the nation's major institutions have instilled "a great deal" or "quite a lot" of confidence in the general population. The military has usually topped the list, with banks and lawmakers at the bottom. Over the last 2.5 decades, confidence peaked in about 2004, when 43 percent of people expressed reasonable amounts of confidence in the big institutions. The low point came in 2014, when just 31 percent expressed reasonable confidence. In 2017, that had crept up to 35 percent – but that's hardly something for organizations to feel proud of: just three institutions registered a confidence rating above 50 percent that year.

In 2020 much changed. The military remained with top billing, and medical systems and schools took remarkable steps up with double digit improvements in perception of the job these institutions were doing. Banks and small business also stepped up.

Confidence in big business, while up three percentage points on 2016, remained very low at just 21 percent – in contrast to small businesses, which inspire confidence in the 70 percent range (second only to the US military). Only Congress, and internet news, inspired less confidence than big business in 2017! In 2020, little changed. Gallup wrote, "Fewer than one in five Americans express confidence in Congress, television news and big business. This is the 14th consecutive year that Congress is the lowest-ranked institution."

While this feedback hasn't necessarily come directly from employees (rather, from the American public at large), it hardly bodes well if the general population holds big business in such scant regard. If employees come to work for an organization that has a poor public perception, it's even more important that the business does its utmost to reverse that sentiment, because our confidence in the company we work for, and our own value, will shape our entire experience of the business – how happy we are, how engaged we feel, how well we do, and how long we stay. We should all take steps to understand and measure employee confidence levels in our leaders and our business. They reflect our overall workforce feelings.

---

[1] Gallup, annual update of Americans' confidence in the nation's major institutions, Confidence in Institutions: 2016 and 2017, June 2017.

We could borrow some tips from the Consumer Confidence Index (CCI, used in many countries to predict future spending). The CCI is a popular economic indicator used by people, businesses, and countries to determine the overall optimism of people toward the state of the economy and their own financial position. For years, economists have measured consumer confidence – and for good reason. While high confidence bodes well for a country's economy and business prosperity, low confidence is an indicator of a more unpredictable buying climate.

The same philosophies could be applied to employee confidence and its relationship to business performance. While consumer confidence in the US is based on various surveys, each with their own questions and methodologies, the questions they employ are quite interesting. Take these from one of the American ABC News Consumer Comfort Index[2], for example:

- "Would you describe the state of the nation's economy these days as excellent, good, not so good, or poor?"

- "Would you describe the state of your own personal finances these days as excellent, good, not so good, or poor?"

- "Considering the cost of things today and your own personal finances, would you say now is an excellent time, a good time, a not so good time, or a poor time to buy the things you want and need?"

Businesses would benefit from having an Employee Confidence Index, which takes the same approach, asking similar questions of their people on a regular basis. In the above example, replace the *nation's economy* with *organization* and you get the picture. Consumer confidence provides a measure of people's intended use of their discretionary income. This should now feel familiar. *Employee* confidence would provide a measure of your people's intended use of their discretionary *effort*; confidence would become a lead indicator of your ability to tap into this effort in the future. Just as consumer confidence is really a measure of doubt (*"I'm not sure we'll all have jobs soon so I better save my money"*), employee confidence could be seen to reflect the levels of doubt in your business (*"I'm not sure my efforts will be acknowledged/ rewarded/meaningful, and therefore I don't think I will invest my discretionary effort into this job."*) Bingo! Low employee confidence equals low levels of effort. Which translates to underengagement.

---

[2] https://abcnews.go.com/images/PollingUnit/m0411Datareport.pdf

I Have Confidence in Confidence Alone

So now let's turn our thoughts away from measurement of confidence to the concept of doubt – the outcome of a lack of confidence. Doubt stops us from acting. It casts a shadow on the new project, the new person, the new product being launched. It stops people from getting excited about the new IT system or app management wants them to adopt. While confidence can power you up, doubt kills confidence. It injects uncertainty and skepticism. It creates cynicism and hesitation. It's the roadblock to that next new innovation to be inspired or the day-to-day culture you aspire to have. Doubt is a strong influencer of decisions and behavior. It's one of the most debilitating emotions humans have to grapple with. While there are notable exceptions, most of the time doubt is a safety signal, a survival instinct to prevent us leaping to our death. If we think about it, much of what we do each day is aimed at eliminating doubt or risk from our lives. As much as it helps us to think twice and perhaps see that oncoming danger ahead of time, doubt is also a powerful source of disengagement.

Managers need to develop greater skills in their ability to help themselves and others eliminate doubt from their work lives. Where curiosity can spark innovation, doubt generates anxiety and can cause paralysis – inaction. So things do not move forward, therefore any bold change is impossible. People self-censor. They plan to fail.

Want to instill confidence? Expose and acknowledge the doubts people have, and then eliminate them. Then you can manage to engage.

Doubt Is Not Resistance

Think about how doubt manifests itself in life, right along the scale – from insignificant indecision to progress prevention. We have a new bonus system coming online; do you think they will ever pay out on it? . . . They want us to start using this new process; I bet it doesn't work properly. . . We've got major problems in this company but the guys in charge are not the ones to get us through a crisis. Yes, our lives are full of doubt, and as a result, we lack confidence in our organizations, in the people who lead them, and all too often, in ourselves. Often, it is this doubt that is mistaken for resistance to change. How many times have you thought about your teams and dismissed their lack of progress as resistance? So imagine how powerful it could be if you were to eradicate unnecessary doubts and enable people to grow their confidence levels?

To thrive, we all need to feel secure and grounded – and that isn't easy in the turbulent times we live in, politically, economically, psychologically, and from a health perspective. We're all feeling the effects of a disgruntled globe. How we feel about our leaders, our peers, and our team's ability to perform is paramount to being successful. Our job is to out the doubt.

St. George Bank: A Visual Workplace in Action

The first personal financial account I ever opened was with St. George, a building society in Australia – an institution owned by its members. I didn't know the difference between a bank and a building society at that time. I chose the building society because it had a mascot that was a big happy green dragon; I was almost 15. Thirty years later, I had the pleasure of taking a guided tour of the call center operations for this same building society that had now grown up to be a bank. I was thrilled to see that the dragon was still alive and well, but I was also captivated by the bank's people in the contact center.

I wanted to see the facility because it had received great press – it had been voted number one call center across the globe at the CCC World Contact Center Awards at the time. As it turned out, one of the leaders over call center operations was a former Proudfoot consultant, Antoine Casgrain, which opened the door for me to see the award-winning work firsthand. It was a living example of how effective and powerful it is to show people how they contribute both to the day to day and to the big picture over time. It was oozing with confidence.

Lesson No. 1: I was immediately faced with giant pictures of people who worked there. The company had used a great visual communication tip, immediately putting faces to the organization. Credibility is a great confidence booster. People listen to people they know, respect, and like. Additionally, the people in the photos felt recognized for their contribution. This in turn gave them a deeper sense of connection to the business; that sense that they *are* the business – that they represent it and can (and *should*) be proud of it.

Lesson No. 2: Take advantage of every communication opportunity. The next thing that struck me was the messaging on the walls – bright, colorful messages. Potentially dull and boring office corridors had been transformed into full-color billboards, like those flanking a freeway. This reminded me of work I had done in a mining community in Indonesia with PT Inco, where my colleague had shown the benefit of painting full-sized buses with work-related themes (just as you might see city buses painted with advertisements anywhere in the world).

Lesson No. 3: St. George used another important communication tactic – *frequency and repetition*. If you want people to recall and connect with a message, say it often, say it in different ways, and say it through different vehicles. Throughout the bank's call center, the same messages were repeated in a variety of phrases and using a combination of posters, wall signs, notice boards, and results boards. It wasted no opportunity!

Lesson No. 4: Be totally transparent and visible. As we moved through the contact center itself, you could easily identify each team. It was a truly visual workplace. It had practiced what I and my teams have preached for years and implemented with our clients. Each team had its own performance board high-lighting the top performers against a variety of indicators and measures. A sense of buzz resonated across the center between the teams, a true sense of involve-ment. The company used visual, real-time team and individual measurement to show progress and results and to make this information available to everyone. This is exactly what performance management systems should be about: real-time, day-to-day feedback. Team members can routinely see both their own contribution and the success of the whole team.

Additionally, dotted around the call center, were the overall results boards—screens with the real-time number. These were immediately visible to everyone. *"People can clearly see that what they do at any point in time has a direct impact on customer service results,"* Antoine reminded me. You can't get more connected to contribution than that.

Everywhere I looked, I saw the results of this philosophy. Focus on your people, so they can focus on the work – and connect better with you and your customers, your products, your services. Focus on the numbers and put every-thing in context, so that everyone knows how he or she is progressing and con-tributing. Provide confidence through transparency.

Lesson No. 5: Remember that your employees are human beings. Added to this personal recognition and performance measurement were some small but important details that reinforced the sense that the bank and its management saw and looked after its people. Fruit and nuts were available throughout the center, free of charge. Quick and easy health tips appeared each week on the back of every washroom door. Health and well-being were front and center in many team con-versations. Childcare was provided onsite. Parking beneath the building was free.

Lesson No. 6: Mentor. The bank's call center also provided "buddies" and accredited trainers and coaches – people recognized as the best at what they do, who can help others to fulfill their potential.

So, was it paying off? Absolutely! Not only had the bank delighted in prestigious call center awards, which reflect back on the employees who work there and reinforce the organization's strong external perception, but St. George Bank (today part of the Westpac Group) also enjoyed an impressive ranking on SEEK, an Australian website where employees rate their organization as an employer. The following feedback provided on SEEK by a St. George customer services employee was typical: "The training was exceptional – I have never worked in a place that has had better training. They make sure you are extremely knowledgeable and confident before actually starting you in your role."

See! Never underestimate the power of employee confidence.

Turn the Lights On

So how might you go about increasing confidence, in a pragmatic and practical way?

Start by increasing your visibility and giving people a clean line of sight to what's happening. In the absence of regular and consistent communication, in whatever form this takes, you know people will fill the void with what they *think* is going on. That is, people will make up their own reality if no one is providing the facts. Missing, incomplete, or buried information affects confidence levels. Make it a priority to clarify and highlight the things people need to know.

This isn't just about transparency – though transparency is a clear expectation by most stakeholders. It's about visible leadership, visible management, visible information, visible discussions, and visible connections between what's being said and what's going on. It must be aligned and consistent.

All too often, poor performance can be traced back to poor visibility. Bosses are not being seen nor heard sufficiently; communication is poor; information is mismanaged or not provided to those who need it, when they need it; communications and actions do not appear to be aligned; and decision-making has become slow and arduous. As with a driver who can't clearly see the road ahead, employees who lack visibility at work may become nervous, slowing their pace and worrying excessively about what may lie ahead. This hardly fosters confidence and best results.

So make it a priority to improve people's visibility of the business, where it's going, what's ahead, and why. Make connections that increase feelings of certainty and reduce feelings of risk. It's no different from when you lodge a complaint with a company or call them to tell them you are unhappy – the first thing you want to hear is "we can fix this." Silence offers no hope and bad communication gets a vote of no confidence.

Continuous Connections

A world-class automotive parts supplier was struggling with its cost base and performance on key production lines – output on the major production line was unpredictable and the three supervisors were as frustrated as their boss. Worse still, there was the threat of a major automotive brand customer reducing orders or even moving business to another supplier. Confidence in their ability to succeed was dropping rapidly from all concerned.

The solution was not new technology or new people, it was gathering, sharing, and making sense of data together: each shift, each team, each supervisor sharing. Data was systematically gathered on production output as well as line interruptions and visually displayed near the line on a performance board and then discussed at the daily check-in (1.5.30).

Production supervisors would meet every morning with the maintenance manager to review root causes of technical failures and agree action plans. The performance board data became an integral part of the shift handover. Higher productivity and consistent delivery was achieved thanks to people engaging with each other and the data. Confidence was restored.

Managing for increased confidence involves helping people to see connections: where, what, how, and why things fit together, giving them context and direction. Employees' confidence also comes from knowing who to go to, where to go, plus what value other people and parts of the organization can add. There's a reason silos don't work: people can't see over the walls.

However tenuously, we are all connected. Our workplaces are social systems. When these connections are broken or not visible, we shut down, confidence dips, and engagement falters. With solid connections, the social system works for us, supporting us and nurturing our confidence levels. So the manager's role is to help create visible connections to indirectly build confidence.

Here are some practical ways you can build confidence and banish doubt:

1. *Personal visibility*. When you are visible you can see, hear, touch, and feel the needs of people, and help make others feel visible too. You bring confidence. Practice HeadsUp, active management behaviors, and 1.5.30.

2. *Information visibility.* In today's digital world, information is more visible than ever. The manager's job is to frame that information – put it in context, make it comprehensible and meaningful – so people can act on it effectively and in a timely fashion.

3. *Visual workplace.* Use the work environment as a communication vehicle, even when this is virtual/at a distance. That's the beauty of technology – Yammer, Facebook, Instagram, Snapchat, whatever your social solution of choice.

4. *Visual impact.* Use visual tools to show the relationship between things (costs, service levels, results) and help people get it. Infographics are not just pretty pictures. They communicate. I'll never forget as a kid, being told how many hamburgers a hippopotamus could eat each day to enable me to see what 88 pounds of food looks like.

Let's consider what all of this might look like, day to day.

Improve Your Personal Visibility

Your own confidence index is determined by how you behave day to day to build trust and respect, removing doubt naturally and routinely through conversation and actions. The 1.5.30 process enables this and *what color is your day* measures it. The HeadsUp High Five is a great tool for confidence: Presence, Vision, Tech Savvy, Coaching, and Influence, while active management builds your visibility. You demonstrate this and you're halfway to taking your team's confidence off the charts. Here's how you use the HeadsUp High Five with active management:

1. *Get out there and engage with people.* Personal visibility as a manager is about *having a presence*; being accessible and actively involved in your world of work. It's not about being seen but being felt. It's also about allowing others to make their presence known, express their views, and get involved.

2. *Check in with people regularly.* This doesn't need to be anything formal, just ask people how they're getting on – not to intimidate them, but out of genuine interest in their work life and well-being, also to find out what might be tripping them up. Technology allows you to do this no matter where you are. Being *tech savvy* is a must.

3. *Hold regular worldview and roadmap discussions.* Have a visible big idea and a plan, and talk about them often. Then turn *vision* into verbs. Macro to micro. Such discussions reinforce people's understanding of objectives

and decisions, plus encourage them to get involved, add their own ideas, become more engaged – so it's important to leave room for employees to bring something to the plan.

4. *Hold joint progress reviews.* On the spot *coaching* goes a long way to establishing confidence – you provide a safety net. As a manager who engages, aim to leave every casual conversation or a formal meeting with a sense that you left things better than before – a sense of forward action and improvement. Routine progress reviews help keep everyone informed and build confidence that everyone is making a valid contribution. Proudfoot was implementing daily team huddles decades ago to keep transformation on track. People need to see and feel progress to help keep them engaged, but they also need to see and feel support.

5. *Communicate creatively, widely and often.* Informal dialogue, using everyday language, is the best means of bouncing ideas around – rather than impersonal emails or formal meetings. Ideally, you should be looking to break down traditional hierarchical relationships and make things more fluid and collaborative to really have *influence*. Get everyone's fingerprints on everything. We know people absorb information in different ways, so use as many vehicles as you can to help people make connections. Soundbites and status updates are easiest to absorb, compared to detailed corporate emails or newsletters. Think Twitter. Make the detail optional onward reading. Visual aids, video clips, infographics – all of these tools can be very effective to frame messages differently or reinforce important points. Consider how people receive information during their personal lives and try to replicate this at work.

Beyond these ways of implementing the HeadsUp High Five, there are a couple more techniques that you can use to improve your personal visibility with your teams:

- *Practice regular, visible reward and recognition.* Don't save up feedback for formal sit-downs. Be generous and visible in your praise, whenever and wherever it is warranted (but don't devalue it by going overboard). Make a big deal of great results when they happen, but also the big effort made along the way.

- *Build your legacy encounter by encounter.* Whether it's providing a comforting word/thanks for a job well done, or establishing a new project around a need identified by a team member, confidence comes when people know what they say and do counts. People will then feel your presence even when you are not there, because of the positive impression – the legacy you leave behind.

And don't stop communicating: the more routine the information flow, the more confidence you build. Use quick video catch-ups and end of week check-ins that are social as well as work related.

Improve Information Visibility: Work on Your Infostructure, the Road to Informed Action

Nothing builds confidence like knowing you're supported by the information you need to make informed decisions. Your infostructure, is a systemic way to ensure people have the right facts, status updates, supporting evidence at their fingertips, where their work gets done. In Proudfoot we call this a Management Operating System – something we invented some eight decades ago. It's the way you move data around a business to be able to plan, schedule, execute work and report, at every level. It's the backbone of an operating model. It drives decision-making. It also drives engagement.

Consider the following when assessing your information visibility:

- How and to whom should information flow?
- Do you have meaningful and easily understood KPIs?
- Is information as visible and available as and where it needs to be?
- Finally, how are you reviewing progress – beyond periodic formal meetings?

A lack of information can be debilitating, causing stress, concern, and doubts. *Timeliness* of information allows people to make the right decisions, to achieve greater results. It's not about poring over data for days – a long wait for information can hinder progress almost as much as having no information.

Real-Time Decision-Making

In this digitally accelerated business era, decision-making needs to be less cumbersome, closer to the action, and in real time. Consider whether, in your organization, a decision can be made and acted on in the same day as a need or problem is raised. If not, work toward that so people can feel change happening. One of the biggest learnings from the 2020 crisis was the absolute acceleration of decision-making. How do you find the right speed for your business that may not be at that same speed but speedier than your pre–COVID-19 world?

Create a Visible Workplace

"If these walls could talk. . ." But they can – and they should! The work environment is your canvas. Use it as a communication vehicle. Nothing builds confidence like total immersion, and visible communication immerses the audience in the message. Here are a few tips:

- *Show first, then tell.* A picture really does paint a thousand words. Wherever you can, present in pictures, then talk.

- *Use space to your advantage.* Look for high employee traffic areas and make them a focal point for messages: look at your entire workplace as a living message board and see where you can take advantage of people's natural presence to help reinforce or disseminate messages.

- *Bring in familiar faces.* If themed posters are your vehicle of choice, customize them; bring employees into photos and videos. We're more likely to take things on board if it comes from someone we know.

- *Think like a marketer: bring color to the workplace.* Take your most pressing message and create an advertising program around it – not an email. And ask your people to do it. You never know who your hidden Banksys are.

- *Use logos to speed up communication.* Logos and icons speed up recognition and let our brains know they don't have to spend time reading a title on a page to determine who or what a communication is about. So take advantage of these useful shortcuts.

Watch out for unintended messages that chip away at confidence. Messages posted up near water coolers or in office kitchenettes, may seem innocuous enough, but they can send out negative messages that undermine or contradict the positive reinforcements you're otherwise trying to get out. At a manufacturing site I once worked at in Canada, I noticed two signs: one was a notice posted above a kettle in the lunchroom, the other, a sheet of paper taped to the front of a fridge. The first notice outlined who the safety committee was and how to contact them – no problem there, except many of the names on the list had been crossed out, suggesting redundancies or a mass exodus of staff! Not very confidence-inspiring for the new joiners down the hall attending their company orientation. This was compounded by the rather unfriendly staff notice on the fridge, which shouted: "THIS MILK IS FOR COFFEE ONLY— IF YOU CONTINUE USING IT FOR OTHER THINGS, WE WILL HAVE TO CEASE SUPPLYING IT!" What it really meant was *"YOU HAVE BEEN TOLD!"*

Sharp Dude and the Energy Vampire

Sometime ago we were asked to help a company that was implementing major change but struggling with a union that was intent on stopping the change process in its tracks. My team was on the ground enabling the firm to lead a major transformation. In keeping with a visual workplace theme, the team felt a mascot was needed to inject good news in a business that seemed dry and dull. They decided to take their program visual. They started with two characters – a mascot and a villain – Sharp Dude and the Energy Vampire – and both had very specific manifestos.

Sharp Dude appeared like the mascots in most advertising: happy, healthy, and helping people to make a quick connection to the program by attaching himself to any communication that was relevant to the change project. He was a picture of the future and carried the message of change, giving comfort that while change was afoot, everyone would survive it. The Energy Vampire, on the other hand, was used to show contrast. He was a picture of the past, holding onto old, worn-out behaviors and processes, and painting a darker picture of doom and gloom. Sharp Dude injected brightness, whereas the Energy Vampire was a brilliantly illustrated bad guy. He ever so softly represented the people who were spending their time sucking the energy out of the business by purposefully working against improvement efforts and injecting doubt into people's minds. The army of the disengaged. As time passed, Sharp Dude was used to illustrate what the organization was doing right and what it needed to do right in the future. The contrast was perfect, and the messages were illustrations of real life in real time – a constant battle between doubt in today and confidence in the future.

It didn't take long for those who might have joined the dark side to question what was going on, and the Energy Vampire gave them the opportunity to do that in a depersonalized way. While it might sound a little dramatic, the visual depiction of good and evil gave people the opportunity to see what happens when people go bad. Sharp Dude had prevailed, but only after people saw the connection between what they do and the bigger picture. The illustrations helped them make those connections and draw their own conclusions that an Energy Vampire would do little but reinforce the doubt that was prevalent in the organization of the past and that the future lay with the confidence that things would change – Sharp Dude.

Provide People with Visual Impact

Storytelling is one of the most powerful ways to allow people to come with you on a journey of change. It's also a brilliant engagement tool – a confidence builder. When someone tells a great story, you start to imagine it in your mind's eye. When you visually put things into perspective for people, you can achieve the same thing – people make a connection, they join the dots. For example, what might *one cent short on price* translate into? A $12 million loss of revenue. That's impact! And that $12 million might be the R&D budget for a new product the business wanted to design. *Make money visible, make numbers come to life, make information understandable.* The late Steve Jobs said it best when describing the iPod. He didn't give a plethora of technical specifications, he simply said *it puts 1,000 songs in your pocket.* Bang!

If people are constantly looking for where they fit in the big picture – in their life, in their relationships, in their families, and of course in their work – then it stands to reason they want to see what kind of an impact they have day to day. We need to make this easier for people to see. Why? Because it removes doubt.

So what are some of the practical things you can do to help create this visible impact?

- *Take a lesson from the digital world: provide real-time data displayed for all to see, in easily understood formats.* This can include hourly flashes and updates, daily results, weekly outcomes. The easier it is for people to see results in real time, the more easily they'll be able to make the connection between the impact they have in their daily work and the results the business is achieving. In our personal lives, we keep people up to date on Facebook and Instagram – but are you exploiting this speed internally within your workplace? Think of your kids' online games with running statistics in the corner of the screen. Now think about how you might do something like that at work.

- *Use scenarios to provide context.* When people can see the impact from selling 3 versus 5 versus 10 units, they begin to see how they make the difference. Providing illustrations and explaining scenarios to people visually allows them to connect their actions directly to cash, break-evens, and profitability. At 3 units we make a loss, at 5 we break even, and at 10 we make a profit. We become confident we are doing the right things.

- *Provide comparisons that resonate.* The examples don't need to be complex. If you're trying to help people understand how what they waste counts in results, convert your product into a visual picture. Remember my hamburger story earlier in this chapter? A hippo eats the equivalent of 385 Big Macs a day. Had I been told what that was in pounds or kilos, it would have meant little to me, but 385 Big Macs was something I could relate to. That's a lot of food.

When I first met Paradigm Learning's CEO, Ray Green, I learned a phrase that stayed with me forever – *people need to learn their way out of a situation.* Presenting a problem to discover your way through is one of the best ways to learn and build confidence. And when people *behave* their way into a new world, they become confident they can change because they demonstrate it to themselves. Paradigm calls this "discovery learning." But the phrase that resonated even more was how people react to your opinions (as opposed to their own). He told me "People will listen to *your* conclusions, but they will only take action on their *own* conclusions." You must look for ways to help the penny drop. Our job in managing to engage is to constantly look for opportunities to create "aha!" moments for our people. That's when they learn best. When they can say "Ah – now I get it!" That sparks confidence and engagement.

Accelerate Confidence Building

One of the starkest contrasts between life now and life even a few years ago, is the emphasis and expectation for everything to happen in real time. Technology has removed the need for many of the delays that afflicted businesses of old – from the slow, physical post system, to the time taken to collate data to build performance reports. Today, from messaging and virtual meetings to status updates, everything happens immediately.

This acceleration of action and reporting can serve us in ways we may have underestimated. Without long delays between requests and responses, we can spare employees from the doubt that can creep in when long periods of time elapse. It is the time when we are in the dark that we often feel at our most vulnerable, the most unsure of ourselves. So the more people are able to learn about performance and success, or see where things may be going off track, in real time, the less of a window there is to worry, and the less likely it is that there will be any nasty surprises.

I wonder if the statisticians could put a value to that anxiety: the cost savings associated with a reduction in anxiety or the moments we lose pondering over the what-ifs; that time spent dreaming of what could be. Whether we arrive at empirical evidence to quantify this, it's clear that speed can substantially reduce the doubt and anxiety associated with daily life, which is something we should all remember when managing people. Leaving people to linger in self-doubt is a fast killer of confidence and engagement.

One Word: When Less Is More

As you start to think in terms of an employee confidence index – i.e., putting a stake in the ground and then charting your progress with people – a handy instant measure is an unscientific yet straight-to-the-point "one-word" test – a quick way to get a feel for the confidence people have in their company by the word they choose. Ask, "What one word would you use to describe your company at this moment in time?" You would be amazed at the widely contrasting perspectives even within the same teams.

These one-word snapshots tell a vivid story. *Confused, learning, improving, chaos, dying, alive, vibrant, boring, dull* are just some of the words people have offered. How confident would you feel in your business if it had been described as *dying*?! What if you didn't ask and never knew?

Workplaces need continuous confidence-building measures. 2020 proved this need. People were spending their time asking, "Will I still have a job next month? Will I be promoted? Will the business stay afloat? Can my team, or the company as a whole, survive this shift?" Fear and doubt need to be eliminated. The general rule is: fill the silence with facts and feelings where doubt could grow. Let people know and understand what's going on. Keep things simple.

In the twenty-first century, the barriers to transformation and improved results are often the barriers to speed and bold action, and these are not necessarily technology. They are, too often, mindset, motivation, and bureaucracy. When you start to manage to engage, confidence builds, mindsets change, and brilliance ensues: boldness and speed to transform follows.

---

1. **Build your own employee confidence index. Determine three key questions that will provide insight into the levels of confidence people have in you, your workplace, or your business. For example:**
   - "Would you describe the current state of your company as excellent, good, not so good, or poor?"
   - "Would you describe your state of mind as highly engaged, not very engaged, or poorly engaged?"
   - "Considering the state of your business and your engagement levels, would you say you're willing to invest extra effort at work a great deal, only if you have to, or not at all?"

FIGURE 7.1   Things You Need to Do Right Now.   (*continued*)

2. Take a tour of your workplace to identify the current level of visibility—to what extent does your workplace use visual aids to get important messages across or to help people see connections?

3. Complete a 'one-word' test. Ask your people what one word they would use to describe your business, team, or leadership today.

Confidence: 5 things you can do today to improve quality of life at work

1. **Go visual**

   Whenever, wherever, however you can, make your workplace visual. Show results, messages, and communications visually first, and then write about them in emails or on company portals.

2. **Banish doubt – tackle people's worries head on**

   Ask the unasked questions; talk openly about what is concerning people. Tell them what they should or should not be concerned about in the business.

3. **Be optimistic – aim for one foot in the present, one foot in the future**

   Keep an eye on your own messages. Be very conscious of your own levels of optimism and strive to raise these wherever possible – everyone is watching.

4. **A quick word – the instant confidence poll**

   Ask each individual for a single word that describes how he or she feels about your company, business, or workplace today. Then address the findings – aim to convert words of doubt into words of optimism in as short a time as possible.

5. **Have presence!**

   Be visible and accessible for your people.

CHAPTER 8

Building Connections: Can You Hear Me?

The real influencers of an organization are the network nodes: the people who most often intersect with the most people.

—Professor Margaret Heffernan, author, CEO, entrepeneur

Value in business today comes from who you know and who and how you connect with them. Connection builds whole new forms of capital – personal, social, intellectual, operational, financial, and reputational.

Connection is about how we relate to other people. You get that sensation that you have someone you can share thoughts and bounce ideas with. When you connect with people at work you feel you've got a buddy or a team who are "in it together." Great connection provides a sense of belonging. We take energy from one another when we connect. We get excited about common interests and common ground. If we don't feel connected to those around us – our colleagues, managers, suppliers, customers – we soon lose our enthusiasm. Without a strong understanding of what links us together and our place in the universe, it's hard to see how who we are or what we do matters. If we feel connected, we understand those around us and importantly, we feel understood. With connection, remarkable things can happen. We engage.

You're the Best Thing about Me

Maintaining an emotional connection is essential to long-term employee engagement. In her powerful TED talk a few years ago, Dr. Brené Brown, a research professor at the University of Houston, Graduate College of Social Work, went so far as to say, "Connection is what gives purpose and meaning to our lives."[1]

How we form and harness connections at work is being rewritten in the modern age. Aided by rich technology, the ability to connect is becoming much more personal, frequent and informal, and less autocratic. At least, that is the expectation. And it makes a big difference to how we feel. Having a deep connection even with just one person at work can influence whether we engage. If it's a positive connection with the boss, it can mean the difference between staying in the job or quitting.

Many leaders would now agree that the human upside of 2020 has been the absolute closeness of connection that transpired as we Zoomed our way through technology solutions to keep close to our suddenly distanced work world. This would have been considered an oxymoron in 2019. How could technology really create closeness, and yet here we are – we've seen one another's living rooms, offices, and kitchens, and many experienced the almost globally famous BBC news reporting of David Kelly when his two small children broke into his office to say hi to Dad as he was interviewed about the impeachment of South Korean president Park Geun-hye.[2] It brought leaders at every level closer to their teams. We felt a sense of connection.

[1] Brené Brown, "The Power of Vulnerability," TED.com (2014). www.ted.com/talks/brene_brown_the_power_of_vulnerability/transcript?language=en
[2] Robert Kelly, "BBC World interview on South Korea" (YouTube, 2017). www.youtube.com/watch?v=0M7679g1BEw

Personal Connection Builds Personal Commitment

The CEO of a major US food manufacturer had invested a significant proportion of its capex budget into plant facilities, upgrading the site in an effort to improve production throughput. Irrespective of the shiny new renovation they were still experiencing high employee turnover and low compliance to production schedules, and line changeovers between product runs were both long and risked contamination. The CEO's disappointment in results was clear. His investment had not paid off. He felt a fresh set of eyes was needed.

When our team arrived, they went about some of the fundamental startup activities for a large-scale change initiative – one was to stand up the Results Hub and form the Results Team. The team reviewed the problem statement – one of which was to reduce downtime in production changeovers and sanitation, while improving quality. The hub tracked the progress the team was to deliver. Within weeks, small changes in results started to track through to senior management and they decided they wanted to meet the Results Team and see what was making the change. They visited the plant, took a tour of the facilities, and then did something they had never done – they had the Results Team and supervisors engaged in the project present their improvement plans – the targets, the timelines, and the actions that were to be implemented. This was the first time these teams had ever presented to senior management. The CEO offered how he could help accelerate efforts and remove traditional barriers to their plans. He was impressed with their approach. He felt confident the team would deliver and did an on-the-spot recognition and reward moment to show it. That one moment of visibility opened the doors to engagement, brought a personal connection between the leadership team and the Results Team, and allowed them to remain in contact going forward, giving regular progress updates.

Playing Push-Me-Pull-Me

To improve our workplace connectedness, we need to review our effectiveness at communication – but understand, connectedness is not just about communication. Since time immemorial and despite all manner of technology improvements in recent decades, communication has remained one of the biggest sources of letdown in annual employee satisfaction surveys. It is an area that managers still get wrong. It is not resulting in the kind of intimacy or connections employees need to feel engaged and self-motivated. But in 2020 for many organizations and leadership teams, much of this changed. It must now be a sustainable change. ~~We can't slip back to the past levels of poor communication that lacked connected~~ness.

The problem is not communication skills – or not solely. It's how we think and frame communication to connect with each other. From the way we throw technology at the issue, or invest in communications training, too many companies clearly persist in the view that communication is a transaction, a linear process. But it is not – certainly not in the twenty-first century. *Communication is an interaction.* It's a verb. We all know the need for improved communication, and in leaderships defence, I think we try. Where we fall over is in two distinct areas: first in the execution of our own communication, which is often a monologue where we simply speak without following up and testing for understanding; and second, in the maintaining of that monologue and forgetting communication is a dialogue, a two-way street that requires our listening and being mutually engaged. It's a game of tennis, not ten-pin bowling. The comms ball needs to come back in real time.

With so much incoming information to digest and respond to, it's easy to feel that we're doing all the receiving and not enough feeding back, or being heard. It's too much push and too little pull. Effective communication recognizes that everyone has a voice and we must provide the vehicle to hear it. But, it is about how we connect, collaborate, and build communities around people and across a business. It is not about being "communicated to." It is as much about feeling included, valued, and listened to as it is about receiving transparent, clear messaging.

Solving the dilemma of poor communication requires that leaders and managers create higher levels of connectivity; seeking out more touch points – more ways to connect, collaborate, and build community with and around people.

The American psychological thriller/science fiction TV drama series *Heroes*, created by Tim Kring and shown originally on NBC, used the phrase "we are all connected" at least 100 times in the first season alone.[3] This was no accident – it's something Kring felt passionate about: our sense of connectedness and its influence in every aspect of our lives. In the workplace, levels of connectivity (including collaboration and community) help cultivate an environment in which people will feel more engaged. Beverly Alimo-Metcalfe, now emeritus professor of Leadership Studies at the University of

---

[3] Tim Kring, *Heroes*, 2006–2010. United States. Tailwind Productions. NBC Universal Television Studio.

Leeds and founding director of leadership consultancy the Real World Group, has done a lot of work examining "engaging leadership" as a predictor not only of productivity but also increased employee motivation, job satisfaction, commitment, and reduced job-related stress.[4] Her work strongly suggests that communication in the broader sense is a "mega need" – linked to overall business performance. While it's old news, we need to address it if we want to manage to engage; more importantly, if we want to achieve remarkable results at work, execute large-scale transformation, and ride the ups and downs of economic activity we will continue to see for years to come.

The three interrelated Cs – connection, collaboration, and community – help achieve this. They are all underpinned by communication. It's when these three interlock effectively that many companies achieve a competitive advantage others find hard to copy. While the study Alimo-Metcalfe was involved with found that an organization's leadership culture positively impacted people's attitudes toward work and their well-being, if it was "engaging with others," it predicted positive attitudes toward wider well-being, including a strong sense of team spirit. Engaging with others requires not just communication then, but connecting, collaboration, and community. So these qualities must feature equally and solidly in the management models we use.

Don't Break the Connection

If we want to improve connectedness in the workplace, look at both the personal connectivity between people, and the vehicles and skills that can improve those connections – the routine way people interact at work. The first thing we need to do is recognize what doesn't work.

One Size Does Not Fit All!

Today, it should go without saying that what makes one personally feel connected and "heard," may be different from that which has a similarly positive effect on someone else. That is, there is no one-size-fits-all panacea management style that will produce greater connectedness, cohesion, and buy-in. So it's a good thing that most things in business, in marketing, are

---

[4] "Engaging Leadership Part One: Competencies are Like Brighton Pier, Real World Group," Beverly Alimo-Metcalfe, *International Journal of Leadership in Public Services* (March 2009).

moving toward the audience of one – the individual. We need to calibrate our actions for each person we lead.

We Cannot Be Assimilated

People at different life stages, from different generations, from different backgrounds or cultures require different connections and different solutions. How connected they feel will be determined by how far you have understood and adapted your approach to connect with them. Unlike the Borg of the famous series *Star Trek,* assimilation is not an option.

Ban Bossy – A Good Boss Keeps You Engaged

By now you should have no doubt that the immediate line manager of any employee has the greatest impact on our day-to-day results, level of effort, and well-being. How they behave influences how their team behaves. This reinforces the fundamental need to get one-on-one interactions right between people at work – but most particularly the boss/employee relationship, how they connect. We know that 80 percent of the variation in engagement levels in the workplace is a direct result of line management. This reinforces the view that a person's most important relationship at work is with his or her line manager. If those manager-employee connections could become a leader's superpower, if connections were stronger, better, fitter for purpose, imagine the results you could achieve with your team. Moreover, if you are embarking on major change, the immediate supervisors' ability to connect with their team to become the organizations transformation catalyst enables you to scale change – the concept of leaders at every level leading change.

Core Principles for Improving Connectivity

Dr. Brene Brown describes connection as *why we're here.* It's why we show up.[5] That's how important connection is at work. That's not to say we want

---

[5] Brown, "The Power of Vulnerability."

to get personally involved with everyone we work with. We hear the phrase "engaging hearts and minds" with such regularity, but really, we "need to touch one another's hearts and minds enough that our conversations resonate, that they mean something." Connection is what we strive for in our lives. With connection comes a sense of worth, linked to other people. We feel valued because another individual demonstrates that value through how they connect with us. This applies in all aspects of our lives, not just at work.

To get there, lets first get the basics right. Below are five simple principles that could help you improve your workplace connectivity levels:

1. *Customization is king* – and it's not just for customers. From the way we interact, our preferred way of taking in information and our learning style, to how we respond to different management and leadership styles, we're all different. So, a good manager will strive to better understand how to relate to the individuals around them. Take notes and make note of what works and what doesn't for each of your team.

2. *The way you connect with individuals shows how much you value them.* Traditional management thinking warned us to keep a professional distance at work, especially as a manager. In keeping with this, we have adopted business speak that seems designed both to baffle and distance people from simple facts and plans but also to depersonalize discussions. *We need to regroup,* we say, when we mean *get together and talk*. We tell our teams we need to *co-create and mobilize* when we mean *get together and get behind something*. Be human. Be personable. It's the concept of authentic – being fair dinkum. When you start from there, connection can follow.

A number of years ago, I attended the funeral service for Kelvin Boyd, a great man and a great work colleague in Proudfoot. During the eulogy, delivered by one of his closest friends, we were reminded of one thing Kelvin always did: *He took the time to ask about you.* I mean *really* ask about you. How was your wife, how were your studies progressing, what was going on in your life? Not a cursory, "How are you?" but a real discussion, and importantly, a discussion held irrespective of the day's demands, the current crisis. When people invest time in learning about you, they invest time in building relationships and making connections. They say, *you count.* They demonstrate they are fair dinkum.

So what kind of conversations should you hold to help you better connect? Think of it this way: if you can't answer three out of five of the following questions about your closest workmates, colleagues, employees (or friends for that matter), then you have some work to do!

- What are their immediate family members' names?
- What do you know about their partner or spouse? If they are single, do they have strong friends and support networks?
- How far do they travel to get to work, how long does the commute take, and how do they travel to work?
- How are they faring financially? (You shouldn't need to pry to learn this: everyday clues should let you know if people are OK or struggling.)
- If they have children, what rough ages are they, do they live at home, are they stars in the community, or are they having any issues?

A connected manager ought to have a feel for this familial/personal context. Unfortunately, in the typical workplace, you may find disappointingly low numbers of people can answer four out of five of these questions about those they spend most of their week with. We have so much coming at us we try to skip the small talk. But is small talk really small? Or is it a means to better connect? Piece together a richer picture of the people around you? The more you learn, the more people in turn will learn about how much you care, improving your mutual sense of connection.

When it comes to how to engage people at work, the point is that a forty-something with young children is likely to have more in common with a twenty-something in the same position than they may have with someone of their own age who doesn't have kids. That is, experience and interests may unite us more than how long we've been around.

3. *We value customer relationship management, so let's value employee relationship management!* Salespeople capture a lot more than customer contact details. Customer relationship management systems (CRM) allow them to add notes about all aspects of the customer's status, interests. Reminders and prompts, meanwhile, allow the salesperson to pick up a conversation where they last left off. As managers, we can capture the same sort of details and prompts about our team members to create our own ERM – employee relationship management. So that we never again need to forget a family member's name, or an important date in a colleague's life – the small things that can make us seem thoughtless and disconnected from each other. Today's smartphones make it very easy to add what you learn into the palm of your hand, filling out people's stories.

4. *Map out who people really are, to help it really sink in and to see the big picture.* This takes your contact information to a more dynamic level. Put all the people you want to build better connections with on one page, with photos and any interesting information about them, such as their stage of life – e.g., are they young and career-minded, building a family, or past that stage? Include detail about what they're known for. Then map who is in contact with whom and to what degree. Include lines to show who else should be in contact with each other ideally, too. Where do interests overlap, for instance? Make it a project, perhaps even a team project for everyone to learn about everyone. Get the different demographics to encourage each other as well. What better way to build engagement than to involve people!

5. *Use what you know to get it right, one person at a time.* Start small and build out. Learn what makes a winning strategy with one person, group, or generation, then expand and adapt this for others as you gain confidence. Take your lead from younger members of staff, who tend to be instinctively well connected. This is a generation for whom nothing moves fast enough. While you may be thinking change management, they're thinking change acceleration – so you'll need to look for ways to manage their expectations or to speed up their world at work. These team members may hotfoot it to their next job if they feel they're in the slow lane at work, and that may come directly from feeling a lack of connection and engagement. But keep in mind that older team members may be slower to form new connections and could be more fearful of change, reinforcing the need to adapt your greater connectivity plan to appeal to everyone in their own way.

Remember, You Don't Know What You Don't Know

Some years ago, I worked with a consultant named Liverson Mdongo in South Africa. He was one of my favorite colleagues. He grew up in Zimbabwe and dreamed of taking a freezer to his little village so the children there could have ice cream. I had no idea about this vision of his until we flew together one afternoon and had the time to genuinely connect. And that's not all I learned.

We were traveling to Cape Town to do some work for a major food manufacturer, a food manufacturer that, faced with redundancies following poor economic results, had decided to set people up in their own businesses rather than simply lay them off. If they were willing, each person was offered the tools and product to become an independent salesperson for the organizations in their villages and towns. Liverson and I spent much of the flight discussing this. It was a great way to extend the organization's reach into their community and while they needed to make economic decisions, they could do it in a way that would engage their people and set them up for success. This was long before the stakeholder engagement themes of today's world. It was, by all accounts quite innovative, particularly in South Africa in the 1990s. But on this trip, I learned about Liverson. It turned out that Liverson had never seen the ocean! A trip to Cape Town meant he was about to.

It was so easy to assume that a university-educated professional man like Liverson had traveled the Seven Seas. He had not. And of course, Zimbabwe is a landlocked country, something else I didn't absorb.

How much we take for granted. Here was someone I'd felt a great connection with during our work time together. What else didn't I know, I wondered. It made me question how much I knew about other work colleagues. Now, when I meet and greet new friends, new work colleagues, or new clients, I think of the ocean of things I need to discover about them.

I'm a Change Junkie – Get Me Out of Here!

When the workplace was made up predominantly of baby boomers (and later Generation Xers), bosses complained regularly about the levels of resistance to change they experienced in the workplace. Everyone ran out and studied change management and a whole industry was spawned. While the boomers in general, we believed, wanted to stick with the status quo, the Gen Xers were somewhat more accepting that change would happen, but highly cynical. Book after business book was published on managing change, motivating people to change, or creating change. As the twenty-first century gathers pace, we've heard it ad nauseum that change is a fact of life.

In this era of enthusiastic market disruption, a younger generation has grown up waiting to seize their moment, hungering for change, chasing the next innovation opportunity. Digital transformation? Bring it on! These forces of nature are entering a workplace that in many cases can't move fast enough

for them. From this standpoint, it's the managem
past, clinging to familiar mantras, and resistant to ch
many of your youngest team members may think).

But perhaps it is here that connections might cc
the different generations, or differing mindsets, car
the way. The uninhibited can encourage older hands to be bold,
tious, more experienced team members can act as the voice of reason – not
curbing progress, so much as guiding it, challenging it, channeling it.

As the world of work evolves and changes, so, too, will the challenges facing managers. Increasingly, you will need to be able to bring to bear:

1. The ability to understand and *enable* the distinct generational differences
   in the workplace so they can better engage with you and each other, and
   connect for mutual benefit.

2. The ability to accelerate change with those who fear it, while simultaneously maintaining engagement for those whose world at work doesn't
   seem to be advancing quickly enough.

3. An appreciation that people may view things from very different vantage
   points, despite desiring the same end result – how they get there will differ.

4. The ability to deal with individuals who appear to suffer from an attention
   deficit disorder, yet require extreme amounts of attention.

5. The ability to inspire and mobilize people in alternative employment relationships (contractors), as well as those who are under someone else's
   leadership yet have relevance and input to your team.

6. The ability to inspire the diverse needs of different people and gain
   support from those who view the world differently.

7. Add to this list a newer one, the ability to inspire people who may have
   been unemployed for great periods of time or underemployed, who may
   feel cynical or simply underinspired by the world's events.

Where once upon a time, an employee may have looked for no more than
clarity and direction from their employers and managers, now their expectations are bolder. They expect to be known as individuals, cared about, and
nurtured to be their best, inspired, empowered and supported. Above all, people want to be free to think, venture ideas, and achieve.

When a manager connects well with people, they become a sought-after
source of inspiration, focus, help, and leadership. People become mobilized
because they want to be.

...1e Is Precious – Use It Well

An assumption that managers can be guilty of is that employees have all the time in the world to give to their job, without full and demanding lives beyond the walls of the business. We sometimes measure commitment based on how late people work. We neglect to respect their private lives; the teams they coach, the scouts they camp with, the tutoring they do when not at work.

I remember a colleague complaining that the younger generation of employees seemed to have no interest in connecting with him, in team building – team dinners were forced fun. To my colleague, this suggested an unwillingness to invest themselves in getting to know their peers and managers more informally, to better connected as a team. Viewed differently, these team members had set their own personal boundaries and were protecting their right to a personal life. As well they should! A good work-life balance is vital to replenishing energy stores.

The lesson my older colleague learned was that people today may connect differently, and may prefer to do it during designated work hours, but this doesn't mean they're any less engaged or committed. While the old-style manager might invite a millennial for a drink after work, the millennial may prefer a caramel macchiato at the local Starbucks between meetings in the afternoon. As managers, we need to rethink what appropriate team building might look like in the modern workplace. For instance, building social time into the working day is likely to be a winning strategy.

If You Want to Understand, Listen

If you only remember one thing from this book, I hope it is this phrase *If you want to understand, listen.* This is a quote from the 2006 movie trailer for *Babel*, starring Cate Blanchett and Brad Pitt.[6] The title (taken from the Hebrew *balal*, meaning to confuse or confound) serves as a reminder of the "human noise" we all must break through to be both heard and understood.

---

[6] Alejandro González Iñárritu, *Babel*, 2006. United States, Mexico and France. Anonymous Content.

The *MacLeod Review*, still considered today as a comprehensive study of employee engagement, outlined a series of enablers of engagement and how to make engagement work. In common with other studies, it highlighted an effective and empowered employee voice as a critical engagement trigger, as manifested this way:

1. People's views are being sought out.
2. People are listened to and are able to see that their opinions count and make a difference.
3. People have an opportunity to speak out and to challenge when appropriate.
4. A strong sense of listening and of responsiveness permeates the organization, enabled by effective communication.

It is about connection. People's desire to be heard at work is no different from our personal desires to be heard in any relationship we have outside the business world. When we enter the corporate environment, the rules seem to change. We forget to be human. Common expectations of people and between people are viewed as something different. So much so that we need government-sponsored reports such as the *Macleod Review* to research and clarify the rules of engagement![7] Humanize. Optimize. Digitize. No matter the work to be done, the first step is always to ensure we understand the human element.

In a crisis, though, it's all too easy to lose your connection with team members. The seriousness or urgency of the situation may mean we strip back the niceties because there are more important and pressing priorities. If all staff hear are crisis and cost reductions, they will soon become alarmed and potentially disengaged. Yet this is a time when the business and its management need all hands on deck, connected and engaged. It's easy to forget that not everyone has access to the higher-level strategy, the company financials, the vision. Helping people to understand "Where are we today?" and "What does the future hold?" is a powerful way to keep connections and reassure that there is a plan. Without that feeling of reassurance and inclusion, they may easily drift away and start looking for alternative job opportunities. When the chips are down, connect more.

---

[7] David MacLeod and Nita Clarke, *Engaging for Success: Enhancing Performance Through Employee Engagement* (UK Office of Public Sector Information, 2009), p. 78. https://dera.ioe. ac.uk/1810/1/file52215.pdf

One Foot in the Present and One Foot in the Future

To keep business moving forward, we all need to be fluid at flexing connections across timelines. We need to be able to maintain a dual perspective, for the purpose of comparison and contrast. We should be able to see how things are now and how we want them to be. If we live too much in the present, or too much in the future, we can soon lose perspective and more importantly momentum. So we need strategies for maintaining our connections over time: the engagement triggers that will keep us on track today, and those that move us forward toward our bigger goals.

The ideal scenario is to have one foot in the present and one in the future: bridging the two by making the connection that what you do today creates your future. That's how progress is made. And progress is something people need to see: why do you think we measure everything? We like and need evidence of movement, that we have made progress, we can see improvement. Without it, we become disconnected, we give up – and managers can be as guilty of this as anyone.

Soul-Searching, a Change Is Gonna Come

If you sense that you may be a source of lost connection for those around you, be conscious of what it is you are doing that might cause people to subtly yet irrevocably disconnect from you. There could be any number of triggers, but here are some common ones you might recognize:

- *Be brief. Stop drawing everything out.* If you can't get to the point of what you need to say, people will switch off. Recognize the cues that people have already flicked to another channel.

- *Stop losing your cool. If you lose your temper at work,* then you have overstepped the boundaries and so people's respect for you will suffer. However challenging things become, try to keep a level head. If you find this happening with specific people and not "everyone" you need to ask, "Do I have the right people on the bus?"

- *Stop underestimating people.* Don't feed them snippets or dress things up: ~~give them reality and detail~~. Let people tell you how much they can handle. Watch for their reactions. Plain, straight speak usually makes better progress.

- *"Don't assume you know where the questions is coming from."?* You can waste a lot of time speaking to what you think the question is rather than what it actually is.

- *Learn from the past by all means, but try to spend more time leaning forward.* Work out the steps to keep moving forward.

When happiness statistician Nic Marks talks about happiness and well-being, he reminds us of the ~~positive – daily – actions we need to take~~. The first of these being to work on connections – increasing our sense of belonging and of having positive, social relationships with people we deem to be important in our lives.[8]

Raising your strength and depth of connection with people at work is not just common sense; it also makes good business sense – and makes for a better society. We need positive social connections just as we need air, food, and water. That's how important this *C* is in helping people get engaged.

Oh, and Don't Forget to Be Human!

It's worth raising this again. When we're under pressure, it's easy to forget that basic life skills apply at work just as they do anywhere else in life.

While I'm reluctant to use this term given our 2020 globally collective experience, the organization of the future will be a *contagious* organism where people connect and thrive. They will feel inspired to give and be their best. Engaged. Enabled. Energized.

---

[8] Nic Marks, "The Happy Planet Index," TED.com (July 2010). https://www.ted.com/talks/nic_marks_the_happy_planet_index

1. **Invest in getting to know your people better.**

   Establish what you know and how much you don't know, and make a conscious effort to fill in the gaps – making notes to help you.

2. **Using your phone, create a contact for each of your team members and complete the fields as you learn more about them.**

   Add unique information: the fact that Kevin has a six-year-old he needed to leave work early for this week because of a problem at school should register as importantly as his birthday, generational traits, or favourite sports. Heather's skills and aspirations should be noted, as should the fact that she needs constant stimulation and should get onto the performance improvement project because she likes to contribute new ideas. Prioritizing the person and getting to know more about them as an individual will help you develop stronger connections and understand how to engage your people. But remember: employee details are dynamic – they need to be updated regularly.

3. **Recall the five groups of questions to know about your people, set out earlier in this chapter.**

   See if you need to adapt them to reflect the demographic make-up of your workforce – but bear in mind that life experiences can override generalizations about people based on age, etc. Once you're satisfied your questions are suitable for the people you work with, and have the answers, add these to your contacts.

Connections: 5 things you can do today to improve quality of life at work

1. **Connect personally**

   Whether on Zoom, in the hallway or over lunch or a coffee break, any opportunity to connect one-to-one with people at work increases that sense of alignment and togetherness. And to the people we work with, nothing quite outshines the feeling we get when we know the boss has taken the time and effort to step outside of his or her scheduled day and invest their time in us.

2. **Connect virtually and visually**

   Consider setting up a team site or other form of social site that people feel comfortable with – remember, it's about connecting and sharing and not just working. Additionally, think of ways you can connect visually – using images, diagrams/maps, photos, infographics, animation, or short videos to get messages across in more effective ways that people can relate to.

3. **Connect as a team**

   Whether it's via an organized get-together or something purely social, nothing beats a team connecting as a whole. Just be mindful of people's willingness to do this out of office hours and respect people's free time and home lives. One option that taps into another human need is to connect around a cause – a charity or just something everyone feels passionate about. This could be something as simple as painting a wall in your building (the more creative, the better) or planting a veggie patch outside or supporting a community project.

4. **Connect with what you learn**

   When you recall during a conversation that Sally's daughter came first in the school swimming competition and ask how she's doing now that the snow has set in, you raise your connectivity another few notches as Sally ponders how good it feels to not just talk about work all the time, but also have the boss remember what's been going on in her life.

5. **Connect beyond your immediate walls**

   Create an ecosystem where connections extend beyond the usual boundaries – including people from other departments or branches of the organization or even customers and suppliers, if you want to be more ambitious. If you've driven process improvement deep into the business, why not open that up to those around the periphery? Give people a way to routinely keep in contact with everyone involved; and watch the connections form and the improvements stack up.

CHAPTER 9

The Strength in Numbers Is Collaboration

If you want to go fast go alone. If you want to go far go together.

—African Proverb

What do Google, eBay, Apple, Intel, Twitter, HP, Microsoft, Ben & Jerry's, Procter & Gamble, and Yahoo have in common? All were born of collaboration. Two people came together to collaborate, they brought yet more people inside the collaboration, and then grew to be highly successful firms of their times.

In a healthy, collaborative environment, the workplace becomes a network of alliances working toward a common purpose – where everyone is giving their best to succeed. If one fails, everyone fails. More importantly, everyone chips in to help them get up: success is a group endeavor. Successful collaboration sees people come together naturally to achieve results. Like any business, it's a team sport.

Collaboration is hardly a novel concept – we understand the intent and intellectually we know the advantages. So how is it that at work, collaboration can still fail? It's not a lack of understanding the common sense benefits? No. Failed or ineffective collaborations tend to be very human ones: politics, power/territory battles, ignorance, or knowledge gaps, all of which need to be addressed. Sometimes, it's the fear that an individual will lose their stardom.

Collaboration reminds us, in the words of Margaret Heffernan, to "forget the pecking order."[1] In her funny yet meaningful TED Talk of the same name, Margaret warns us against super chickens and encourages us to look to build a constellation of stars. She encourages us to look what happens when people connect – we develop a culture of helpfulness, and a culture of helpfulness outperforms individual intelligence every time. She reminds us it is "the collaborators who last" – "you don't want stars." When you manage to engage, you lead to make everyone successful. You develop social capital.

While politics is a noun, it's really a doing word. Worse still, a dirty word – we see it as the debate or conflict among individuals or teams having or hoping to achieve power. That's how the term made the leap from a profession to a verb used to describe the dark side of behaviors at work.

If *politics* is in your culture, stop it! Don't participate! Don't create ground for it to fester. The only outcome is a toxic workplace that plays people off each other and causes teams to take sides. Worse still, it sees good people thrown under a bus. People leave. *Power,* though similar to politics, creates a different environment – one ruled with iron fists and stifled cultures lacking innovation or creativity. One person is the star, the rest must follow. Power is a very personal play and one that people need to see in themselves and stop. The more you crave power, the more people will be deaf to what you say. If *ignorance* is your excuse for a workplace lacking in collaboration, get smart. You should be the catalyst for collaboration. Not believing in the need to collaborate or seeing its merits, continuing to allow silos and walls to divide the business reduces your chances of finding real success. If gaps in your own knowledge are preventing you from letting your teams collaborate and work in the right space, get up to speed. Learn who as well as where and how your people can collaborate more effectively.

A Person Is a Person through Other People

Ubuntu is a concept that says it is not just being among other people that makes us human, but our efforts to be humane and benefit others that defines our own humanity.

---

[1] Margaret Heffernan, "Forget the Pecking Order at Work," TED.com (2016). www.ted.com/talks/margaret_heffernan_forget_the_pecking_order_at_work?language=en

Ubuntu offers a powerful lesson on the road to engagement. It helps explain an individual's fit with others, within communities, in our organizations and within the world in general. Ubuntu is about the relationship between the thumb and the fingers. It underscores our relationship with each other at work: *a person is a person through other people*. It is the basis of social networking today, reminding us that long before digital social networking permeated our lives, we harnessed our instinctive social nature every day.

A Thumb Working Alone Has Little Value

Africa is a great place to find stories that reinforce the need to balance our broader team focus with our individual team members. I love the stories of the Shona people of Zimbabwe and their wonderful tales to bring life lessons to their young. There is a marvelous story I've used to demonstrate the need for the many to help the few. It goes like this: An older man in the tribe is teaching a young boy to hunt. Although he was barely old enough, the young boy was eager to learn the weapons and the thrill behind hunting. But the elderly gentleman was less interested in teaching the art of weaponry and much more interested in first, teaching the lessons of community and the boy's role in it. To illustrate this, the wise old man taught the would-be hunter an old African Shona proverb: *Chara chimive hachitswane inda*. Broadly translated, it means that "A thumb working on its own is useless." The man explained: *"It has to work collectively with the other fingers to get strength and be able to achieve anything of lasting value." We* is better than *me*.

We Are Social Butterflies

The spirit of Ubuntu captures the inherently social nature of humans – our need to be connected through the interdependent relationships we have with each other. But it also accounts for how we trade our time with others and the value of this to our quality of life. All sorts of health and well-being studies confirm that humans don't do well in isolation; that so often people's longevity correlates with the number of people they have in their lives and the value they provide to each other. We see similar trends in the workplace: people staying longer and thriving more if they collaborate with others. We don't just enjoy interacting with others; we need to. So there is every reason to make the most of this, by fostering healthy and productive collaboration at work.

Collaboration Conquers Conflict

Collaboration at its finest engages people and achieves remarkable results. Consider this: Only 44 percent of work packages for small construction projects at a large government military facility were being issued on time, causing significant delays and lost time for construction crews. A deep dive as to why this happened found that the Planning department uniformly scheduled work package issuance dates six weeks after the initial request for the work without regard for any engineering drawing requirements. Planning did not check with Engineering to find out when drawings would be ready. The Planning department blamed Engineering for not delivering drawings on time, and the planners believed that the engineers were not very productive. It was a vicious cycle of underperformance and underengagement, until everything changed when the head of the Planning department asked the head of Engineering to partner with them and together improve the process. What they learned was invaluable to address the issues. Planning learned that Engineering did in fact set due dates for every set of drawings, so the Engineering department gave Planning access to the schedule so that they would know when to expect drawings. The Planning department then began to schedule the issuance of work packages based on the planned availability of drawings. This resulted in much more realistic schedules for work package development, which, in turn, led to more realistic scheduling of construction crews. On-time release of work packages increased to 92 percent within two months of the change. A win-win for cross departmental collaboration and for employee engagement.

Think Big

We find ourselves in an age of extreme complexity. At work there are overlaps between responsibilities, people, departments, our company ecosystems, and across our companies, into communities and even whole economies. It seems natural that we should capitalize on these, that we should collaborate wherever this feels right.

When major change happens, whether triggered by global recessions brought about by global pandemics, or triggered by complete shifts in technology as we've seen in the unfolding of today's mobilized digitally advanced, AI-enhanced business environment, opportunities to do things differently often present themselves. Today we see the interdependencies of business more clearly than we did even a few years ago. Teams that once thought they were islands and happily compartmentalized away from the rest of the business, can no longer be viewed that way. To stand out in a brutally competitive, dynamic market where disruption has become the norm, companies must actively seek out new ways to collaborate, as a source of not only greater efficiency and productivity, but as a means of boosting inspiration, fostering innovation, and expanding idea dissemination, taking creativity to new levels. It is a competitive advantage.

Collaboration can also be a source of simplification – of cutting through organizational barriers and internal process complexity. Today's technology makes it easier than ever to spontaneously form and coordinate teams, virtual and others, with no limits to location, to do this. These are just as likely to include freelance contractors, customers, and suppliers, as well as people from across the organization. Thanks to digital collaboration platforms, social networks, instant messaging applications, and conferencing tools, we all know location and distance are no longer a barrier to getting together and sharing work.

Today people outside work instinctively collaborate across traditional borders without even thinking of it in those terms – crowdsourcing solutions – organizations are catching on quickly. People know exactly what technology can do ("there's an app for that"), and should leverage things they usually do intuitively outside work.

Make Your Mark

Marketing experts have long understood the importance of collaborating across traditional boundaries. Cross-promotions, where companies bring a variety of products, sponsors, services, or offers together to reduce the price of the promotional activity and make the proposition more attractive to the consumer, are commonplace. A simple example would be a restaurant and a movie theatre joining forces to combine a pizza promotion with a two-for-one movie pass, and a mobile phone company distributing the offer. It's this cross-creativity we now need to see more of in other areas of business.

Promoting collaboration involves giving people access to other people, expertise, information, and knowledge to arrive at the best possible outcome. As well as improved, expedited results, successful collaboration also gives people the bigger picture, a chance to see what others do and how they work. It can be a positive, stimulating, and inspiring multidimensional learning and development experience.

For the business, facilitating combinations of diverse skills and experience can result in alternative solutions to problems, and expanded skills and capabilities. It can reveal new opportunities, open up new markets, inspire the creation of new products and services, and enable a new competitive edge. We're already seeing whole value chains change, through greater collaboration and joint ownership between parties once confined to customer-supplier relationships.

At its best, collaboration is exciting. It brings novelty, variety, and possibility to people's working days; it gives people new insight, a chance to shine in a new capacity. These new ways of working, new experiences, and new faces around our tables offer promising new ways to engage people. And that can be a multiplier.

An Opportunity Shared Is an Opportunity Doubled

It's increasingly hard, and costly, for organizations to do everything themselves, and to do it well. Companies that spread themselves too thin often see profits spiraling downward because their only option is to compete on price: their business model doesn't allow for them to differentiate on quality and special features. As opportunities to collaborate increase, businesses have more options – to meet all of the customer's needs, but while remaining focused on the thing they do best. For everything else, they can use a strategically chosen partner. They can collaborate.

Such partnerships are becoming increasingly creative. We now see large corporations partnering with or 'incubating' smaller, more dynamic businesses – a mutual trade of the smaller company's specialist expertise with the scale and resources of the bigger player.

Supersize Me

Consider again a professional services business like mine in management consulting. The consulting firm provides a service to a client – let's say a transformation project. We know we can engage people, reduce costs, release cash, and help the client grow their business. The client is looking for a variety of components to gain the best value from the consulting firm. The consulting firm knows it can provide all the elements of a great project for the client and do a great job with its existing offer. But it also knows it can access specialist skills for one or two components of the service, say key digital transformation or technology skills – e.g., activities that aren't its main area of specialization – and execute a project that is of even greater value to the client. Partnering with a technology provider enables the offer to become more valuable, but it also ensures technology solutions are seamlessly built into the change management component to ensure user adoption – something we call behavior change.

We have been partnering with a series of specialist firms since 2000, so that collectively we are able to add greater value to a client's project. For example, we partner with scoutbee sourcing AI to deliver major procurement transformations. Scoutbee supplies the technology of speed to source, we supply the consulting of procurement transformation. Together, we reduce the client consulting spend and results. Apart from the sizable investment required and the competition for specialist skills, emerging opportunities won't wait around, so speed to market is vital. Partnering allows that.

As we supersize our capabilities through strategic collaboration, the world gets bigger and smaller all at once. So why, then, don't we see more creative collaboration in everyday working life? People hate to lose control and partnering, real deep collaboration, requires the loosening of control to tighten the outcome. Just as businesses in the twenty-first century shouldn't try to be all things to all people, nor should we as individuals. Collaboration makes it okay that we don't know everything or can't do everything ourselves.

Beyond Borders

But collaboration isn't as easy as it sounds. It isn't just a modern spin on team-work. It's about harnessing people in new ways. This introduces some special challenges:

- *The call to collaborate can stir doubt and erode confidence as people con-template the unknown.* People are partnering with those they don't know or haven't worked with before. The speed with which you build and sus-tain trust between the various parties is critical. The quicker you're able to put people at ease with the desired combination of people, resources, and technology you bring together, the faster the collaborative effort will get down to business.

- *Collaboration routinely introduces new parameters as you consider whether to create or buy-in the skills you require.* You must develop relationships where payment and contracting doesn't get in the way of teamwork and collaboration – a feeling of oneness still needs to override contracts.

- *Collaboration requires a project management approach.* As you dynamically form and reform collaborative teams to involve different voices, and a greater range of skills and experience with different skill sets, be prepared to manage the diverse complexities of differing loyalties, reporting lines, remuneration and reward systems, cultures, and expectations. Identifying who should sit around the table also becomes a challenge, as will making sure that others, who haven't been included, don't feel passed over. Early involvement and communication is a critical success factor.

- *Collaboration creates organizational change.* You can expect your organization's structure to change as the weight of responsibility and accountability shifts, during cross-party collaboration. While ownership of the result may remain the same, execution may be weighted differently by different partners along the way.

- *Collaboration changes people's roles and relationships, with greater emphasis on skill, ability, expertise, and reduced observation of traditional hierarchies.* How you develop this model will determine how your people adapt to it. New forms of organization will need to be developed to accommodate the involvement of people at both the core and fringes of the team or the business. Enabling people to see where they sit and when they will be called on is key. The concept of "first among equals" becomes a leadership tool. People step up or out, depending on the stage of the work.

- *Collaboration stimulates movement in the organization.* As people swap in and out of teams, and move between and across business units, even between companies, people may feel unsettled and at risk of slipping between the cracks. You need careful management to maintain engagement. 1.5.30 becomes even more important.

- *Collaboration requires different management skills.* Managers brought up in the command-and-control style of management are likely to feel threatened by the shift to more dynamic and collaborative styles of working. Businesses will need to rethink their talent management models to bring on collaboration friendly managers who have the energy and skills required to harness the opportunities that dynamic co-operation makes possible.

- *Enabling people to move between departments and beyond company boundaries at speed requires agile, adaptive organizational capabilities.* For dynamic collaboration to succeed, it must be possible for those involved to connect on demand and hit the ground running. Red tape and rigid policies will need to be rethought to accommodate the flexibility and speed of movement now needed.

- *Collaboration will affect career paths.* As collaboration becomes the norm, there will be new opportunities for the multi-skilled while average performers may find it harder to get ahead. Other career paths will open up as chief collaborators replace department heads and team leads – those who can engage and lead diverse groups of people, those that provide the enabling interfaces.

- *Collaboration could produce a blame culture as people look for ways to protect themselves if things go wrong.* If something goes wrong during a collaborative initiative, individuals may become defensive and revert to their original allegiances, passing blame to those from other departments or from outside the company. A strong team identity will be important to guard against this, along with a culture that encourages admission of errors, with a view to overcoming them and moving forward. The growing prevalence of the 'fail fast' mentality (experiment, fail, learn, move on), associated with driving innovation across all sorts of industries, should help here.

And these are just some of the more obvious challenges associated with proactive collaboration; there are likely to be many more. But the benefits unlocked by a positive approach to collaboration will make any teething trouble well worth it.

Preparing the Way for Collaboration

Before we explore how to create a workplace that encourages collaboration, it's a good idea to reflect on how conducive your environment, culture, and mindset is right now. Consider the following:

- Are you open to collaboration?
- Does your organizational hierarchy allow for collaboration in its fullest sense?

- Does your ecosystem, your operating model, allow collaboration? Are your current processes and tools enablers of or barriers to collaboration?
- Are your people *ready* to collaborate?
- Is your physical space, IT setup, and digital work tools collaboration friendly?
- Are your people attuned to other work cultures?
- Are you developing communities of expertise, practice, and experience, for others to readily tap into?
- Is there an intrinsic incentive for people to collaborate?

If you want to harness any and all collaboration opportunities, your people will need to be able to adapt to, mix and match, with different organizational cultures: public sector with private; research and development cultures with manufacturing; learning cultures with those geared more to speed of delivery.

Putting It All Together

A new head of Supply Chain for a fast-food company had been promoted to take over a failing department. He had been given the role to turn the function around. Costs needed to be reduced and the lead times for product promotions had to be shorter so that the company could exploit market share intelligence. The company needed to become more effective and agile.

The Procurement department was very well established with many years of experience in a group of six people. After a number of years of success, the department had become complacent and had ceased to chase suppliers so hard for cost reductions. Processes existed, but were not well defined, and the company never knew when a project might be delivered. It was the cultural norm for every issue to be listed but without providing a solution or commitment to a deadline.

Promotions were taking more than 10 weeks to organize and there were examples of the competition stealing market share due to slow execution. Culturally, a gap had developed between Procurement and the rest of the company – specifically Marketing, Operations, and Finance.

The new head of Supply Chain recognized the head of Procurement had lost his way and lost his Cs. He needed to recognize they could not perform in isolation any longer. They were also culturally closer to suppliers than their colleagues. He needed them to see they were part of a company with a bigger plan, and objectives that needed to be delivered. An unreliable department of ill-defined procurement projects and increasing costs needed to change.

The head of Supply Chain embraced the full suite of tools within the 7 Cs. It was time to reengage the team to reach once high-performance levels.

So the new head of Supply Chain set up team-building exercises directly between individuals in his own department and Marketing, Operations, and Finance to build connections, collaboration, and a community spirit. This created stronger relations between the staff and their colleagues. This created a huge time efficiency because some of the sub-teams started to take decisions for themselves, and trusted certain decisions could be taken, which reduced the process time still further. He addressed the ecosystem, ensuring key processes were defined, standardized, and published between the departments so that deadlines could be predicted by all employees.

The shorter processes created the time for the Procurement team to increase the number of tenders with suppliers. The stronger sense of discipline also resulted in negotiation strategies and tactics being integrated into the tender process. This resulted in savings of £11m for the first year, when savings had not been seen for a couple of years.

The net effect of the better-quality working culture meant that Procurement also became an attractive place to work with good career opportunities.

Curators of Curiosity

By assessing your readiness to embrace richer collaboration, you'll begin to get a picture of the steps you need to exploit this powerful opportunity and engage your team in new and exciting ways – and, in so doing, bring a whole new level of energy to your business, one that paves the way to the results you need.

Above all, you will need to review your own approach to management, making sure your focus is on how to *curate* success rather than how to manage it. Become a guardian, not a director. Guardians are the keepers of the keys – the protectors and guides who see what needs to happen to enable people to cooperate and thrive. The priority should be to enable and energize, to facilitate.

Getting the foundations right for collaboration is not just about getting the right people around the table, it's also about having the right framework and attitude on board. Teaching people that collaboration is a skill, bringing an "everybody-wins" atmosphere to business, and challenging the bad attitudes that infect collaborative efforts are just as crucial. Remind people that if you keep doing the same things, you'll keep getting the same results. Breaking out of our comfort zone is essential for growth.

Collaboration Takes Energy

It takes perspiration and inspiration to view and do things differently, so this is a further consideration as we lay the foundations for increased, instinctive collaboration. To inject this enthusiasm for trying something new, think about ways to promote it, such as generating curiosity, refreshing perspectives, and reinventing yourself.

Bring Curiosity to Life

Helping people be curious is a great way to fuel their appetite. Researchers tell us that the more curious we are, the more engaged in life we'll be. This is why lifelong learning is so critical to our well-being and longevity.

Create a platform through which people can ask questions to better understand why things are happening, how things work, who does what. Encourage probing. Stir people's interest. Make them want to know more. For instance:

- *Make interviewing routine.* The last time you interviewed someone was probably when you were looking to hire them. This may also have been the last time they got to ask you candid questions about the business. Set up interviews for people to learn through questions.

- *Take a documentary approach.* Make it a podcast. You could record these informal interviews or have someone act as a host or reporter and share the findings in a short, informal work-based documentary.

- *Interview you.* Everyone should take the opportunity to interview their boss when they start a new job – to learn about their priorities and expectations, what makes them tick. In fact, they should have a chance to go right to your C-suite to understand more about the workplace, its culture, and the people in key leadership roles.

Why shouldn't employees be encouraged to find out:

- What one thing, more than any other, their leader or manager is concerned about at work
- The first word that comes into their head when they think about work
- How they stay excited about and engaged in what they do
- How they keep up to date with the things that interest them most
- Where they go for inspiration and ideas to keep work fresh and new
- Where the business's real value lies, in their opinion
- When they feel at their best at work
- When and how they know they need a break from work
- The person they find most interesting in the business
- Who keeps them sane at work
- What they value most in their job
- What is most important to them in their work life

Take a Wider Angle Lens

There are few better ways to change the way people feel about something than to change their vantage point – e.g., from focusing on what's wrong to seeing what's right. So throw on a wide-angle lens. Let people step back and see things anew.

As a leader or manager, you can provide a vehicle for people to view their work from a new vantage point. You can help them volunteer for new programs and projects, give them more of a sense of control over their own knowledge and development path, help them see more of what they can do instead of what others might do for them. Encourage people to become part of the revolution rather than a bystander. Put them into experiences that shows work performed differently.

Use Selfie Superpower

Most people love a chance to focus on themselves, and we should embrace this. Let your people sit back and think about what they really want to get out of work – e.g., the stability of an income, the chance to learn new things, help others learn, meet new people, and make a difference. As they tune into their own hopes and needs, get them to note these down and then to start looking for ways to fulfill them. Help them identify opportunities to break out of their mold and collaborate.

Collaboration 4.0

New forms of collaboration are already taking off across the globe, as linear ways of connecting and doing business are replaced by more dynamic, mesh-like formations and digitization. This is part of the *ecosystem,* placing an emphasis on mutual cooperation rather than each party fulfilling a particular obligation within their designated role. It is when people can move out of their traditional boxes and form new and different connections that we pave the way for exciting things to happen. Bringing down traditional boundaries and structures promotes innovative thinking and new competitive advantage.

Diversity – It's about Collaboration, Not Just Race and Gender

The more diversity – of people, roles, perspectives, voices – that can be included in a collaborative effort, the better the end result and the shorter the road to engagement as new energy and momentum usher in a sense of the possible. While many of us are talking about gender diversity, it's also about diversity of thinking. If all your team members come from your school, your last place of work, your small community of thought leaders, chances are, you don't have enough diversity of thought, no matter the diversity of gender or race.

But some shape will be needed to get the best out of these expanded scenarios. Advanced collaboration isn't about letting control fall away and inviting in chaos. It's about having a different *kind* of structure, one built on dynamic networks and easy interfaces – allowing people to connect quickly and seamlessly when they need to. In this context, structure acts as the enabler – making it possible for people to find and harness the knowledge and expertise of others, supported by appropriate technology and the guardianship of an enabling manager.

If we want to harness energy, talent, experience, knowledge, ideas from wherever these qualities might be, then we must stop thinking, acting, and organizing in the mindset of silos and job compartmentalization. We must learn to be more open, more willing to share, to contribute to the whole. This includes taking combined responsibility when things are going less well.

In the old world, progress was all about planning, rollouts, and rolldowns; things moved in a linear, sequential, hierarchical way. Today, progress is much more fluid and dynamic. The emphasis is on launchpads; spontaneous co-operation, prototypes, engagement, and creation. The many are just as able to empower the few as the few are able to power up the many. Energy and ideas are free to flow in all directions.

Where collaboration goes, engagement flows, and results follow. One conversation could change your world of work. Curating the collaborations is a vital skill of managers who engage.

---

1. **Review the questions posed in this chapter to determine your preparedness for a more collaborative workplace:**

   a. Are you open to collaboration?

   b. Does your organizational hierarchy allow for this in its fullest sense?

   c. Are your current processes and tools enablers of or barriers to collaboration?

   d. Are your people ready to collaborate?

   e. Is your physical space and IT setup collaboration friendly?

   f. Are your people attuned to other work cultures?

   g. Are you developing communities of expertise, practice, and experience for others to readily tap into?

   h. Is there an incentive for people to collaborate?

2. **Conduct a series of re-energization exercises with your team prompting:**

   • Curiosity: through informal interviewing of key people to understand where they're coming from

---

FIGURE 9.1 Things You Need to Do Right Now. (*continued*)

- Selfies: help team members find projects or other vehicles to help them change their vantage point or revitalize their work experience
- Personal reinvention: encourage some soul-searching to help people reassess what they really want to get out of work – so they can make it happen.

Over time, give everyone the opportunity to complete all three exercises.

Collaboration: 5 things you can do today to improve quality of life at work

1. **Spread the pain!**

   Take unsolved problems to a bigger audience. Who said the boss was the only one who had to bear the brunt of the stress at work? Don't just ask the usual suspects for input: think laterally. The more ideas you get, the more chance there is that one will be a winner, even a game changer.

2. **Redefine 'team'**

   Beyond your immediate team are all the other people who touch and feed into it. So why not harness this greater group to capture ideas and solutions? Make sure this works both ways – get your people to contribute to (and learn from) teams beyond their traditional parameters. Everyone stands to benefit from a more rounded perspective.

3. **Share your subscriptions**

   If you're a regular subscriber to business magazines, industry reports, specialty newspapers, and targeted news feeds, share the

FIGURE 9.1 *(Continued)*

best reads with others. Leave finished publications in communal areas, and share relevant and timely digital content via common social forums or the company portal. Be inclusive. Shared insights could prompt new ideas and spark collaboration.

4. **Redesign your workspace**

   Find ways for your workplace to open itself up more physically for collaboration – by removing physical barriers available or providing common spaces for casual collaboration, pandemic friendly of course. Make sure you do something similar for remote and virtual team members via online collaboration forums and messaging platforms.

5. **Bring the outside in**

   Bring speakers in to address your teams. This could be a fellow manager visiting your site, a customer, a supplier, or an expert from the community. Once they've spoken, invite questions. Consider: "How might we collaborate for mutual benefit?"

CHAPTER 10

Building Community: 1 + 1 = 3

Community is much more than belonging to something; it's about doing something together that makes belonging matter.

—Brian Solis, digital analyst, author, speaker

I f there is one thing that binds people together, it's the spirit of community. A shared sense of understanding. Sporting events, concerts, cooking classes, computer games, even cities demonstrate this. Common links. A sense of belonging is important if people are to feel that what they do has context and meaning. Joint knowledge to solve some of the greatest problems facing your business bring people together. Community spirit can have a strong influence on people's inclination to do well, improve, and shine. It can also enable large groups of people to achieve remarkable results. If we feel part of a wider community, we feel seen, supported, and validated. We don't feel alone: we know there are people we can call on, who will help. It may be our immediate community, or a more virtual community linked by mutual interests or a common purpose.

In our home lives, sense of community was dwindling – people's transience and increased self-sufficiency has brought disconnection. This is an opportunity. We strive to feel part of a community, to be with the in-crowd. How you bring that to life at work to perhaps fill the gap at home could become your own secret weapon. People love to be in the club. Why not make it yours?

Belonging to a community doesn't only starve off loneliness and isolation; it also offers us a chance to grow as people and develop by learning from others more experienced or knowledgeable in an area that interests or is important to us. Being able to use our own knowledge and experiences to give back and help others is also rewarding.

If, as employers and managers, we fail to foster this craving for community in the workplace, we are missing a tool in our engagement kit. When we value and respect the people around us, and feel enriched by their company or connection, it will affect how we feel about coming to work each day. If we feel included, recognized, inspired, and stretched, by our colleagues and our management it's a multiplier – we are more likely to step up to achieve more. Our sense of community becomes an important source of engagement.

As managers, we should consider ourselves "community spirit champions" or chief community officers. Someone who will cultivate and promote an environment at work (however virtual) that connects people with common goals, interests, or concerns so they can support, help, and inspire each other.

Communities' Role in Riding Out Bad Times

Communities aren't just about common interests; they also provide a source of support for people when the going gets tough. We see this after natural disasters and through the pandemic of 2020. Similarly, our communities at work provide ideas and support in times of distress. Digital technologies have brought about a community revolution to enable this, particularly through the isolation protocols – social connection while physically distancing.

Cognizant is a US-listed IT services firm, with a significant offshore capability in India. Before providing advanced digital solutions became a core tenet of its own business and prior to the likes of Yammer, the company wanted to improve its pan-operations communications to bridge the long distances separating its team members. It built a system based on the principles of social networking, and soon found that the younger members of the workforce were migrating to it en masse.

But crucially, it wasn't just communication that improved: it was the sense of increased community that really paid off. This was demonstrable too: among those people using the system, attrition dropped by a third compared to those who rarely used it. The virtual networking enabled through the digital social tools didn't replace the need for face-to-face meetings, but provided an important reminder that communities are vital to inclusion and sustained engagement – and need to be proactively built and nurtured.

Community Is King

When companies view community building as a steppingstone to engagement and therefore as a way of creating new levels of performance, it's a sign they have recognized the power of the "home-team advantage." It's an accepted phenomenon that sports teams win more often at home than they do when playing away. Why? Because their community comes out to applaud them. They feel support, uplifted – as though they can't fail.

We hardly need empirical evidence to recognize the power of community:

1. *Community builds camaraderie.* It is a highly collaborative, connecting process that moves focus away from the self. People work with others toward something that's good for everyone and where everyone looks out for each other.

Community Collaboration

At Proudfoot, our global change management team had known each other for years and worked together on projects regularly, but seldom had they stopped to really consolidate their efforts. They had become individuals with the same function/role, scattered across the globe, doing remarkable work with their teams but often reinventing their materials over and over again bespoke for each need, and yet there were common principles they could leverage.

Suddenly they were given an assignment to jointly develop solutions for the Global Transformation toolbox. After initiating a weekly call, that, to quote one team member, "quite honestly, started off rough and mostly complained about the nerve to toolbox 'us' creative folks where we have different audiences, different ways of presenting, different cultures, etc.," they got to work. That same team member recalls the process now with passion and pride: "Through brainstorming and realizing we HAD to do this, we came up with a brilliant plan to develop the content with 'must haves' and include our 'individual variations' to allow for the different audiences, cultures, presentation styles.' We quickly allowed each other and granted each other permission to stop each other from derailing the work, and came back to constructive progress. The final products were brilliant. A huge improvement in content with the collective brain power unleashed. We've now continued our weekly meetings, and it's turned into a really fun, collaborative working session. The agenda is mixed and varied, depending on the latest hot task; and, more importantly, throughout the week, we are sharing and asking each other for help much more often (and GETTING the help). It's been an amazing community built through a forced action, that has created a really special team."

2. *Community builds mutual ownership.* It builds a collective sense of responsibility for the end result – and also its upkeep. Participants instinctively assume ownership and accountability. No one says, *"Hey, you built this, you'd better maintain it."* Instead, people are saying, *"Hey, I was part of this, and I care that it succeeds. Let's make it work and keep it working."*

3. *Community members feel responsible to each other.* People generally have a natural inclination to chip in and help. When a building is burning, they don't leave the firefighting to the guy who owns the building alone, nor to the guy who is trained to fight fires; everyone chips in.

4. *Communities offer greater protection.* There are more eyes on the ball (think Neighborhood Watch), so members are less vulnerable to incident or failure.

5. *Communities bring commitment.* Not letting others down becomes as important as not letting yourself down. Walking away from something becomes a community discussion, not an individual's decision.

6. *Communities help us focus on what unites rather than divides us.* When we feel surrounded by kindred spirits, we feel a stronger sense of belonging so our enjoyment and satisfaction levels peak.

7. *Communities accelerate progress.* With joint agendas, where more people are taking proactive steps toward something and feeding each other's passion, they achieve more in less time.

8. *Communities build leaders.* Natural stars rise. People offer support to the people who have the talent and can do the job; everyone gets behind the people and teams who will win or get the job done.

9. *Communities attract and nurture experts.* People get to know who the go-to people are. Arrows point to the experts and everyone comes to the aid of people who need it.

10. *Community triggers engagement.* Context, success, concerns, and ideas are instinctively shared. People feel supported rather than alone. It's an environment where people can give freely and thrive as their confidence grows. It's a breeding ground for engagement.

The Great Liberator

It was this understanding of the power of community spirit to inspire and bring out the best in people that influenced my time leading the People Solutions team at Proudfoot. Proudfoot at the time had spent more than six decades advising businesses about operational improvement and change – with a strong reputation for getting the results but also making change happen and stick. But there came a point when Proudfoot's market position appeared under threat: copycat companies were suddenly claiming to offer a similar proposition. At the same time, clients were making it clear what they wanted: what they really needed was for employees to engage in the *process* of getting to that new way of operating, to ensure that any change would be sustainable, and to make sure their own people could do it themselves the next time.

Proudfoot had a great deal of experience in this area but struggled to get this across to the market – making it clear how our approach stood apart from our would-be competitors. Which is when we coined People Solutions, emphasizing our ability to help organizations reduce the pain of change for their people and accelerate measurable results. While there were many aspects to this, one critical component was the building of a global community to drive home the change management approach and build excitement behind it across the business. Despite geographical spread, we built community using technology, meetings, and centers of excellence.

The power of this community was evident a few years later when, at the annual People Solutions Conference, the entire community gathered to share its accomplishments, learnings, and client success stories. The conference became one enormous people solutions, show-and-tell event; booths were used to display the tools, products, and processes they had developed, innovated, and produced to move and engage their client's people. Moreover, the community left no doubt of the difference it was making through the competitive advantage it gained. I will never forget the CEO of a competitor consulting organization telling me how disappointed he was the day one of his key and longtime clients said it was moving its business to Proudfoot, which "did change management better, with this thing they called People Solutions." The community we had created had become something much greater than the sum of its parts.

Community Is a Unique Selling Proposition for Employers

Until the wider business world cottons on to the value of proactive community fostering, the sense of community you work to create in your organization will stand out to potential employees. People want to work somewhere welcoming, somewhere that has energy, somewhere they can thrive but also in today's highly competitive world, they want to work somewhere they feel they will be "known for something." They want a sense that their superpower will develop and become a career power tool. It's an important differentiator in attracting and keeping desirable talent. The communities you develop can become your superpowers.

In the age of the crowd, a company's ability to tap into the benefits of community at work will be a strong determinant of its level of employee engagement. Community is the outcome of collaboration is the outcome of connection: 1 + 1 = 3. When individuals connect and collaborate, communities can form. With community comes people who are the best for a team, not the best on the team. You develop concepts like first among equals. You surround yourself with the people who lift you up. You work outside the traditional company borders and silos. You create new, more engaging ways of working. You go further, faster, together.

---

1. **Assess the current levels of community in your organization.**

   a. Do your people feel part of a community or is their primary alignment and allegiance to their immediate team?

   b. Do they have access to greater knowledge banks than their closest colleagues?

   c. Are they community-minded, or motivated mainly by their own achievements?

2. **Assess what may be needed to improve the sense of community in your workplace:**

FIGURE 10.1 Things You Need to Do Right Now.

a. Do you have a person who is focused on building community spirit at work?

b. Does the organization share the role community could play in your business?

c. Do you look for ways to bring community into a work setting?

d. How well do people support each other when things aren't going well?

e. How well do people share responsibility and feel a duty to each other?

f. Do you harness technology to promote workplace community?

g. Is the everyday work environment and rhythm conducive to community building?

h. Have you considered using professional approaches – e.g., events, meetings – to foster internal community?

i. Is the company's emphasis on managing knowledge as much as it is on sharing, capturing, and hoarding knowledge?

Community: 5 things you can do today to improve quality of life at work

1. **Encourage mutual interests**

   Let people own the process of community building – and throw the net wide. Gather your people and invite them to come up with three communities they'd like to build around your business. For example, one focused on a cause you all care about, one focused on a problem you're all looking to solve, or a skill you all want to improve; and, perhaps, one that the team chooses without prompting.

2. Be part of the community, but don't try to lead it

Just because you are the boss doesn't mean you have to lead a community. Simply be part of it. Make your contribution as valuable as that of the other members of the community. Learn from them as they will do from you.

3. Create a 'friend finder'!

Make it easy for like-minded people to find each other or for people with a problem to find people with solutions. Use social media as a reference point for how easy this should be. Set up a way to connect people across boundaries and businesses through the virtual world and create a way they can communicate about their world. This will help expand your community beyond traditional boundaries. Connecting people who traditionally would not be in contact, but have things in common, is a great way to build a strong and diverse community that will add real value for its members and their shared purpose.

4. Community spirit awards

Recognize and reward community-building initiatives and contribution. Whether it's someone contributing to the knowledge base of the business or taking the time to nurture a teammate who's been struggling to acquire a new skill, show appreciation when your people go the extra mile in the interests of the greater good.

5. Get among the local community

Nothing makes us feel better about an employer than seeing that company in a positive light in the community. Look for ways your business can be present and of use in the local area – from giving talks in schools, providing teaching and apprenticeships, to volunteering and helping in practical ways. Who knows, you may even find some new employees!

CHAPTER 11

Growing Capability: We Yearn to Learn

$$Happiness = \frac{Needs}{Capability}$$

—Anonymous

There is nothing worse than that clumsy, awkward feeling of not being able to do something. It's why people drag their feet to engage in new projects, processes, or technology. Not because they don't want to but because they don't feel capable enough to give it a go. They don't want to feel like they will screw up or just plain underperform. We've all been there.

We also hate the thought of not learning. Of going through the same proverbial motions day in, day out. It's why people take night school, it's why we engage in community activities like volunteering at a school or helping build houses at Habitat for Humanity. Most humans want to learn, and they want to learn new skills that add value to their personal brands, no matter their roles. They want to develop their employability. While firms may be reticent to set people up for success for their next job, the average employee expects it. Recalling the response to the famous question, "What if we train our people and they leave?" and of course the answer is, "What if we don't train them and they stay?" Investing in people is a no brainer. There are now so many studies that tell us to keep our brains engaged and learn new things after we retire, reinforcing the need to do this as a life-long adventure. It can only benefit everyone.

We've learned that engagement comes from a whole host of triggers. Many are table stakes in that they don't necessarily engage but when absent they disengage: fairness and freedom, clean workplaces. We've also learned that engagement comes from a cause, confidence, collaboration, and a sense of community.

Many of these have their roots in a sense of being capable, being able to do a job well. Capability development is an engager. From our work with clients across 50,000 engagements, we know, the more people learn particularly through coaching and application, the more engaged you become. Having the chance to observe, experience, and learn from others across and beyond the organization is part of that: a chance to be surrounded, inspired, and encouraged by capable people. To stay engaged, it's important to feel that we are growing – and to see this growth, and wider growth around us, reflected in business results, promotions and rewards. Success breeds success: we need to feel our job allows us to be in a company that is growing, one in which we are all learning as we go.

Apply Learning Liberally

When I was very young and living on the south coast of New South Wales in Australia, I remember a local fisherman teaching me how to pick up a gigantic crab. It was the size of my entire torso. The fisherman was showing me how to hold the crab, first with his demonstration – big, fat hands wrapped around the crab. *Get your fingers on his underside, wrap your thumb on his topside, and* – with a huge smile, he yelled – *then hold on!* After a few tries, holding this crab with both my hands, I did it. I was holding an enormous crab. I was absolutely chuffed with myself, holding it high above my little head to show my Dad. I'd mastered a skill that could sit at the top of my resume. I was 11.

It was only later, on a subsequent visit to the harbor side, that I learned the lesson of application and practice. I didn't know that this initial encounter had been weighted in my favor. What I'd not taken the time to do was count how many legs the crab actually had. Perish the thought that someone may have been eating him one leg at a time! The crab was missing a few of his legs! When I tried to show off my newfound skill to my mother with a different crab, I was horrified at the result. The crab I now chose was not only slightly bigger but he had all his legs. As I picked him up, following all the instructions from my previous coach (who was no longer there), this gigantic crab was having none of it. He broke free from my wispy grasp and took flight up my arm, wrapping himself around my neck, his claws dangerously close to my fear-stricken face and perfectly positioned in my line of sight. Thankfully, Dad leapt to the rescue! He grabbed the crab, carefully unwrapping his legs from my neck, closing his claws and moving them away from my eyes, holding the crab as my now defuncted instructor had trained me. Hurt ego and a few scratches, I lived to

tell the tale, but between the shock, the outcome, and the fear
body, crab carrying would not be something I would try aga

Unthinkingly, we expose people to this kind of situation an ᵁᵁ￼
at work. How often do we bring in already-skilled people to do jobs, rather
than coach less-experienced team members so they know what to do and can
thrive? Worse still, how often do we give someone a go, but then when they
don't step up and immediately outperform others, we tell ourselves they will
never improve and that we made a poor decision to try to train someone new?

Opportunity is the greater engager. People step up for opportunity, they
stretch themselves for it, they get excited by it, they go the extra mile for it.
Opportunity lays the foundation for so many things in life. We crave opportunity. But when the going gets tough, our tendency is to reduce risk by doing
tasks ourselves rather than helping the inexperienced develop their skills.
Better do it ourselves than waste our time teaching others who are less capable.

But when we do that, we stop being managers. We demote ourselves and
our people, literally taking the position below us rather than allowing our
people to rise above.

Coaching Is Another C

As we know from our own careers, experience is the mother of all teachers.
Putting people into experiences to discover their way out is the great developer, so however risky it might feel, we should seize chances to expand people's comfort zone, and let them (and us) see what they are capable of. Their
engagement and long-term loyalty depend on it. This includes coaching and
guiding people through the rough times – the times when we might most
want to step in and seize control. Our role as leaders is to find ways to safely
enable people to step up, even in storms. That is how you manage to engage.

This is also about taking learning out of the training rooms and into the
real world, and being prepared to trust people to test out their newfound
knowledge in a live environment. At some point, new pilots have to take over
the controls and new surgeons have to operate on real people. Unless people
have opportunities to apply what they have learned soon after the training
has taken place, the investment in their development may as well have been
for nothing, just as a new driver should take to the roads immediately or risk
forgetting the techniques and real-world tips they've been taught.

Coaching Is a Capability Multiplier

Throughout this book, I've used the word *multiplier*. I believe engagement is a multiplier effect. When you focus on engagement, you scale outcomes. The more you engage, the greater the outcome. People engage people who engage people . . . it goes on. Capability development, more specifically coaching for capability development, is a multiplier. But coaching is one of the toughest skills to get right as a manager One of the foundational workshops we provide our clients during a transformation program is coaching: how to accept coaching and how to be a better coach with your own people, peers, and, even boss. But coaching can be tricky, so managers sometimes avoid it. It's a balance: you can't step in and grab the crab, and you need to ask the right questions. This is pretty difficult for some managers or supervisors. But when done right, it can change your relationship with a team member. When you manage to engage, there are two places you may need to coach: as a reaction to a result – a gap in performance; or proactive – where you want to tap into potential for the betterment of an individual or company.

In a heavy industry client, one of our senior transformation consultants had spent much of the pandemic conducting coaching training remotely – literally on line. Like telemedicine, our consulting assignments moved remote for several months. She had gotten to know one manager well. Let's call him Steve. He had been having trouble with one employee who was slow, not picking up skills rapidly enough, seemed to have a negative attitude; and, he had been suspected of causing some damage on the floor and not owning up to it. The coaching training was well timed for Steve to apply the skills to this live situation. Steve and the consultant agreed to have an after-workshop conversation to detail out his assumptions and during that session, they developed a plan to address the situation and came up with questions for Steve to ask to allow the employee to contribute to the conversation and be part of the solution. Steve was reminded that since he was asking these questions, he needed to make sure he listened to the responses. After the coaching session with the employee, Steve called in to debrief with the consultant and described a completely different and more positive outcome than he expected to achieve. Based on his employee's responses, Steve was convinced that the employee did not cause the damage, had very little experience in the industry, and was really trying to do the right thing. The action plan they developed together was a much more positive and skill-based plan than the disciplinary ultimatum Steve originally had planned, and likely a step on the way to engagement.

Indeed, gaining experience and feeling we are making progress is a critical aspect of engagement. Building capability stimulates that state of mind in which we choose to proactively invest our discretionary effort at work.

Supply Floaties

Teaching someone to swim is not about throwing people in the deep end to sink or survive, certainly not without floaties (flotation aids for the non-Australian readers) to prevent them from drowning. In the workplace, people need to be similarly supported as they brave new situations – if we want them to succeed or persevere, feeling good as they rise to the challenge before them needs to be well thought through. Coaching and feedback is key.

While I was president of People Solutions at Proudfoot, I felt as though I had been thrown in the deep end when the CEO at the time decided I should do something new; that I should step into a line management role in Europe and run Operations. My gut reaction was No! I had no experience!

Suffice to say, I took the role. Three things happened. The first was already in place. I was a member of the Executive Development Program (EDP) and, in this capacity, had access to board members and other leaders. Second, the CEO telephoned me regularly to discuss the challenges of the role, situations I was facing, and what he had done when he had been in the role. This gave me a chance to sound out what I was planning and test the logic with him prior to execution – a great luxury. Third, he assigned me a coach who sat in on many of my more challenging meetings. This provided an opportunity to talk about my progress and how I had managed; it built my confidence that I was starting to ease into the role. A seasoned professional showing confidence in your progress can be a powerful boost. Another way of coaching is to provide shadowing opportunities – the new incumbent shadowing the experienced hand and seeing how it is done – something far more effective than mentoring. Real-world learning trumps hypothetical discussions every time.

Somewhere over the Rainbow

As organizations are realizing more and more, developing people's capability needs a flexible approach: a combination of formal and informal learning, and the chance to experience new situations and try out new skills. Helping people to grow is as much about recognizing what people may be capable of as it is about giving them a chance to thrive, by inviting them to push themselves and face their fears – as long as the support and encouragement they need is there to underpin any transition. If we fail to develop people, we risk them stagnating, losing confidence and disengaging – because they no longer feel stimulated, stretched, and on a clear path to a brighter future. And if we waited for everyone to feel "ready" to go to the next level, or take the lead in an intimidating live situation, we wouldn't get very far – because that day might never come. Ultimately, without development you leave yourself with fewer resources you can lean on, your own engagement suffers.

How Are You Developing Your People?

As we enter into the third decade of the twenty-first century, we need to focus on *how* rather on *whether* to develop people.

So how do you keep people in that cycle of self-improvement, which in turn keeps them intellectually stimulated, even when money is tight, and budgets are cut? Engaging people in interesting projects and discussions is a good place to start, as well as exposing them to new information, people, and insight – to open their circle of knowledge and resources. Community and collaboration go a long way to assisting here, providing connections to other capable people.

Improving engagement through capability development is about spotting peripheral or latent talent that perhaps isn't being used to its full potential in a current role. Adopting a *talent is everywhere* mantra is a valuable approach, helping us to keep our eyes open to clues we may have missed, talent that isn't yet being tapped and developed.

It is for all these reasons that we need to focus on the triangle of *training, application,* and *experience* – enabling people to truly develop their capability.

Everyone Stop Learning, Please!

I'm heartbroken when training is stalled, cut, or canceled in the name of saving money. It's one of the first to go, next to consultants and marketing, when a crisis hits. While understandable (I've had to make the same terrible decision), it is never a good solution. I still recall an Accenture study that asked middle managers in the UK about training: fewer than 1 in 10 rated their training to be excellent and 1 in 5 found it poor. But the killer stat was this: 1 in 7 middle managers received *no* training at all. And we wonder why people at every level are underengaged!

As the UK wrestles with the transition of Brexit and the aftermath of border controls from a pandemic, and sees many EU nationals returning to the home countries due to the job uncertainty that abounds, the lack of investment in homegrown skills is glaring. A 2017 report[1] from the UK's Chartered Institute of Personnel and Development (CIPD) left little doubt of the impact this would have on the economy.

The report, which highlighted flagging learning and development in the workplace, suggested that UK employers spend around *half* of what their counterparts in other major EU economies do on training – a gap that continues to widen steadily.

The US has similar issues, but for different reasons. The past few years have seen a tight job market with large skill shortages. Whole industries are struggling to attract and retain talent. If firms don't invest in engagement, including capability development, they will neither retain nor attract the right talent.

In times of crisis, we need good people more, not less! While training budgets may be cut, application and experience should never be. The key is to look for opportunities to provide application and experience in lieu of training spend. These cost little. During our turnaround at Proudfoot, we implemented a weekly call named "What if you could?" People from across our globe prepared and presented a one-hour session online, taking people through a project, a skill, a client story. In the five years it's been running, only six have been canceled and some 75–100 people join each week. It costs nothing but our time.

Work: When People Get into It, They'll Get More Out of It

Intellectual *challenge* differs subtly from intellectual stimulation. The former may keep us interested, but mastering a new intellectual challenge keeps us productive. This is about *application* – pushing ourselves or being pushed to learn continuously. When we are challenged – as long as we don't run from it – we move into a situation where we feel we are doing something that is causing us to *get into* our work. We also start to produce different results.

If we think of capability development from an engagement perspective, in addition to the productivity and results perspective, we can identify ways to

---

[1] CIPD, "From 'Inadequate' to 'Outstanding': Making the UK's Skills System World-Class," CIPD Policy Report, April 2017. https://www.cipd.co.uk/Images/from-inadequate-to-outstanding_2017-making-the-UK-skills-system-world-class_tcm18-19933.pdf

help people get *into* their work so that they in turn can get more *out* of it, and along the way, achieve better results. It's a win-win for both the individual and the business.

When what we do gives us the right balance of interest and skill, intellectually stimulating and intellectually challenging, we really do *get into our work*. Some people call it *the zone* or getting into *the flow*. That is where we see engagement boom when all other triggers are equal. When we sit solely in an underchallenged or understimulated zone, it can create anxiety, as does underchallenged and overstimulated. We can also feel the stress of understimulated and overchallenged. Even apathy can surface, in the case of the *understimulated* and *underchallenged*, when boredom sets in. The issue is skill versus interest when it comes to engagement. Balance the two.

Change Your Vantage Point

Think back to my personal anecdote: my early enthusiasm for doing the best job I could in a basic role at McDonald's when I was young, bright-eyed, and bushy-tailed. How can we encourage more people to relish the *experience,* even if what they're doing feels beneath them? If we look at this as an issue of being understimulated (and overskilled) for a role, we could encourage people to view a job from a different vantage point – instead of being the lowly person who wipes tables and takes out the trash, they are responsible for customers' first impression of the business. Stuck in the old way of thinking, the manager might think: *don't put them in the role or don't keep them in the role.* An alternative is to make the role more intellectually stimulating or intellectually challenging, for example by *adding responsibility or accountability to the role.* If this is an option, the next step in my experience might have been to introduce some additional training so the front-of-house table wiper and floor sweeper can shine and take new pride in their reimagined Meet and Greet capacity.

But what about when the star employees find themselves floundering in a new role, barely keeping their eyes above the water line? These are the team members who qualify as intellectually stimulated category but don't yet hold the requisite skill. Or they are stimulated but not intellectually *challenged.* Anxiety can flourish here, as vulnerability and self-doubt come to the fore. Gaining experience is a process, but becoming good at something can hurt – physically, mentally, and emotionally. It's embarrassing, it can injure our ego, and the harder the journey appears, the more chance there is of disengaging from the activity – you might consider giving up.

So how can we help people feel great about their level of skill, build on it, and help them eventually feel they have mastered their field, no matter how tough the skill is to acquire? Play to their strengths. Find the bright spots. Look for fit. Encourage dialogue, a problem shared is a problem halved, provide safety nets, reward intent and progress, engage in solidifying connections. Encourage collaboration and create community around the skill development.

Visible support (creating a rah-rah team around the learner) and helping him or her understand the value of perseverance creates skill, but it also creates engagement. This way, capability development becomes a stop on the road to engagement.

The more people feel invested in, developed, and that they are making progress, the more engaged they feel. The more balance we strike between intellectually stimulating and intellectually challenging, the more we remove disengagement triggers such as anxiety, lack of confidence, and other performance derailer's. Through this lens, capability development is everyone's responsibility.

Sometimes It's Just about the Company We Keep

Continuous learning isn't just good for business; it's good for people's health and well-being and is a key to life satisfaction. Social capital creates economic capital.

People love the chance to meet and be among others as part of the benefits of training – the social experience. Our contact with people is a stimulating and a welcome break from routine, and it provides the opportunity to share knowledge and practices. But with limits on in-person engagement caused by the pandemic, this became a legitimate impact on our social capital. We must find other ways to build and maintain relationships with others at work. We need the chance to be in a room with peers or experts – even if virtually – to exchange stories and experiences. If we don't respond to the challenges of distant work experiences caused by a pandemic or a global workforce, we could ultimately lose the ability to generate that next new breakthrough idea or innovative product.

Don't lose this aspect – create it in other vehicles. If you must cut training, consider replacing existing training sessions with roundtables or informal sessions where people can simply meet and mingle, even virtually, hearing from and being inspired by those they look up to and share solutions to the key performance indicator (KPI) that needs to move. But even these events should be built up to and built on from, not isolated events: create follow-on opportunities backed by appropriate support and coaching. You must help people process and talk about the experience to ensure the newly acquired knowledge beds in. And when working remotely during a pandemic, social distancing cannot mean feeling remote. We must find other touchpoints no matter how virtual, formally or informally.

Test Your Capability to Build Capability

Capability development is an art: it should capture people's imagination and trigger new passion. Importantly, capability development is not the responsibility of a learning and development team. It's everyone's responsibility, starting with the line manager. To deliver the intended results and stimulate engagement, learning opportunities need to include:

- Interesting, relevant, and up-to-date content, sincerely presented and put in context
- A focus on the individual, not just the group
- An element of fun or entertainment
- Interactive, participative, and active elements
- Coaching and feedback
- Follow-on discussions to make connections to the workplace situation

To review how well you're setting your people up to build capability, addressing their innate need for learning, and paving the way to engage people through skills development, assess your current efforts:

- *Do you make sure your development activities actually lead to learning?* Effective learning is full of dialogue, conversation, and checks and balances to make sure activities and processes are effective – that knowledge is being taken on board. Bringing people together to read a PowerPoint deck isn't training. If this has to be your approach, distribute the deck ahead of time, then bring people together to talk about it – or turn the training into distance, self-paced, or online learning – and then ensure you build in learning discussions with colleagues, bosses, experts, trainers, and coaches.

- *Are you making your training interesting and engaging wherever you can?* There is a reason gaming has become the time-stealer of whole nations: those games are utterly absorbing and fun to play. Now translate that approach to the way your people learn at work.

- *Does your training balance work, life, and value driver skills?* Doing well at work isn't just about having the right skills to perform a particular activity. It also requires that people have a good set of life skills – the ability to get on with people; function as part of a team; build confidence, drive, and create value; cope in a crisis; manage stress; make informed decisions, etc.

- *Do you look for pockets of learning that could be spread to the entire organization?* This is about reverse engineering – spotting what is working well in a part of your business and extrapolating from that so the whole company can benefit. Do you actively seek out areas where performance is achieving outstanding results, and work backward to see why and how these pockets of brilliance come about, and then share them?

- *Do you consciously provide people with learning experiences?* Providing experiences – job changes, special projects, assignments, travel, meetings with people outside the normal networks – counts toward providing development opportunities, as long as the checks and balances of feedback, coaching, and follow-up are in place to support them.

- *Is learning part of people's everyday conversation at work?* "What did you learn today?" should be a question people hear frequently, irrespective of their level, age, or position.

- *Can you feel people being stretched?* Can you see sweat pouring off the brow of your learners? Just enough sweat to test that the stimulation and challenge test can be passed – just enough stimulation and challenge to make it meaningful learning.

- *Are you giving people a taste of something outside their current remit?* Companies that excel at developing their people let individuals build an appetite for new challenges or next career moves – they provide the opportunity to immerse their own people and teams by embedding them in other teams such as a consulting team – future-proofing the business.

Future-Proofing the Business

Capability development is as much about yours as it is your teams. Below are just some of the current capabilities leaders and managers should have on their own development agendas, as they repurpose themselves to manage to engage:

- *Fringe management:* The ability to lead and influence people beyond your current team – those whom your team needs to deal with regularly, from other internal functions, sister organizations, to teams within customers or suppliers.
- *Guardianship:* The ability to inspire, guide, and foster collaboration. This is greater than mentoring individuals; it is about developing links and networks across the organization where unrelated teams find common ground and determine they are related.
- *Management innovation:* Alternative or more creative management processes and models can be designed to actively promote employee engagement and volunteerism.
- *Community development:* The ability to encourage and build connections around common causes, across the organization or with those outside your organization to solve problems common to larger groups.
- *Confidence building:* The ability to banish doubt and build confidence within the business, across teams, and within individuals.
- *Decision facilitation:* The ability to enable people at the front line, where work gets done, to make more meaningful decisions and have an impact on the running of the business.
- *Employee well-being management:* Passion for improving people's quality of life at work is built by creating a more meaningful and challenging experience.
- *Talent spotter:* When Kate Moss, the UK supermodel, walked through JFK Airport as a teenager, she had no modeling capability, but Storm Model Managements founder Sarah Doukas spotted her potential and knew how to develop it. That ability to glimpse future talent paid off for Doukas: to this day, Kate Moss remains one of the world's best-known supermodels.
- *Future thinker:* Determine tomorrow's skill needs today, so you can start to develop the skills ready for what the future holds.

The Power of Pride

When Proudfoot worked with a major seafood company on the West Coast of the US, we saw the true meaning of engagement, of making a difference. The firm was growing double digits and needed to keep up and build a business that could flex to increased volumes. As part of the project, we trained supervisors in the use of active management tools to best execute their 1.5.30s. The supervisors were taken through the content and had a schedule of "on-the-floor" coaching, to embed the new behaviors into habits. At the completion of the training, we awarded certificates for each supervisor, and we asked them to share the experience in front of the class and pose for pictures. It became obvious that one particular supervisor, who had done a great job embracing the new skills, had been especially thrilled to have been part of the program. This supervisor had worked up to his current position from humble beginnings. He had never completed high school, was never part of any management training, and this was the first time he would receive a diploma! The class witnessed how sincere he was, and coupled with the feedback from the assessments, we all knew the new skills he had acquired would be sustainable. While production improved, sales improved, delivery/logistics became better coordinated, it was the engagement of that one man that brought tears to some of our consultants. One man's life was brightened because he could go home and show off to his kids the diploma he had received at work that day.

Understanding the impact of capability development on people can be easy to measure – you see it in their results and in your business KPIs. They apply the skills and achieve, or not. But understanding the impact of capability development on engagement can be an eye-opener, if not a tug on your heart strings. People love to learn. Learning means more than the action, it means growing personally.

1. **Cast fresh eyes over your capability development practices, challenging your existing activities using the prompts set out above.**
2. **Consider what self-fulfilling prophecies you may have perpetuated – e.g., "He can't do that because . . ."; "She would not be**

FIGURE 11.1 Things You Need to Do Right Now. (*continued*)

good at that because . . ."; "They could not do that because . . .".
Are you sure those assumptions weren't shortsighted?

3. Reflect on how well you're adapting your development priorities and learning content to reflect the needs of tomorrow. What new skills and experience will be needed in future, and are you doing enough to prepare for that now?

4. Ask all your people before they go home today: "Did you learn anything new today? If so, what?"

5. As a collaborative exercise with the team, conduct a 'future talent' review, looking at the latent talent in your business. Compare your list with theirs – who made it and who didn't make it on to each list? Why?

Capability: 5 things you can do today to improve quality of life at work

1. **Make learning a sharing experience**

   Find out what people are learning each day and find a way to share this, so more people can benefit. Giving people the opportunity to really think about what they have learned or what capabilities they feel they are developing at work is a valuable exercise in its own right too – encouraging them to reflect on how far they've come and any needs that remain unmet.

2. **Lower the barriers that bind people**

   Let people put their hand up for promotions, positions, training, development, and experiences. At a minimum, take the time to learn what people wish they could learn or experience at work.

FIGURE 11.1 *(Continued)*

3. **Let people shadow other roles**

   Devise a program that allows people to experience other people's jobs with a view to expanding their appreciation and understanding, but also to increase their own capabilities. Make sure people feed back what they have learned.

4. **Fire up people's imaginations**

   When you're in discussions with people, how thought-provoking are they? Are people responding with straightforward information in answer to a specific question, or are you prompting them to be a bit more reflective? Make a conscious effort to ask 'what if' questions or share some interesting thoughts of your own. Stir people's brains.

5. **Learn from your team**

   Letting people teach is as engaging as creating the conditions for them to learn. Letting your people teach you new skills or outlooks is a way to build stronger connections and show you are looking to learn as well.

CHAPTER 12

Freedom: The Great Facilitator

Build a world that is different from the . . . one they've always known. . . but if you use them (dragons) to melt castles and burn cities, you're not different, you're just more of the same.

—Kit Harington, actor in *Game of Thrones*

Imagine how people would *feel* if they could control their own destiny. Freedom. Wars are fought over it; countries are built on it, and people die for it. We strive for market freedom, political freedom, freedom of speech, and freedom through democracy. One of life's bitter stressors is feeling you are not free – to think, to speak, to act. The question for leaders is, do our people feel they relinquish their freedom each day they enter our workspaces or work hours? Do our teams feel they leave their true selves locked away? Do we free people up to create remarkable results or tie them down to tradition and the way things have always been?

Whoever said that when we come to work, we should leave ourselves – our hopes, dreams, desires, and who we really are – at home? No one. And yet people feel this is what's expected; but what if you could become a better version of yourself through what you do for a living? What if your managers inspired that?

Freedom Comes from Being Empowered

It's disappointing when the only way people think they can have free rein at work is if they go off and set up their own business, but that's what the surveys show. It is the entrepreneurs who feel the most engaged, not even management feel they get free rein. We all have a boss. If you think about your role as a manager, it's an odd situation – your ability to gain a sense of freedom at work can often come from controlling someone else's sense of freedom – having power. But freedom and power are not the same thing. We should not be looking to gain freedom by taking power from someone else. Real freedom comes from being empowered. It comes back to managers needing to learn how to be curators, guides, and enablers rather than data collectors and directors.

If we know people crave autonomy in life, why should this be any different at work? No one likes feeling things are out of their control; that their opportunity to contribute to decisions, to drive direction and make a real difference is suppressed.

Freedom Shouldn't Be Filtered through a Boss

Unwittingly, our hierarchies and divisions can give a sense of entitlement or take it away. They can police information, consciously or otherwise. The boss stands up front, sits at the head of the table, runs a meeting or holds the data. She hosts the call or asks for the update. Recall your "what color is my day?" log. How much of it was really focused on you rather than your team? We do this to stay in control, in the know, to be in the loop. But is this causing others to feel out of control, out of the loop?

As managers, we spend an inordinate amount of time validating, checking, and reviewing data. Why? Why can't it filter to us with the right commentary from those who know it best, rather than filter from us awaiting a response? Why not reframe the flow? Why not invert the pyramid? Why not give up control?

Freedom Is Not a Threat

If you're concerned about anarchy breaking out or perhaps just worried chaos will ensue by giving people freer rein at work, here are some strategies to help you maintain creative order.

- *Embrace and learn to function in a flatter, nonhierarchical world.* Let go and let your teams get on as they see fit – remove your need to control it. Handing over more of a sense of personal responsibility and accountability helps your team grow. It doesn't mean relinquishing accountability. It means freeing up others to assume more responsibility. As long as people feel they are doing something because someone has asked them to, rather than because they know they own the task and it's theirs to make the best of, their inclination toward the work is likely to be more dutiful than eager. Let people tell you the expectations. Let them report their progress routinely, with action plans and resolutions. Let them lead the daily meetings. Let them be in control.

- *Information and education are the way to freedom (not power).* Having the right information at the right time driven to the people who need it most, with or without the boss knowing it first, are the ultimate conditions to cultivate freedom. People can get on with their jobs and use their own discretion based on the facts they need.

    As a newbie consultant some 25 years ago, I learned how the true power of information lay in its ability to allow people to make decisions, and not the information itself. At Proudfoot, we call this flow of information the Management Operating System (MOS). It is the backbone of a business, and allows people to better make and execute business decisions. This is part of a good business ecosystem. Many of the people who cloned this approach and opened their own businesses loosely based on the Proudfoot MOS misunderstood its intention. They called their systems "management control and reporting systems," or "systems for managing," and various other names that reinforced a sense of command over someone. But really, the purpose should be to build information flow into the operating model of a business so it becomes a source of collective knowledge – which can be called on at the point of need, accessible as a natural part of someone's job – the "infostructure" of a business. When you use data to let your people manage their own work, you set them free to be remarkable. You engage them in becoming part of the infosystem, not just receivers and reporters of it.

- *Lead a collaborative effort, rather than manage individuals.* Teams today are more fluid than ever: they're as likely to include external people as internal employees. Roll with that, and be the person who steers and connects people for success. Instead of controlling what everyone does, focus on the links between people – the handoffs between collaborating parties. Be the bridge maker – be there for support and guidance, and then trust people to do their best and ask if they need help. When you master the handoffs at the team level, learn to master them at a department level and beyond, breaking down your business silos. This is what managing at the fringe is all about.

- *Create listening posts to foster freedom of speech.* When activists want to rally support, they paint, write, and tell their stories, continually finding ways for people to access, see, read, and retell them. Nothing gives a sense of freedom like knowing you will be heard, and nothing is more engaging than knowing you have been listened to. Provide your business with listening posts – points of contact where everyone can hear each other's opinion and comment – then look for ways to capture and act on these posts.

   At the birth of the internet (then chat rooms and company intranets), management was often afraid to allow people to openly give input online without designing a mechanism to approve (manage) what was written. This wasn't very enlightened thinking. You can't manage opinion, you can only learn from it and change it through the right action. Make sure you provide open access to allow anyone to have a voice and to visibly provide input in different ways, then respond. People will sensor if their colleagues are out of line or go rogue.

- *A schedule can free or tie people depending on who's set it.* Control over our own time (the *when* part of our life) gives a sense of freedom that comes from feeling we have control not only over our destiny (the *why* part of life) but also *when* we will arrive.

In the early days of my career, I worked with a dynamo man by the name of John Williams. John liked to keep to his own schedule. But the people he worked with preferred him to adhere to their schedule. They parted ways fairly quickly. As John put it: "Why would I want to sit in traffic for an hour and half to be here by 8:30 when I can power-work during my morning's peak hour, accomplish much of my to-do list before everyone else gets out of their cars and off their buses?" John's thinking was ahead of his time, and pretty logical, too: neither his job nor his responsibilities required him to be in a designated building by 8:30. It just happened to be the rule. When this suggestion was blocked, he felt no inclination to stay. He didn't feel heard or trusted.

- *Make strategy and improvement programs routine and accessible to anyone.* Give people a vehicle through which they can regularly voice what cheeses them off, explain the bad-hair days, offer their ideas to improve the business, and see ideas acted on. Add nontraditional people to your strategy exercises and conversations. Invite team members to attend your management meetings. Most critical to this is the communication of where ideas come from – nothing sparks more ideas than the knowledge that people are paying attention.

Sometimes we limit improvement programs to those we can immediately quantify, those that save money. Acting on ideas that will help your *people* to grow is especially likely to become self-perpetuating. A clean infrastructure will open the door to engagement, while growth and development opportunities will foster their enthusiasm. Innovation stimulates everyone into overdrive.

Freedom Frees Up People to Be Remarkable

Our ability to confront this moment in time when change proliferates every conversation, every part of our organizations, requires us to grant ourselves the freedom to think differently, to dare to be different in the way we rise to challenges, to act boldly. *Ordinary* is the last thing we need in business today. When we manage to engage, we are looking to lead people on a different journey, one punctuated with thoughtful debate and wild curiosity. One where our people can see themselves free to be remarkable.

Above All, Trust People

This sense of freedom in business is grounded in trust. Nothing is more empowering and liberating than knowing you are trusted; conversely, few things are likely to prompt disengagement more than feeling you are *not* trusted. The bosses of the twenty-first century are facilitators. They go Heads-Up. They practice active management. They exercise their management muscle through 1.5.30s. All of which is constructed on trust.

In the twenty-first century, the need to know, trust, empower, and develop people is giving rise to a new type of boss: one who does much less "bossing" and much more enabling. Success in this role can be measured at the end of each working day by posing the question, "Did I give people the freedom to act?" Because that gives people the freedom to develop and grow. If we want to cultivate remarkable people, we must first free them to be exactly that, so that they do not leave their remarkable, community-enhancing selves at the door when they come to work but are instead free to continue being those remarkable people right across the working day.

Freedom: 5 things you can do today to improve people's quality of life at work

1. **Free people from rigid office hours**

   Where you can, change the hours of your business to suit people. Some like to rise early, others late; some get stuck in traffic. Reestablish start and finish times to suit your people as well as your business. Free them from schedules that don't work.

2. **Create freedom of information**

   Open your books to everyone: let them see and be part of what's really going on. Enable everyone to see, contribute, and provide feedback to the monthly report. Be inclusive. Make collective knowledge richer.

3. **Free the police force**

   In place of the traditional policing of people (with follow-up that feels like micromanagement), agree jointly with teams what discussions are required and when. Then show you trust them and get out of their way.

4. **Free up decision-making**

   Let people make decisions. Seeking approval costs money and engagement. Give people the freedom to move forward.

5. **Create freedom of choice**

   This could be about what projects to work on, which career paths are of interest, the suppliers that should be awarded contracts, who gets hired, and so on.

FIGURE 12.1 Things You Need to Do Right Now.

CHAPTER 13

Making a Difference: Engage. Enable. Energize.

Just because you fall on your ass, doesn't mean you have to stay there.

—Jack Quaid, *The Boys* Amazon TV Series

As we reflect on the nine triggers of engagement identified as being critical in our new reality, and to twenty-first century management innovation (the MI-9, for short), it now falls to you to determine which need more attention than others as you move deeper into your own workplace transformation.

Context is important. The priorities for one organization will differ from another, based on the type of business, its ethos, and its current state of performance – financially and culturally, including your existing levels of employee engagement. So, emphasis will need to be adapted accordingly. But the beauty of the MI-9 (our 2 Fs and 7 Cs) is that they can be turned up or toned down as you see fit for your people. You must calibrate – you must experiment until you get it right. No one has a clear plan, but you need a road-map to navigate through the MI-9, constantly recalibrating as team members change and company and industry conditions change. Your ability to look, listen, and learn, will impact how you influence.

re change was driven by a pandemic, depending on your already calibrated your business models and operating ably had to make great transformation, starting with a .... ui paper, rebuilding, reshaping, and changing how you run your business. But it could not be your business or operating models alone that changed. You needed your management model to change as well – the way you manage to engage; the way you lead to achieve your results.

Monetizing Effort: Creating a New Currency with MI-9

As managers and leaders today, our greatest challenge is to reshape engagement, and it starts with these basic tools. The MI-9. We must use them as a gauge, a compass. They create a new currency – your team's discretionary effort. It is invested, held back, banked, or used. Engagement is how you monetize effort. Your ability to create an engaging workplace, an engaged workforce, and teams of people who create value each day will be the difference between teams working together for a common purpose or just a bunch of people simply trying to get stuff done. The difference is profound.

Value has come to be much more than the products or services your firm produces and the results they achieve. As people, we know we gain a sense of value in the context of those around us. Value becomes priceless. We all want to see our worth. Without that visible link to worth, we lose sight of our value. As a leader and manager, how valuable your people feel will affect their desire to lend you their discretionary effort. Their value will become yours. The ability to create a sense of worth in others will be our most priceless skill. That's how you become a magnet for talent, ideas, innovation, and growth. That's how you manage to engage and achieve remarkable results.

Achieve Your Leadership License to Operate

The MI-9 help power our people's emotions to lend their effort at work. They enable managers to earn a license to lead in the eyes of their people. The concept of *license to operate* has long been in use where businesses impact communities; the mining industry is just one example. Firms earn their license to operate in a community through their ability to effectively engage and "do the right thing" – stakeholder engagement. This license to operate concept is not dissimilar from that of a doctor who is sworn to "first, do no harm." In business today, our ability to earn our leadership license to operate is as vital as that of a community license to operate. If you don't earn it, you won't engage. The MI-9 becomes the foundation for your license. Use them poorly and you underengage, you stall, your brakes lock up, you slow down, you lose points, you lose your license. Use them wisely and you move forward; changing gears, you can accelerate; safely, you earn your license.

To do this, you must build time into you schedule to continuously look for ways to improve how you engage, ways to apply the MI-9 to better interact, trust one another, create confidence, and work together. Humans are at their best when we do this. The investment you make in engagement is a multiplier – a triple bottom line effect. It enables people to make productivity gains and companies to achieve profitability gains. Engagement enables and energizes people to bring ideas and innovation, which brings competitive gains. It also helps you. No one person can lead alone; we simply have too much coming at us today. Instead, the more we engage, the more we distribute leadership responsibilities and create leaders at every level, if only to prevent ourselves from becoming overwhelmed. It's an "all-eyes and all ears" attitude.

But there is no one formula.

Flatten the Workplace Hierarchies

Fair trade and freedom are expected; they are the table stakes. Getting this right first is the only time it's about you. Traditional hierarchies, position power, and inflated egos belong to the business archives of old. In the new transparent, ultraconnected world, employee structures are much flatter and fluid. Your personal capabilities impact fair trade and freedom. Take these personally. For those brought up in old-school management environments, this may feel far outside your comfort zone. But it should – and this is healthy. It's a sign of our own growth, and the rewards will be worth it. Finding your people's sweet spot could mean solving retention issues, driving new revenue, and honing your company's unique selling proposition through new management innovation. What's good for our people becomes good for business.

So we must start with the way we manage. Our job as leaders is to discover what triggers engagement in each individual, one person at a time, and then build those triggers into what we do every day. This feel-your-way approach goes against old management styles where the leaders set the agenda and the team obligingly falls into line. But as we acknowledged at the outset, there is no exact prescription for success – no magic formula. Every business, every workforce, every employee is different. The challenge for the manager, then, is not to follow a rulebook but to learn to take time, tune in, and respond as appropriate.

Pull up a Seat at the (Kitchen) Table

To move beyond table stakes are the rest of the MI-9 – the 7 Cs. You need to be really creative in how you apply them. You must push the envelope.

The challenges that lie before us as businesses and as leaders in the current age are unprecedented. No one has all the answers. Experience is all well and good, but it doesn't outdo fresh thinking. We cannot try to get the old to fit the new.

As a result, the few can no longer monopolize the many into compliance; instead, leaders and managers need to mobilize *everyone* to work together to find solutions. We are bursting at the seams with bright, intelligent people who understand where markets are going and what customers need. It's time to be much more proactive and systematic about tapping into that.

When you recalibrate your boardroom table in the spirit of a kitchen table, you engage in conversation and debate. You allow people to put their thoughts on the table, not their positions. You help everyone make sense of what is happening around them. You let them have a voice in a safe and productive way to respond to that environment; as people engage in points of view, find common ground, and move forward. Connection and a fair dinkum interest in people can drive more change than traditional lines of communication ever will. Our brains are built for kitchen tables; it is unlike any other organ in our body, it is social. It requires a social context. We know the greatest turn-on for people is other people. We know we cannot survive long-term isolation, nor can we live without a sense of belonging. So we must build more kitchen-table conversations into our organizations – the concepts of connecting, collaborating, and community to help bring our social needs to life. We know this will bring our people to life.

Engagement: The Future of Business Is Still People

No amount of technology in an organization will replace how you engage people in their work. While technology platforms and innovations will help, and they may even make it easier for you, true engagement comes from true leadership: the ability to utilize our technology effectively, to be tech savvy, and then lift our heads up and engage in real discussions with our people and teams, to move them to want to invest their effort in your business, in your objectives, in your customers. On the ground, leadership brings this by harnessing technology to reimagine work so people can be freed up to think, act, and perform; so they can raise their hand to solve problems and participate in change. Technology is only as smart as the people using it.

Indeed, in the future we can expect to see management effectiveness become more visible still, as markets start to recognize the importance of measuring employee participation more formally, alongside companies' carbon footprints – with expectations that this will be reflected in companies' annual reports. Employee confidence indexes will paint refreshingly open and honest pictures of the way businesses are run and how employees really feel. This is how brand equity will be built in the future.

The Change Imperative

But there is a lot of work still to do to get to where we need to be. CEOs and senior managers the world over speak of the need to gain buy-in from their people to the latest corporate initiative, of the need to deliver sustainable change and fundamentally change the way we engage people. We expect our people to be different and deliver diverse results, yet how can they, why would they, if they feel exactly the same as they did yesterday?

These are conversations we should be having, *wherever* our businesses are right now. We need to be asking ourselves, and our people, every day: are they really getting into their work? Are they all-in? Are we anywhere near a point where they are *engaged* rather than disengaged? Without addressing the great people crisis and making it a priority, our economic ups and downs, our woes will continue. Our crisis will deepen. Our superpower as a species is our ability to engage. It's what makes us different from every other species on the planet. We need to use this power wisely. It will enable us to survive epic disruptions such as COVID-19. It will enable us to thrive no matter what the next disruption throws at us.

Right now, I guarantee there are management teams across the globe discussing where they need to reduce their costs. They are considering outsourcing and onshoring, consolidation strategies, or just plain redundancies. But are these same management teams considering what they can do to better engage their people in helping solve these problems and therefore osts? Are they considering fundamental management change, management innovation? Or are they persisting in the quest for productivity at the expense of employee engagement, inadvertently reducing well-being and satisfaction of people at work? I hope not.

Lead Generously

You can apply the MI-9 engagement triggers as widely and creatively as you like: they can – and should – have a far-reaching impact. For instance, they should influence how and who you hire, how you form teams, and how you design and implement change in your business.

The MI-9 triggers of employee engagement are a challenge for leaders to embrace how they manage, how they spend their time and on what, to look for ways to innovate their own management approaches, and to evolve themselves into leaders.

Employee Engagement Is the Best Investment You'll Ever Make

Investing in people is never a waste. You know people are a company's competitive advantage; they always have been. How you build your management models to release their latent talent and energy is up to you – as long as you do. When you understand what truly engages people, you're able to design a better business, a more effective organization, one that works *for* people and not against them. You are able to develop managers who appreciate the impact they have on others, and leverage this to enable and energize people to be remarkable.

One thing is for sure. People will no longer put up, give up, and shut up. They will simply walk out, in body or just spirit. We want more from and out of our work. Fair trade must take its place at the table as *the* table stake of choice, first among equals. We must obsess about fairness and build our businesses on a fair trade society; one where everybody has the opportunity to be remarkable and the exchange rate for effort is equitable. We must expect an infrastructure that works for us and not against us. We must feel confident in ourselves and those around us, including our leaders. And while we may not literally fight for freedom at work, we will vote for it with our feet and eventually exchange our lack of freedom for another job, another boss. Yes, ultimately, we want to be engaged.

The twenty-first-century leader and manager must learn a new craft and become true movers and shakers – the movers and shakers of people, not power. Management toolkits must explode with ways to better engage. It is new ground, and it should be groundbreaking. We must look for ways to master our trade, not our people. *Work* cannot continue to be viewed as this four-letter word.

As kids we say, "Get ready, get set, go!" yet in business we all too often jump to the go. We must spend time on the ready and set to better prepare for the go. This is how you use the 2 Fs and 7 Cs every day.

The Past Will Never Again Predict the Future

The world has always been judged by its last actions. Countries, companies, teams, and individuals have always been only as good as their last results. But this is where change begins: the packing away of the past and the unpacking of future potential. Blowing away the practices that no longer work and finding new ideas that may work in the future by experimenting with them today.

Nothing is certain, but it's time to start placing our bets on new and different approaches instead of the tried and tested.

Engagement will come as management helps trigger it one heart, one mind, one spirit, one person, at a time. This is a grassroots-to-global (G2G) movement, as Professor Anil Gupta calls it[1]. He founded the Honey Bee Network to facilitate the spread of groundbreaking practices and technologies among the world's poor. The Network is an open-source structure that mimics the behavior of the honey bee, cross-pollinating ideas. This is how engagement must be viewed. We must share ideas and experiments to innovate the way we manage and lead our businesses.

Every organization and workforce is different, and no two employees are the same. Innovative management styles must be designed. The MI-9 including practices such as HeadsUp, 1.5.30, and active management offer a launchpad for making positive changes to the workplace – a guide

---

[1] Anil Gupta, "India's hidden hotbeds of invention," TEDtalk (video and transcript). https://www.ted.com/talks/anil_gupta_ind"ia_s_hidden_hotbeds_of_invention/transcript?language=en

to improving employee connectedness, banishing doubt, inspiring growth, and building passion, which will be the bedrock for long-term business prosperity and renewed job satisfaction. Forward-thinking leaders and managers are encouraged to apply these for the people they work with, and build their management ecosystems, practices, and processes around them. But what becomes evident as you move through the engagement journey is the need to view engagement as the first step and not the outcome. The scorecard is clear – 2 Fs and 7 Cs, the quality of life index at work is available. The tools are usable. Great things really can happen at the intersection of people and technology.

So with this in mind, what will your personal legacy be as a manager? How will you become a leader? Will it be the systems and processes you improved, the costs you reduced, and the products or services you sold? Will your record be judged on those results alone, or will it also be based on the minds you inspired, the spirits you moved, the people you prompted into action through passionate, uninhibited engagement?

I know which I would rather be remembered for.

Conclusion

Good, better, best. Never let it rest. Until your good is better and your better best.

—Unknown

My mother had a small sign near our kitchen table my entire life. Today I still recall the words. . . *good, better, best.* . . I don't believe we get to best when it comes to engagement. How can you when it concerns people? We always want more, different, better. But I do believe in the spirit, in the need to continue the quest. You never know what is around the next corner.

2020 changed the way we look at work, the way we look at resources and assets, the way we look at our businesses, the way we look at value. It was the greatest disruption of our generation. No one escaped its impact – not the rich, not the poor, no country, or industry. It was a catastrophe for many or a welcome growth injection for a few. It was hard work and high stress for still others. It created the B2P that leaders at every level know in their hearts they need to achieve – a business made up first and foremost of people connecting with people.

If it didn't change your world, it likely should have. The challenge for most firms was to maintain business continuity while executing reparative and restorative strategies and initiatives. And clearly, to do this effectively required a change in the way we engaged people. The globally underenthused could not create the needed safe, productive, purpose-driven new reality.

So How Engaged Should Your Organization or Team Be?

I am asked this question a great deal and in many different contexts. For example, when you work in mining, you are looking for community engagement. Managers blind to the real outcome see engagement as an end grade rather than the journey and will ask, "What score should I achieve in my community engagement levels?" My answer is, are you happy with a 100 percent failure with one individual? When you don't shoot for 100, that's what you get. A 50 percent engagement score means 50 percent of the people are not engaged. Given the damage a disengaged person can wreak on your workplace, infecting your team, would you be happy with a 50 percent score? You can't say raising engagement to 50 percent from 30 percent is a win. It's only when you start aiming for 100 percent that you start to close the gaps. That you look at every option available to you to make great change and allow people to really show up at work.

Organizations that prioritize people and their engagement will not only drive their own performance but also positively affect their community, their economy, and society. After all, the best ambassador for a company in a community is an engaged employee. Healthy and fit businesses are better for everyone. When you look through the engagement lens, you create a better working world where jobs are designed for the better of people and not just profits. That will drive business and people outcomes of wellness. It also drives higher living standards. Engaged workforces engage in productive work. With productive work comes growth. With growth comes jobs. With jobs come a better economic reality for the many.

The conversation must elevate beyond the immediacy of coping with today and move into the pragmatic solutions to last through tomorrow.

Managing and Leading

One of the first things I learned from Jon Wylie, our global president of Natural Resources, was the time differential on leaders versus managers and the value of storytelling:

> *Leadership is a future focus. It links the here and now with the future and communicates how what we are doing today supports where we are going in the future. Intentionally or unintentionally as a leader you are constantly communicating and teaching how to close that gap or progress toward the future state. . . . When you use storytelling in a "teach don't tell" model, you create engagement by creating understanding. People can see the world in their mind's eye. Our job as leaders is to tell the story of the future and then engage people in the journey to get there.*

I believe we now have an opportunity to rethink why we serve our customers and, therefore, what work should be done, how and when, as well as

Acknowledgments

As a first-time author who has a passion for learning, it's our clients who often teach us the greatest through the living-lab that is their workplace and the challenges they entrust in us to help solve. I thank the many I have worked with in my 30 plus years of consulting. Each day that I engage in work I also learn from the many teams I am fortunate to lead and the people I have been fortunate to work with; support goes a long way. Special thanks to Jon Wylie, Lorena Schoenfeld and Alan Steelman as well as Fiona Czerniawska, Pernilla Fransson, St John Cameron, Emilio Di Spiezio Sardo, Greg Moore, Neil Maslen, and Julia Malasaga. Thank you to Zach Schisgal, Kelly Talbotingy, Dawn Kilmore, Cheryl Ferguson, Jayaprakash Unni, Dawn Kilgore, Shannon Vargo, Ashley Edwards, Sally Baker,Abirami Srikandan, and the team at Wiley & Son's. And a thank you to the people who at various times enable a book to keep moving forward through their support or sometimes just a brief conversation; Judy Newcombe, Bianca Okros, Sue Tabbitt, Gemma Manning, Lana Abraham, Millie Booth, Daniel Budd, Marija Bacic Main, Judith MacCormick, Annie Tignol, Christine Perrin, Diane Chaput, Betty Leitch, James Wong, Marty Sheetz, Antoine Casgrain, Manfred Stanek, Jonathan Clegg, Liverson Mdonga, Crispin White, Rouge Sana, Edward Le Pine Williams, Christopher Juul, Tom Cook, Stuart Mills, Sir Richard Shirreff, Mike Critelli, Mike Michael, The Honorable Steve Bartlett, Honorable Bernard Lord, Gordon Peeling, David Turnbull, Ray Wilcox, Franklin Feder, Linda Glendinning Roseman, Bronwyn Covill, Summer Dean and the late Kelvin Boyd. All of whom offered a word of encouragement or a thought that brought ideas. And Team Proudfoot with special thanks to Christine Branston, Monique Jackson, Emily Sollitt, Zuki Liang, Andrew Xu, Michael Kirsten, JJ VanPletzen, Cay Mims, David Braithwaite, Scott Staunton, Paul Batten, Angus Maclean, Peter Damm, Guerau Carbo, Bruce MacConnell, Ted Binkoski, Edward Corey, Juan Lizarraga, Brian Olsaver, Nelson Miller, Tony King, Richard Briggs, Stephan Laurent, Al Logie, Tim Gaffron, Andreas Paetz, Reza Ram, Alex Davison, Roger Hedman and Isabelle Le Bec. Not forgetting some of the people I take inspiration from – Gary Vaynerchuck, Patrick Lencioni and Fareed Zakaria. And of course, Mum, Dad, Peter, Paul, and their families who never fail to engage.

About the Author

Pamela Hackett is the CEO of Proudfoot, an expert in business and operational improvement and transformation, founded in 1946, and the first implementation management consultancy of its kind. The firm works with clients to engage, enable, and energize their entire organization in the pursuit of large-scale, measurable results that are meaningful for all stakeholders. For more than three decades, she has worked with clients to transform hundreds of organizations in dozens of countries in most major industries, including manufacturing, retail, financial, insurance, mining, oil and gas, and aerospace. She has worked in the trenches with people at all levels of organizations, learning firsthand what works and what doesn't.

Pamela is a dynamic thought leader who is passionate about the power of people in transforming an organization. She believes people engagement is the driver of sustainable change and improved productivity, whether it is across an entire organization and culture or within teams. She also knows it starts with the manager and their ability to manage to engage.

As digitization has taken hold and leaders at every level are wrestling with chaos in an ever-more rapidly changing world, Pamela is fanatical in her view that great things happen at the intersection of people and technology. To support that, she has launched #HeadsUp – a movement that reinforces the need to raise your head from your technology and connect with people – at home, at work, or in the community.

Pamela continues to guide her teams and clients to help them innovate and grow, culturally, organizationally, and profitably. She continues to be a visionary change maker, guiding organizations around the world into a stronger, better future.

Index